The Change Agent's Guide to Radical Improvement

The Change Agent's Guide to Radical Improvement

Ken Miller

with special contributions from
Robin Lawton

ASQ Quality Press
Milwaukee, Wisconsin

Library of Congress Cataloging-in-Publication Data

Miller, Ken, 1970-
  The change agent's guide to radical improvement / Ken Miller.
     p. cm.
  Includes bibliographical references and index.
   ISBN 0-87389-534-7
   1. Organizational change. 2. Management. I. Title.
   HD58.8 .M528 2002
   658.4'06—dc21

                                        2001006577

© 2002 by ASQ

10 9 8 7 6 5 4

ISBN 0-87389-534-7

Acquisitions Editor: Annemieke Koudstaal
Project Editor: Craig S. Powell
Production Administrator: Gretchen Trautman
Special Marketing Representative: Dave Luth

ASQ Mission: The American Society for Quality advances individual, organizational and community excellence worldwide through learning, quality improvement and knowledge exchange.

Attention: Bookstores, Wholesalers, Schools and Corporations:

ASQ Quality Press books, videotapes, audiotapes, and software are available at quantity discounts with bulk purchases for business, educational, or instructional use. For information, please contact ASQ Quality Press at 800-248-1946, or write to ASQ Quality Press, P.O. Box 3005, Milwaukee, WI 53201-3005.

To place orders or to request a free copy of the ASQ Quality Press Publications Catalog, including ASQ membership information, call 800-248-1946. Visit our Web site at http://www.asq.org .

Printed in the United States of America

 Printed on acid-free paper

American Society for Quality

Quality Press
600 N. Plankinton Avenue
Milwaukee, Wisconsin 53203
Call toll free 800-248-1946
Fax 414-272-1734
www.asq.org
http://qualitypress.asq.org
http://standardsgroup.asq.org
E-mail: authors@asq.org

Table of Contents

Introduction

Your mission, should you choose to accept it . . .

This is the book I wish I would have had before I embarked on my career as a change agent. (Actually, nobody sets out to be a change agent; it just happens.) I wish I would have had it before I:

- Tried to solve world hunger
- Got double crossed by a team sponsor
- Improved a process for a product nobody wanted
- Let a team present their ideas solely on the merits without any compelling data to convince decision makers
- Facilitated the team that would never end (I think they are still working)

In short, this is the book I needed before I learned what it really takes to be a successful change agent. My pain is your gain. This guide is everything you need to know to survive and thrive as a change agent. It goes beyond the current wisdom on facilitation, tools, and teams. It goes beyond the current and past management fads (TQM, reengineering, surveys, and so on). It goes beyond these by integrating them all. That is, at the heart of each of these change methods are some useful principles and excellent tools that when used at the *right time* in the *right way* can create radical improvement. Rather than preaching a single dogma, I have chosen to integrate them all and then to provide ways for you to decide the right tool for the job.

I hope you find this book comprehensive enough to succeed right away and stimulating enough that you begin to pursue additional ideas, methods, and tools not covered within. At the back of the book is a resource guide, a portal of sorts, that links you to some of the best thinking of today and yesterday on how to improve performance.

I'd like to acknowledge the people who have made this book possible:

I first must thank my lovely wife **Jennifer.** Without you, I never would have had the confidence or character to become a change agent. I shudder to think where I would be had I not caught even a little of your enthusiasm, energy, integrity, and way with people. You are the most beautiful soul on earth.

Robin Lawton, you are truly a genius. I said almost 10 years ago that you were 10 years ahead of your time, and today you are still 10 years ahead. You deserve to be the Dr. Deming of the knowledge age. Your concepts, principles, and methods for customer-centered organizational change are both revolutionary in impact and elegant in their simplicity. I thank you first for enlightening me, then for mentoring me, and now for supporting me. I can never repay my debt to you.

To learn more about Rob Lawton's work and that of his firm, IMT (International Management Technologies, Inc.), visit www.imtc3.com. Important concepts used in this book have been excerpted or adapted from IMT's workshop, "Creating a Customer-Centered Culture"® and Lawton's text, *Creating a Customer-Centered Culture: Leadership in Quality, Innovation and Speed,* Milwaukee, WI: ASQC Quality Press. 1993. (See appendix A.) Specific IMT tools adapted here include Team Charter, Product Self-test, Customer Roles Matrix, Focus Group, Focus Group (new product), Voice-of-the-Customer Table, FACT Sheet, Product Flowchart, Process Analysis Checklist, and Project Selection Matrix.

Quentin Wilson, you are the master of guerilla warfare. Your confidence in me has allowed me to grow in ways I never could have imagined. You gave me free reign to try out new ideas and methods. You threw me into situations where you were the only one confident that I would come out alive. The fact that you empowered a 20-something kid to radically remake a highly visible organization of which you were in charge astounds me and is a real testament to your character. The secrets and survival tips that I outline in this book are a direct result of chances you allowed me to take and our Friday afternoon debates about management theory. Know that I will follow you into any battle.

Thanks also to all of the teams, clients, organizations, fellow change agents, and enlightened managers I have had the pleasure to lead, facilitate, train, support, counsel, and learn from. I would especially like to thank Kay, Mellodie, Greg, Stan, Glenda, Bev, Carolyn, Carolyn, Blake, Bill, my father, Lisa, Lisa, and Lesa.

Becoming a Change Agent

What separates excellent organizations from the truly ordinary? What allows some organizations to rapidly change and continually reinvent themselves while others have trouble turning the boat even slightly? The best-selling business books and management gurus offer a dizzying array of silver bullets and panaceas. While all are sound theories, they continue to overlook the fundamental ingredient that must be in place for the improvement to work: the presence of change agents.

Change agents are individuals who have the knowledge, skills, and tools to help organizations create radical improvement. In short, the people that get tapped to make *it* happen, whatever *it* may be (leading the strategic planning retreat, facilitating a reengineering team, managing the new project, and so on). Rarely in a position of authority, they achieve results with their keen ability to facilitate groups of people through well-defined processes to develop, organize, and sell new ideas. They challenge teams to get outside of the box and utilize innovative tools to harness that creativity to make improvements that matter to the bottom line. Change agents are the invisible hands behind the scenes that turn vision into action. They are a leader's best friends. While it is true that you can have change agents and not have success, *you cannot have success without change agents.*

Change agents are individuals with the knowledge, skills, and tools to help organizations create radical improvement.

There is nothing more difficult to carry out, nor more doubtful of success, nor more dangerous to handle, than to initiate a new order of things. For the reformer has enemies in all those who profit by the old order, and only lukewarm defenders in all those who would profit by the new order, this lukewarmness arising partly from fear of their adversaries, who have laws in their favour; and partly from the incredulity of mankind, who do not truly believe in anything new until they have had actual experience of it. Thus it arises that on every opportunity for attacking the reformer, his opponents do so with the zeal of partisans, the others only defend him half-heartedley, so that between them he runs great danger.

Niccolo Machiavelli

The Change Agent Body of Knowledge

The role of a change agent is to *help*:

- Decide what to change
- Facilitate what to change to
- Sell the change
- Implement the change

The key word is *help*. Change agents do not ride in on a white horse to solve the organization's ills. Rather, they work *with* and *through* people to make improvement happen. They live by the credo that people only support what they help create. In order to carry out their role successfully, change agents must be skilled in five areas: business knowledge, change processes, change agent tools, facilitation skills, and the politics of change.

Business Knowledge

The foundation of a change agent is business knowledge. This knowledge is not so much what one might learn in an MBA program, such as marketing, accounting, or manufacturing; rather, it is a deep understanding of how work gets done. Change agents must understand the *system of work* (Figure I.1), its components, and their interactions in order to know where a change is needed and what change process is required. From a few known symptoms, the change agent must be able to diagnose what system to change and where in the system to make the change and must have a process to help a team change it.

There are three environments[1] in which the change agent must work, each with its own set of change processes and tools (see Figure I.2). **Organizational-level change** deals with the larger systems that help the organization set direction, develop plans, set priorities, and allocate resources. **System-level change** improves all of the components of the *system of work model*, whether that be determining customer expectations, redesigning products, or reengineering processes. **Individual-level change** deals with the products and systems that help employees excel and grow, including performance expectations, development plans, positive reinforcement, and training.

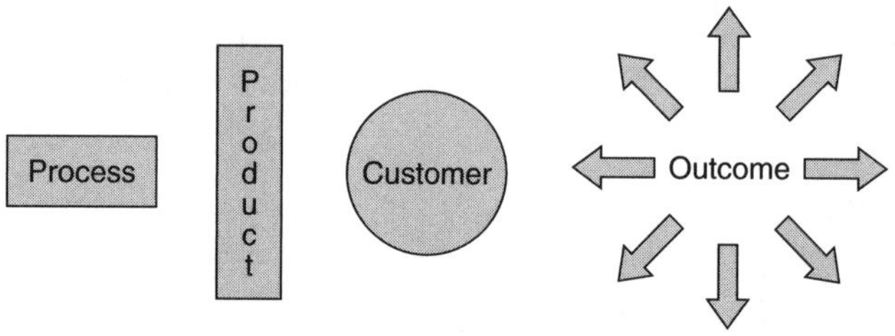

Good Change Agents

- *Are passionate*
- *Are knowledge seeking*
- *Have access to power*
- *Are respected by the organization*

Figure I.1 The system of work.

Source: Adapted from IMT's workshop, "Creating a Customer-Centered Culture."® Used with permission. (See appendix A.)

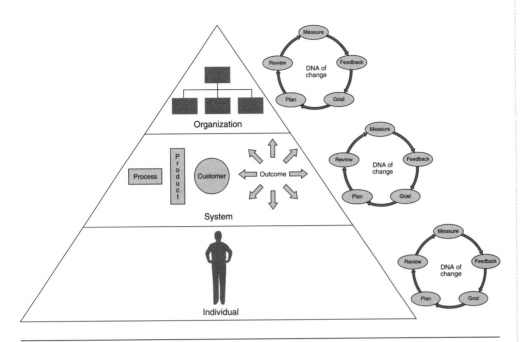

Figure I.2 Three levels of focus.

The change agent must be able to move freely between all three environments, applying the methods and tools to enhance performance at each level.

At the core of all three environments is the DNA of change (Figure I.3). Individuals, business processes, and organizations as a whole must have this DNA to make improvement continuous. The change agent understands this and knows how to implement it in all three environments.

Change Processes

There is an old bit of cautionary wisdom that says if you give a man a hammer, everything looks like a nail. Unfortunately, this is how too many organizations and change agents function. They apply a seven-step problem-solving method to every issue that presents itself, whether applicable or not. Reducing errors by 25 percent calls for problem solving; cutting process cycle time by 80 percent does not. Whether the objective is improving customer satisfaction, reducing absenteeism, improving on-time delivery, or developing new innovative products, a different process with a different set of tools is required for each.

Change Agent Tools

Associated with each change process is a set of tools. When used correctly, these tools make the change processes systematic, effective, and quick. They are designed to ensure that team members are asking the right questions and arriving at the best answers. However, it is important to stress that they are just tools. Without an organized change process, they accomplish little. The change process drives the tools.

The Change Processes

- *Customer satisfaction*
- *Process improvement*
- *Problem solving*
- *Planning*

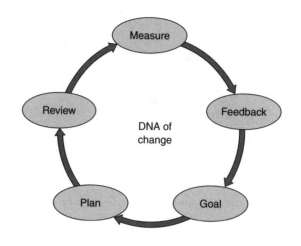

Figure I.3 DNA of change.

In addition to the tools that support particular change processes, there are common sets of tools used by each process. These tools help organize projects, analyze data, and cultivate, express, and implement ideas.

Facilitation Skills

All change is difficult, and most projects fail before they even begin. A change agent must understand how to organize a project so that it has the best chance to succeed. Tantamount to this is uncovering the project's success criteria, securing management support, and building the right team. From there, a change agent must be able to keep that team motivated and focused to accomplish its mission. Finally, the change agent must be able to make the group of individuals function like a team by building consensus, resolving conflict, and cultivating participation. The change agent must push the group members to think of what they never thought possible.

Politics of Change

Brilliant ideas are produced every day in organizations. There are shelves full of binders with wonderful team recommendations, new product ideas, and cutting-edge strategies. Unfortunately, these things are rarely implemented. Successful change agents have the ability to navigate the politics of change. It is their job not only to make sure that the team generates dazzling ideas but also to build the compelling case for change and the sales pitch to close the deal. The change agent must understand the six layers of resistance and how to overcome them. They need to know the tactics for reducing resistance to innovation. Most importantly, they need to know who has the power and how to hit their hot buttons. The outcome should be determined before a team ever makes a presentation.

Table I.1   Change agent skills.

Business knowledge	Change processes	Facilitation skills	Tools	Politics of change	Result
✔	✔	✔	✔	✔	Radical improvement
0	✔	✔	✔	✔	Minor improvement with little bottom-line impact
✔	0	✔	✔	✔	Wrong solution for situation
✔	✔	0	✔	✔	Mediocre ideas with little consensus or passion
✔	✔	✔	0	✔	Lots of talk, little progress
✔	✔	✔	✔	0	Good ideas that never get implemented

It is the rare few that possess all five sets of skills (Table I.1). The rest of this book, through use of the change agent model, is designed to create a well-balanced change agent who is adaptable and successful no matter the challenge.

Change Agent Model

Anybody who has ever been a part of a change project knows the journey can be a harrowing one; rife with drama, pitfalls, and fleeting moments of exhilaration. The success of these projects is often in the balance, hinging on many factors like scope, team-member selection, management support, fate, and so on. Despite all of these factors, many projects succeed and produce astounding results.

The change agent model was developed after observing hundreds of teams, many of them successful and many not. The truly successful projects consistently had three things in common:

1. The team was working on the right thing
2. The team was using the right change process
3. The team made a compelling case for change

Working on the Right Thing

The problem with many teams can best be summarized by a headline that appeared in a recent newspaper: "University Team Attempts to Solve World Hunger." Too often team projects tackle a scope so large and so nebulous that success is nearly impossible. Successful change projects need to be focused on specific things such as outcomes, products, and processes (that is, systems) that will lead to tangible results. Teams cannot solve world hunger (or "improve communication" or "raise morale"), but they can improve the speed of a process by 80 percent or redesign a core product/service to improve customer satisfaction (ultimately improving morale and

Change Agent Skills

Diagnose issues to determine proper change strategies

Work with senior management to pinpoint key areas for improvement

Organize project teams

Lead effective meetings

Manage group dynamics and maximize team participation

Create a compelling case for change

Collect actionable data

Analyze data for improvement opportunities

Conduct customer focus groups

Measure customer satisfaction

Facilitate innovative solutions

Eliminate 80 percent of process cycle time

Get to "yes" by managing the politics of change

Orchestrate large-scale change initiatives

Successful change projects need to be focused on specific things like products, processes, and systems.

communication in the process). The change agent model equips change agents with the ability to diagnose the real issue affecting the organization, to scope the project accordingly, and to select the right change process that will lead to dramatic results.

The Right Change Process

It is amazing how many teams try to fit square pegs into round holes. Although one size rarely fits all, too often teams try to apply a seven-step problem-solving model to every situation they face, or they define everything as a process and try to flowchart their way to improvement. A change agent has to truly understand how business works, how to determine what is preventing the organization from succeeding, and how to apply a change process that makes sense given the situation. Most improvement projects tend to fall into one of four categories: problem solving, process improvement, customer satisfaction, or planning. The change agent model teaches change agents how to manage each type of project. The model also recognizes that no matter what change process is required, the front end and back end of the project are the same. That is, a process-improvement team or a problem-solving team still must have a team charter, team sponsor, and team-member orientation. In addition, these teams will follow the same process once the solutions have been identified; that is, they will sell the ideas, implement the ideas, document their impact, and celebrate success. The change agent model diverges at the change processes and converges after the solutions have been rendered.

A Compelling Case for Change

Most seven-step team processes leave out two crucial steps: diagnosis and creating buy-in. While these models provide great guidance on how to solve a problem or improve a process, they do little to help the organization pick the right things to work on; equally as important, they do not teach the teams how to get their ideas implemented. Change does not happen because it is the right thing to do; rather, a team must be able to make a compelling case for change targeted at the right decision makers and supported by facts that matter to them. The change agent model ensures that teams work on projects that matter to the bottom line, produce dramatic results, and win the support of people in power.

The change agent model integrates the best practices in organizational development, team building, voice of the customer, reengineering, problem solving, creativity, innovation, and project management. In short, it is the whole elephant. By integrating all the pieces, it ensures that teams:

- Identify the right issues to work on
- Scope the project properly
- Identify the right team members
- Use the right tools and processes
- Make compelling cases for change
- Generate breakthrough ideas that get implemented
- Achieve results that are tangible, measured, and celebrated

The Change Agent Model

Diagnosis
Organizing the project
Change processes
- *Customer satisfaction*
- *Process improvement*
- *Problem solving*
- *Planning*

Managing ideas
Creating buy-in
Implementation
Evaluation
Celebration

About This Book

This book is designed for use in meetings as you facilitate teams through the change agent model. Each of the chapters in this book pertains to one of the components of the change agent model. The text of each chapter explains the concepts, provides real-world examples, and enumerates the step-by-step procedure to implement that phase of the change agent model. At the end of each chapter is a series of tools to support the phase of the change agent model. For example, chapter 3 discusses focus groups as a means to determine customer expectations. At the end of chapter 3 tools are provided to help set up and actually conduct a focus group. Snapshots of each tool appear inside the chapter text, and each tool is briefly explained, including the appropriate time to use each and possible pitfalls.

Each of the tools at the end of the chapter consists of four pages. They are laid out in such a fashion that you can use them while facilitating meetings. The first page explains the tool's purpose to you and gives you talking points to explain the tool to the team. The second page provides step-by-step directions for using the tool. An example of what a flipchart page will look like while you are facilitating the tool is included on the third page. The fourth page contains a quick checklist that you can use after completing the tool to see if you did it correctly. If your flipcharts look like the pictures from page three, and if you can affirmatively answer each of the checklist questions, then you probably have done a great job.

In addition, in the appendix you will find a series of project maps. These maps give you a general idea of how you can expect a project to go depending on which change process you are using. I have attempted to give you sample meeting agendas and tools you can use for each step in the process. As we all know, life never goes as planned, and neither will your projects. It is unlikely that your projects will be as linear as these maps, but at least you will have a general idea where you are (and where you should be).

You will notice throughout this book that there is little reference to manufacturing examples. This is by design. There are endless books on improving the manufacturing of a widget, including SPC, Six Sigma, Lean manufacturing, and so on. However, there are very few books that focus on how to improve the work the other 85 percent of us do. Fewer than 15 percent of people make widgets anymore; even inside manufacturing companies, less than 15 percent of the staff are personally manufacturing the product. Most of you are engaged in knowledge or service work in the public, private, and nonprofit sectors. This book is for you.

You will also notice that I reference a particular example, a government team working on improving income tax filing, repeatedly throughout the book. Customer research with change agents new and old revealed a desire to see one example used all the way through the process being described. So you will see a consistent example used to illustrate each tool as well as some real-world anecdotes to illustrate each chapter's core concepts. The reasons I have selected this example are as follows:

1. Tax forms and tax refund processes are not manufacturing.

2. Even those who do not work in government are familiar with a tax form and all of its associated joys. Everybody can relate to this product.

3. I wanted to show that if you could improve what is often considered the worst process on earth, then the principles and tools can work anywhere.

4. It was an actual project that produced actual results: tax refund checks were produced 80 percent faster (fastest in the nation) at less cost, tax forms were made simpler and customized to customer segments, and the organization was one of the first to market with Internet filing.

I know that some of you may feel this example does not apply to you because your organization is free of bureaucracy and politics, but I beg your indulgence.

Endnote

1. The concepts of three levels of improvement are also discussed in *Improving Performance: How to Manage the White Space on the Organizational Chart* by Rummler and Brache (San Francisco: Jossey-Bass, 1995). However, we arrived at our theories independently (that is, I had not read their book until someone pointed out the similarities).

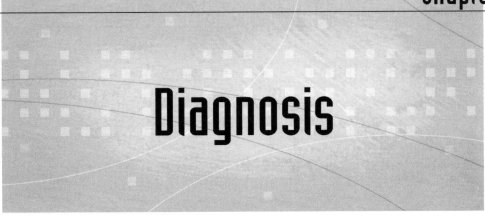

Chapter One

Diagnosis

Tell me where it hurts . . .

Ideally, as change agents, projects would come to us crystal clear. We would know what the issue is and who needs to be involved, and we would have a clear idea of the definition of success. Unfortunately, things seldom work that way. Change agents are often recruited by someone (we will call them a sponsor) who has only the vaguest idea of how the project should unfold. (Note that not all projects are reactive. Many times change agents help the organization proactively identify projects for improvement. See chapter 12 for these methods.) Sponsors typically speak in three languages:

The solution is not the solution because the problem is not the problem.

1. **Symptoms.** They can tell you the pain they are in and the effects it is having on the organization, but they do not know what to do. Examples might include low morale, losing customers, always firefighting, turf wars, and so on.

2. **Objectives.** They can tell you what results they want (like improved customer satisfaction, more productivity, or less rework) but again do not know what to do to make it happen.

3. **Solutions.** They know the solution they want and want your help to get people to "buy in." This is usually a dangerous proposition. Experience has shown that the solution is rarely the solution because the problem is not the problem; that is, you end up treating the symptom and not the cause. For example, I was approached by a sponsor to deal with the "phone issue." Customers could not get through, and once they did, they had to wait an eternity on hold. The sponsor told me that he needed my help to prove to the people upstairs that he needed more staff and more training. By applying the diagnosis methods, however, it became clear that the real problem was not the number of employees but the number of calls. Further diagnosis pinpointed why those calls were happening, and a team was formed to improve the document (product) that caused so much customer confusion.

The relationship between change agent and sponsor is similar to that between doctor and patient. The patient usually comes to the doctor and says either "my stomach hurts" (*symptom*), "I want to feel better" (*objective*), or "give me some morphine" (*solution*).

Once the symptoms or objectives are uncovered, a change agent follows a similar process as a physician:

1. Identify the system.
2. Check vital signs.
3. Select appropriate treatment (change process).

System—*A process (including suppliers, inputs, and people) that produces a product for customers in order to achieve some desired outcome(s).*

Identify the System

Change agents work on the systems in the organization.[1] An organization is actually a collection of systems all working to achieve some desired outcome(s). These systems are independent of any organization structure (which is why most reorganizations rarely produce the results promised; the boxes on the organization chart are different but the systems that produce the work remain the same). Systems usually cut across an organization horizontally. A critical skill of a change agent is to be able to listen to the symptoms being described by the sponsor and to isolate which system is the culprit (see Figure 1.1).

A quick way to find the system is to isolate the deliverable or "service product" to which the symptoms relate. Common troublesome service products include purchase orders, instruction books, forms, performance appraisals, sales forecasts, policy manuals, and so on. Once the products are identified, the rest of the system falls into place.

The *sponsor's interview* tool is a helpful resource during the diagnosis phase of a project. By interviewing the sponsor and other key people related to the issue, you can quickly uncover symptoms, objectives, the product, the system, key players, and potential obstacles.

The *sponsor's interview* tool is a series of questions designed to uncover the following:

Service Product—*A deliverable created as a result of work activity.[2] It is:*

- *A noun*
- *Countable*
- *A unit of output that is given to a customer*
- *Packaged in discrete units*
- *Expressed as something that can be made plural (with an* s)

Examples:

PC Repairs
Purchase orders
Financial audit reports
Grant applications
Strategic plans

- The nature of the problem or issue, including symptoms, objectives, and possible causes
- The importance to or impact on the organization
- Who is affected by or cares about the issue
- The urgency/time frame for resolving the issue
- Project scope and constraints
- Potential players
- Who has the authority to say yes to any recommendations

While you ask the questions, you also should listen for hints that will help you uncover:

- The system
- Where in the system to focus
- The appropriate change process

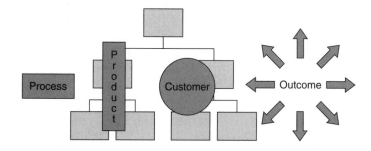

Figure 1.1   The system of work.

Source: Adapted from IMT's workshop, "Creating a Customer-Centered Culture."® Used with permission. (See appendix A.)

The *diagnosis worksheet* (Figure 1.2) is a helpful tool to assist in this endeavor. By completing each of its blanks, you can see the scope of the situation and prepare yourself for the next step: checking the vital signs.

Check Vital Signs

Once the system needing improvement has been identified, you need to identify where in the system to focus (Figure 1.3). The symptoms and objectives (and even the solutions) provided by the sponsor should point the way. However, it will be

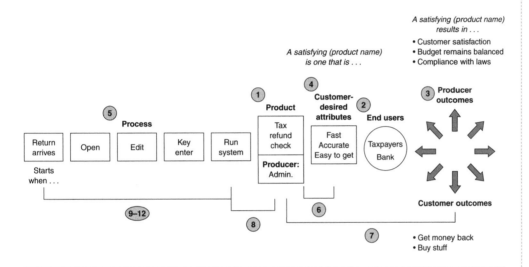

Figure 1.2   Diagnosis worksheet.

Source: Adapted from IMT's workshop, "Creating a Customer-Centered Culture."® Used with permission. (See appendix A.)

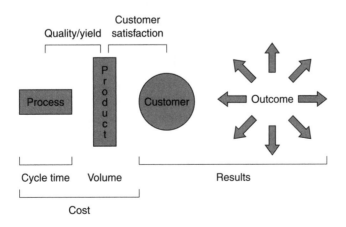

Figure 1.3   What to measure.

Source: Adapted from IMT's workshop, "Creating a Customer-Centered Culture."® Used with permission. (See appendix A.)

helpful to validate these symptoms. You should collect vital data about the system to help pinpoint where you should direct your improvement effort.

In an ideal world, data will be available; in most cases, it is not. If you are able to identify where in the system to focus without the data, then proceed. The team can collect data as part of its project.

Table 1.1 can serve as a guide to some of the more common symptoms and objectives and where in the system they fall.

Select Appropriate Treatment [Change Process]

Once we know where in the system to work, we need to decide which change process to apply. Table 1.2 identifies which change process corresponds with common project objectives.

Table 1.1   Common symptoms and objectives.

Symptoms	Objectives
• Too many phone calls (product)	• Increase customer satisfaction (product/customer)
• Too many customer complaints (product/customer)	• Increase productivity (process)
• Takes too long (process)	• Reduce errors (process)
• Everybody is upset	• Cut costs
• Have to keep redoing it (process)	• Improve communication
• No one cares about quality (process)	• Better results (outcomes)
• Losing customers (customer)	• Speed things up (process)
• Poor communication	• Boost morale

Table 1.2   Change processes.

Objective	Problem Solving	Customer Satisfaction	Process Improvement	Planning
Reduce errors	P		S	
Reduce time (increase speed)			P	
Increase on-time delivery	S		P	
Reduce cost	S		P	
Reduce complexity		S	P	
Increase sales		S		P
Increase customer satisfaction		P		
Increase productivity			P	
Increase the volume of . . .				P
Decrease the volume of . . .	P			
Reduce customer complaints	P	S		
Reduce phone calls	P	S		

P = Primary change process   S = Secondary change process

One project may require more than one change process. Consider, for example, the symptom of *customers cannot get through on the phone.* Further diagnosis may produce the objective to *reduce phone calls.* This objective first will require using the *problem-solving process* to identify the root cause of the phone calls. More often than not, the root cause will be a service product that is difficult to understand (like an instruction book). Redesigning the service product to meet customer expectations is the domain of the *customer-satisfaction process.* Further, data collection may reveal that another large source of the customer phone calls is the question, "Where's my stuff?" This question is typically the result of a slow process with many rejects requiring the assistance of the *process-improvement process.* It is easy to see how one project may require several change processes (Table 1.3) and how critical it is that the change agent not only be proficient in all four but know which ones to use as well.

> *It is easy to see how one project may require all four change processes and how critical it is that the change agent not only be proficient in all four, but know which ones to use as well.*

The Wrong Things to Work on

If I had a dollar for every team project I have seen that was chartered to "improve communication," I would be a very rich man. Improving communication is number one on the top-five list of things *not* to work on. The top-five list, the reasons to avoid the items on the list, and what to do instead follows:

1. **Improve communication.** Exactly what does this mean? People are quick to label all sorts of organizational dysfunction as *communication problems.* Some of those dysfunctions include a horizontal process being managed by a vertical silo organization, a process with numerous handoffs, constant inspection, and no clear definitions of success. Other dysfunctions labeled as *communication problems* include no interaction with the end-user customers or unresolved competing customer interests. A manager who paternalistically withholds "bad news," someone being passed over for a promotion, or co-workers who simply do not like each other are other examples of common dysfunctions labeled as *communication problems.* These latter situations are all quagmires to be avoided at all costs. You will endure much heartburn and have little to no

> *People are quick to label all sorts of organizational dysfunction as communication problems.*

Table 1.3 The change processes.

Customer-satisfaction process	Process-improvement process[3]	Problem-solving process	Planning process
• Define work as a tangible product	• Observe the process	• Define the problem	• What do we want to accomplish?
• Determine customers/roles	• Flowchart the process	• Verify the problem	• How will we know we have accomplished it?
• Segment customers into relevant groups	• Analyze process performance	• Write the problem statement	• What do we have to do differently to accomplish it?
• Determine customers' prioritized expectations	• Improve the process by:	• Look for root cause	• Who will do what by when?
• Measure the degree to which those expectations are achieved	• Reducing cycle time	• Develop the solution	
• (Re)design the product to meet customer expectations	• Increasing precision/certainty		
• Develop innovative new products that better achieve customer-desired outcomes	• Reducing complexity		

impact on the outcome. The other two sets of dysfunctions, process issues and customer issues, can be addressed using the change processes. However, the change agent must complete a skillful diagnosis to pinpoint the system causing the communication issues. Further, the change agent has to sell the sponsor that poor communication is the effect, while a dysfunctional work system is the cause.

2. **Employee satisfaction.** I could go on and on about the reasons not to work on employee satisfaction. In many cases, the reasons are the same as those listed previously. Employee satisfaction is directly related to the science of motivation. Motivation is a science. A body of research exists that has validated what works and what does not. Unfortunately, team after team dabbles in this area with no understanding of what the research has identified. Nine times out of ten, the team recommends an employee of the month program, more parties, and increased pay. Whether you fall in the behavioralist or the intrinsic motivation camp, you can quickly see those solutions are hollow and ineffective. Refer to Frederick Herzberg's seminal article "One More Time: How Do You Motivate Employees?" from the *Harvard Business Review* for a good synopsis of motivational theory.

   Rather than work on employee satisfaction, direct your improvement attention at the systems in the organization where those employees work. By fundamentally improving the systems that satisfy customers and deliver organizational outcomes, you invariably end up improving the lives of the employees.

   For example, I worked on a project in an area of an organization referred to as "the beast." This area had chewed up and spit out some of the best managers I have ever met. Employee dissatisfaction was high, and turnover was rampant. Management and employees had reached an informal stalemate where neither talked to each other. It was no surprise to discover that this area was also the highest source of customer dissatisfaction, rework, cost overruns, and customer-complaint calls. So where is a change agent to start? Boost the employees' pay? Hold a management-employee powwow to create a shared vision? No. None of these would change the system of work that was causing these ill effects. The process still would have 10 handoffs. The work would still be simplified to the point it had no meaning, and customer expectations would still be unclear and unmet. Experience has shown that improving the system and therefore improving customer satisfaction and organizational outcomes ends up improving employee satisfaction. In the case of the beast, all 10 handoffs were eliminated; the functions consolidated into one requiring more judgment and increased skills. The end result was a process that was 80 percent faster, a 50 percent reduction in errors, and higher employee satisfaction because their jobs involved human functions like decision-making, collaboration, and research. Low and behold, higher pay resulted because the jobs had increased complexity. Mission accomplished.

3. **Turnover.** See Number 2.

4. **Projects with no support.** These projects usually occur when an organization decides that "that unit" needs to get better, and they ask "that manager" to form a team and improve it. "That manager" goes through the motions to satisfy the bosses and has no interest whatsoever in seeing anything change. The end result is a frustrated team with good recommendations that go nowhere. *A successful project must have a supportive sponsor.* If the person in

Movement is a function of fear of punishment or failure to get extrinsic rewards. It is the typical procedure used in animal training and its counterpart, behavioral modification techniques for humans. Motivation is a function of growth from getting intrinsic rewards out of interesting and challenging work.
—Frederick Herzberg

charge is not supportive, then either pick another project or find another sponsor higher in the food chain.

Another way this project manifests itself is a team trying to change "those people." That is, a project is undertaken to improve somebody else's system. This is not only unfeasible but also is a quick way to start a war. Projects need to be limited to the team's sphere of influence. While there may be other organizations or units that constrain your success, you cannot arbitrarily change them without their involvement. I have seen many successful projects that involve interagency or interdepartmental cooperation. They were successful largely because the change agent was careful in how the project was organized, including a clear charter, clear roles (including who will approve recommendations), and careful team-member selection.

5. **Projects with no impact on the bottom line.** Countless organizational change initiatives have withered on the vine because they decided to start with "low-hanging fruit." This low-hanging fruit inevitably has no impact on the systems that produce value for customers and the organization. Since all change, no matter how small, seems to take at least six months, management gets bored and moves on to the "next big thing." It is okay to work on some low-impact projects like the employee newsletter or the expense account process, but they should not be the core of your initiative. These projects can supplement the projects that will fundamentally impact the bottom line of the organization.

It is okay to work on low-impact projects like the employee newsletter or the expense account process, but they should not be the core of your initiative.

Take your time doing the diagnosis. Get a second opinion. Just like a surgeon, you do not want to cut into the patient until you are sure of what is causing the pain. Change agents have to live by the same Hippocratic oath: *first do no harm.*

Endnotes

1. This book uses a fairly narrow definition of a system for the purpose of facilitating performance improvement efforts. For broader ideas about systems see the works of Russell Ackoff or Peter Senge.

2. Adapted from Robin Lawton. *Creating a Customer-Centered Culture.* Milwaukee, WI: ASQC Quality Press. 1993.

3. The concepts of the customer-satisfaction and process-improvement processes are adapted from IMT's workshop, "Creating a Customer-Centered Culture."® (See appendix A.)

Sponsor's Interview

What is the issue?

Objectives

- Understand what needs to be improved.

- Understand why it needs to be improved.

- Develop a feel for what the project might entail, who will need to be involved, and how difficult it might be.

Prework

Review the questions and customize.

Think of additional questions to ask.

Research the environment (who is in charge, what does the unit do, how does it fit into the organization, and so on).

Estimated Time

45 to 60 minutes

How to Introduce It

Explain to the sponsor that you want to understand the situation and would like to pick that person's brain about a few things.

Diagnosis
Organize the project
Change processes
Customer satisfaction
Process improvement
Problem solving
Planning
Managing ideas
Creating buy-in
Implementation
Evaluation
Celebration

SPONSOR'S INTERVIEW

Action Steps

1. Describe the situation. What is going on?

2. Why is this an issue?

3. What evidence do we have that the issue exists?

4. Where and when is the issue happening?

5. Who else cares about or is affected by the issue?

6. What have you already done to try and resolve it?

7. What do you think the solution is?

8. How soon does the issue need to be resolved?

9. If we worked on this issue, what results would you hope we could achieve?

10. If we worked on this issue, what undesired results would you hope we could avoid?

11. What obstacles or problems would impact us being successful on this project?

12. Who needs to sponsor the project? (The person that can say yes to recommendations)

13. Who needs to be involved on the project?

14. What materials can I read to get some background on the issue?

If you are still uncertain of the project scope, start asking system questions from the diagnosis worksheet.

Example

1. Describe the situation. What is going on?

   Citizens are complaining about tax refunds taking too long. The phone never stops ringing. We have piles of tax returns waiting to be processed. No one communicates with each other. No one takes responsibility for quality. So much of our time is spent fixing mistakes (our mistakes and the citizens' mistakes). The computer system is antiquated.

2. Why is this an issue?

   We want to please the citizens, because when they are happy, their legislators are happy; and when they are happy, we are happy.

3. What evidence do we have that the issue exists?

   We can produce charts showing size of backlog, number of phone calls, average processing time, and so on. All trends going in the wrong way.

4. Where and when is the issue happening?

   It covers many units inside the Tax Division. Things are pretty calm in January and February, but from March through May it is a nightmare.

5. Who else cares about or is affected by the issue?

   The legislature, accountants, the budget administrators, and treasurer are all affected.

6. What have you already done to try and resolve it?

   A task force was created last year to develop performance standards for processing employees. Also, we have been researching ways to outsource to get more help and currently are exploring new technology.

7. What do you think the solution is?

   We need more people and a better computer system. We also need citizens to stop making so many mistakes and the legislature to stop changing the law.

8. How soon does the issue need to be resolved?

   By next tax season would be great.

9. If we worked on this issue, what results would you hope we could achieve?

   We hope for fewer phone calls, avoiding the need to hire more people, faster turnaround time, and fewer errors.

10. If we worked on this issue, what undesired results would you hope we could avoid?

    Do not make the turf battles any worse. We cannot compromise our legal responsibility.

11. What obstacles or problems would impact us being successful on this project?

    The computer system, the sheer volume of tax returns that come in, and the turf wars are all potential problems.

12. Who needs to sponsor the project? (The person that can say yes to recommendations)

    Stan should sponsor.

13. Who needs to be involved on the project?

    The following departments need to be involved: processing, legal, error correction, forms, phone center, budget, and customer service.

14. What materials can I read to get some background on the issue?

    We will send a strategic plan.

Checklist

❏ I have a good idea what the issue is and what the sponsor wants to achieve.

❏ I am pretty sure about what system needs to be improved.

❏ I have a good feel for the scope of the project and who needs to be involved.

❏ This project is worth doing.

❏ The sponsor is excited and thinks I can help.

Diagnosis Worksheet

What needs to be improved and what change process will we use?

Objectives

- Identify the system needing improvement.
- Identify what part of the system (if not the whole thing) to improve.
- Determine the appropriate change process.
- Identify the right project sponsor.

Prework

Complete the sponsor's interview.

Estimated Time

30 minutes

Diagnosis

Organize the project

Change processes

   Customer satisfaction

   Process improvement

   Problem solving

   Planning

Managing ideas

Creating buy-in

Implementation

Evaluation

Celebration

DIAGNOSIS WORKSHEET

Action Steps

Describe the System

1. Identify the product and the producer around which the symptoms/objectives seem to be centered.
2. Identify the end users of the product. End users are customers who actually use the product to achieve a desired outcome. They are the people we had in mind when we created the product.
3. Define the outcomes expected of the product for the end user and the producer.
4. List the key product attributes likely to be expected by the end user.
5. Describe the major steps of the process that produces the product.

Check Vital Signs (look at data for each of these)

6. Does the product meet customer expectations?
7. Is the product achieving the desired outcomes?
8. Is the process able to produce the product accurately? (If not, do we know the cause?)
9. Is the process able to produce the product in a timely manner?
10. Does the process take too long?
11. Does the process cost too much?
12. Is the process too complex?

Select Appropriate Change Process

Objective	Problem Solving	Customer Satisfaction	Process Improvement	Planning
Reduce errors	P		S	
Reduce time (increase speed)			P	
Increase on-time delivery	S		P	
Reduce cost	S		P	
Reduce complexity		S	P	
Increase sales		S		P
Increase customer satisfaction		P		
Increase productivity			P	
Increase the volume of . . .				P
Decrease the volume of . . .	P			
Reduce customer complaints	P	S		
Reduce phone calls	P	S		

P = Primary change process   S = Secondary change process

Example

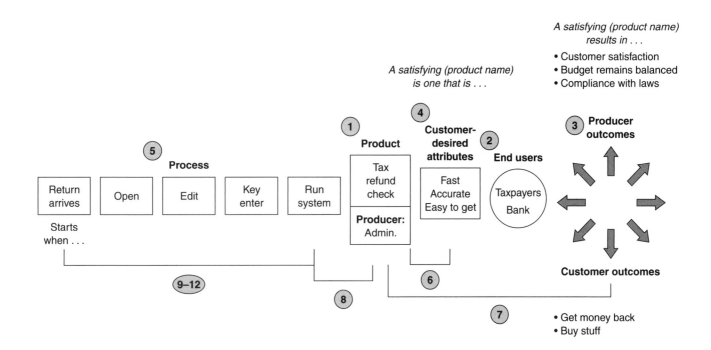

A blank diagnosis worksheet can be downloaded at www.changeagents.info

Checklist

- ❏ The system is clearly defined, including the following:

    - ❏ The product

    - ❏ The producer

    - ❏ The end users

    - ❏ The major process steps

- ❏ I can get my arms around this system.

- ❏ I have a pretty good idea (backed up by data) of what part of the system needs to be improved.

- ❏ I know which change process(es) I will need to use to complete the project.

- ❏ The project is feasible. (I'm not trying to solve world hunger.)

- ❏ I have a pretty good idea of who should sponsor the project and feel they will be supportive

Chapter Two

Organizing the Project

People! People! Work with me here . . .

After diagnosing the situation, identifying the system to be improved, and selecting the right change process, the change agent then plays a crucial role in organizing the actual project.

Change agents work with and through people. There are times that outside agents are needed to give perspective or expertise, but most often change is more successful if it comes from the people inside the organization. People tend to support what they help create. It is not the role of the change agent to ride in on a white horse with guns blazing and solve the problem. Rather, the change agent's role is to:

- Help decide what to change
- Help facilitate what to change to
- Help sell the change
- Help implement the change

Quite often a project is dead before it even begins.

Who is the change agent helping? Teams. Teams are one of the best ways to create change. The type of teams necessary are those that come together to accomplish a goal and then disband. When led properly and when working on the right things with the right change processes, these teams can produce extraordinary results that no individual could produce alone. Teams provide diverse opinions, expertise, and insights. If organized well, teams have a tremendous ability to build on each other's ideas and have a strange way of creating an infectious enthusiasm that spreads throughout an organization like a virus.

Quite often, however, a team project is dead before it even begins. Countless teams have embarked on projects with no clear goals, no readily identifiable roles, little support from management, and no time or resources to accomplish their task. The change agent must ensure that the project is set up to succeed by following four steps:

1. Chartering the team
2. Orienting the team
3. Training the team
4. Conducting the first meeting

Chartering the Team

All teams need a sponsor, the person who is able to say yes to the team's recommendations. It is the sponsor's role to:

- Provide initial direction to the team
- Support the team and help remove obstacles to project success
- Approve the team's recommendations
- Ensure the team's recommendations get implemented
- Celebrate team success and spread the message

Since the sponsor plays a crucial role for the team, it is essential that the right person be selected. First and most importantly, the sponsor must have the authority to approve what the team recommends. Although some recommendations might stray beyond that authority, the sponsor ultimately must have authority over the system being improved. Nothing is more disheartening to a team than to work hard for months to produce excellent recommendations only to find out that the person they are pitching them to cannot do anything about them.

Secondly, the sponsor must be supportive of the change initiative. This cannot be faked. The team members and the rest of the organization will know when a sponsor is not serious about making a change. You do not want to wait until the team presents its proposals to find this out for yourself. It is about commitment. The sponsor does not serve as a team member, so it is not a question of time commitment. The sponsor shows commitment by allowing the team to push the envelope and to think outside the box, by allowing people the time necessary to be productive team members, and by clearing a path through the organization so the team can get what it needs to do the job.

The first responsibility of the team sponsor is to charter the team. A *team charter* (Figure 2.1) is a powerful document that serves two purposes:

- It helps the sponsor clarify expectations and understand what will be necessary to achieve them.
- It provides direction and guidance to the team and proactively answers the most important questions team members have of a project:
  - What results are expected of us?
  - How long will the project last?
  - How much time can I spend on it, and who is going to do my real work?

In addition, the *team charter* serves as a valuable resource for the change agent to keep the team focused and on track.

The *team charter* helps overcome many of the reasons teams fail by doing the following:

1. **Defining the desired outcomes of the project.** The more specific the goals, the better. Ideally you would like to be able to quantify the level of improvement expected, such as 80 percent improvement in process speed, 20 percent increase in repeat customers, and so on. However, this is not always possible. It is important to note that the purpose of the charter is not to define the solution (sponsors really want to do this!). Rather, it should specify what is to be accomplished and should leave how it is to be accomplished up to the team.

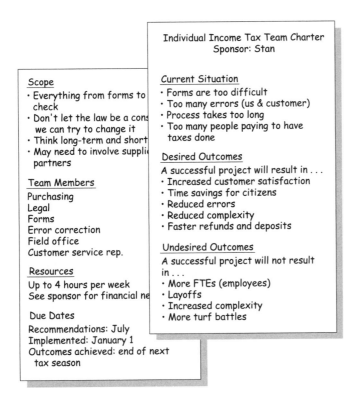

Figure 2.1   Team charter example.

2. **Clearly defining the scope and boundaries of the project.** The charter should communicate what is on the table and what is out of bounds. If the team is looking at a process, the charter should specify where that process begins and ends and what part the team can examine. The size of the scope determines the length of the project. The change agent must ensure that the scope is not so large that it cannot be accomplished (solve world hunger) or so small that nobody cares (install a candy machine in the lounge).

3. **Delineating the right team members.** The right team members are:

   • Familiar with the system being improved

   • Ready (that is, they have the time and want to do it)

   • Open-minded

   • Able to play nicely with others

   Anyone who has ever led a team or has been a team member knows how excruciating the experience can be if the team members do not meet these criteria.

   Picking team members is actually a three-stage process. First, the sponsor (and anyone helping the sponsor brainstorm the charter) should identify the functions that need to be represented on the team. For example, a team chartered to improve the cycle time of ordering and purchasing supplies will need representation from the purchasing department, the accounting department, employees who order supplies, a manager, and any other functions of the process. Second, for each function identified, the sponsor should nominate several people who, in the sponsor's opinion, meet the criteria of a good team member. Third, the change agent needs to interview these people and make recommendations to the sponsor about which ones will work best (see Figure 2.2).

Sound like a lot of work? Try skipping steps two and three and see how you do. (I will send you some aspirin and bandages). There is no substitute for picking the right team members, as you have to live with these people for several months. You cannot pick your relatives, but you can pick your team members.

As you interview people, you will quickly gauge who is ready and who is not. For people that are ready, no obstacle is too large. For people who are not ready, no obstacle is too small. No matter how much expertise people might have, if they do not have the time or commitment level, do not put them on the team. Their absences and inability to carry their share of the load serve only to demoralize the rest of the members who have made a commitment.

Similarly, no matter how much expertise a person may have, if that person is not open-minded to change, do not put him or her on the team. Too often sponsors put someone on the team in hopes that they "get religion." People will invoke the Lord's name all right, but not in a constructive way. Team projects are not rehab centers. Another common team-member pitfall is putting the person with strong ownership over the product or system on the team. Sometimes these people can be good team members; more often than not, however, they resent that a team has been formed to fix their work (and there is no way a bunch of know-nothings—especially those dumb customers—are

1. Have you ever participated as a team member, either at work or in your personal life? Was the experience a success? What made it successful? Unsuccessful? Would you participate again if you have an opportunity?
2. How did you respond the last time a coworker, friend, or family member pitched a new idea to you that you thought was unusual, offbeat, or "outside the box"?
3. What do you think are the most important attributes of a team member?
4. Which of these attributes do you believe you possess? Why?
5. Would you be interested in participating on this team? Why?
6. What assets could you bring to this team?
7. What do you think about change in organizations? Give an example of how you have dealt with change in the workplace.
8. Describe your knowledge/experience with the system this team will be working on.
9. Teamwork requires a commitment of time. Are you willing to commit a minimum of three hours per week for approximately four months?
10. What obstacles may prevent you from being a contributing part of this team?

Figure 2.2   Team member interview questions.

going to tell them how to do their job). For your health and for the sanity of your team, do not include these people. (The team-member interview should help you determine who these people are.) If their expertise is critical to the project, then consider adding them as advisors to call on when necessary (and not vice versa).

Team size should be limited to between six and eight people. You can stretch the number to 10 if necessary. Teams are not a Constitutional Congress; it is not crucial that every precinct is represented. The more members that are added, the more difficult it is to bring the project to successful conclusion in a timely manner. Consider using the advisor role for functions that "just have to be represented" but are not, in your opinion, crucial to the team completing its task. Advisors get called in from time to time so the team can tap their expertise and get their ideas. This gives you the benefit of their knowledge without them coming to all team meetings.

4. **Preapproving the amount of time team members can spend on the project.** Many team members are picked because they are the "stars" in the organization. These stars tend to volunteer for many things and carry a heavy workload. Team members need to know that they have the time to devote to the project. Far too many teams have failed because a key member could not keep up the commitment level. It is not the team member's fault; rather, the sponsor needs to step in and reassign some work to others in the organization so the member can fully contribute. It is vital that you troubleshoot these situations before the project begins.

Team members should plan to devote four hours per week to the pursuit of project goals. Two and a half to three of the hours will be spent in team meetings, while the rest will be spent doing research and supporting the team tasks. Experience has shown that teams are more effective if they meet weekly for at least two hours (see Figure 2.3). Teams commonly want to meet for an hour every week or two hours

Too often sponsors put someone on the team in hopes that they "get religion." People will invoke the Lord's name all right, but not in a constructive way. Team projects are not rehab centers.

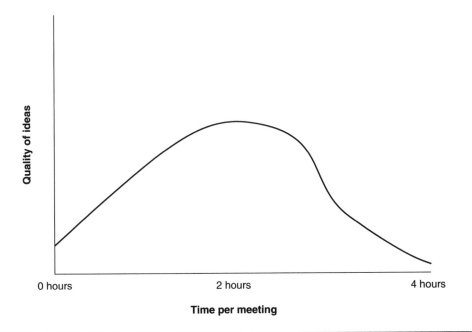

Figure 2.3 Team meeting times.

every two weeks. Both cases are strongly discouraged. Meeting every week encourages commitment from the team and allows for continuity of the project. Biweekly meetings cause many problems. Usually the group spends a great deal of time trying to remember and rehash what was discussed two weeks ago. In addition, members who miss a meeting are a month removed from the project. Meetings that are short in duration can shortchange the brainstorming and innovation you want from the team. Team members feel that they do not have the time to challenge or really discuss an idea because time is running out. The following are observable effects of meeting too infrequently or for too short a time period:

- High team turnover
- High absenteeism
- Members "withdraw"(lose interest but continue to show up)
- One or two people carry most of the load
- The team feels like it is "spinning its wheels"
- Little data are collected to present a compelling case for change to the sponsor
- Final recommendations are simple, with little depth of analysis
- Final recommendations do not get very far "outside the box"

If the organization cannot commit to this time investment, then you obviously are not working on a project that matters to the organization's bottom line. If a team member cannot make this time commitment, then you need to pick someone else. This stage in the charter is a real test of how high a priority the project you are handling is to the organization.

Orient the Team

This step is done to allow the team to learn about the project from the team sponsor. Team members are invited to ask questions about the project and to gauge the level of commitment expected of them as well as the commitment level of the project's sponsor. Many team projects are won or lost at this step. What happens at this meeting can greatly affect the motivational level of the team and the enthusiasm to proceed.

While the main purpose of the orientation meeting is to share the team charter, other critical issues need to be addressed:

- **Introducing the sponsor and the sponsor's role.** The sponsor needs to give all the right vibes. Hopefully the sponsor will avoid saying things like, "this project is important, but I don't want you to forget you have real jobs," or "I want you to be creative, but I want you to be realistic." The team sponsor needs to give every sign that he or she is in favor of this project and will bend over backwards to support the team. It is okay (and quite common) for the team to be skeptical of the sponsor, but it is not okay for the sponsor to be skeptical of the team.

- **Explaining how the project fits into the larger initiative, strategic plan, and so on.** It can be quite motivational to team members to know they are an integral part of the organization's strategy. If possible, try to have the champion of the overall improvement initiative present at the orientation meeting to make this explanation. If the project you are working on is not part of a larger initiative, then the sponsor should spend this time explaining why this project is important.

It is okay (and quite common) for the team to be skeptical of the sponsor, but it is not okay for the sponsor to be skeptical of the team.

- **Maintaining the self-esteem of the people in the area being improved.** It may come as a surprise that not everybody likes change. Not everybody will appreciate the team's efforts, especially those who have pride in the status quo. This can be a sensitive issue and one that needs to be handled delicately by the sponsor. It has been proven effective if the sponsor downplays the problems that have led to the project's creation and instead stresses the opportunities. Comments like "something doesn't have to be broken to be fixed" or "we want to make our best even better" go a long way toward maintaining the self-esteem of the workers and team members.

- **Discussing the time commitment asked of team members.** It is important that this message come from the sponsor. The sponsor should give each of the team members a chance to voice any concerns about this time commitment and should begin the troubleshooting process. All team members should leave this meeting confident that they can devote time to this project without having to work after hours to do their other work. The sponsor should also make it clear that it is perfectly acceptable to opt out of the project. Events happen in people's lives that affect how much commitment they can make to any project. Hopefully your interview will have uncovered this; if not, the team members should know that they can talk to the sponsor after the meeting if they have concerns.

- **Making the team members feel special and honored to be part of the project.** The team sponsor should explain why the various members were picked and what high expectations he or she has of them.

- **Introducing the change agent and his or her role.** A ringing endorsement from the sponsor makes the change agent's job much easier. The team should understand that the change agent will be leading them through a structured process that ensures they are asking the right questions and coming up with the best answers. The change agent is there to manage the team process, allowing the members to focus on the content.

When notifying the team members of the orientation meeting, it helps to ask them to bring their calendars. This allows you to discuss dates for any training you have planned and to book the team's first meeting.

Train the Team

To train or not to train, that is the question. It is not essential that every team be trained before every project. So long as the change agent knows the process and tools, the team may only need to know the change process from a broad perspective. However, team training can be helpful in the following circumstances:

- **When there is a need to introduce a common language to the team or introduce principles with which the team is not familiar.** (Upon reading about the customer-satisfaction process in chapter 3, you will see where this might definitely be the case.)

- **When the team strongly exhibits behavior contrary to the principles of the change process.** For example, team members might have a reputation for not being customer focused and now are going to be undertaking a customer-satisfaction project. Other team members might be legendary for their bureaucratic tendencies and are now being asked to radically streamline a process.

- **When the team needs to have its assumptions challenged.** Oftentimes team members come to a project with a solution in mind and are hell-bent on seeing it through. Team training that broadens their perspective, challenges their assumptions, and lets them see they do not have the problem licked can be very beneficial.

- **When the team is skeptical of the project, the method being employed, each other, and so on.** A credible training program delivered by a skilled and effective presenter can help turn the tide and move skeptics to at least a neutral position.

The real test of whether to train or not to train is this: *Will the team follow you now without it?*

It is helpful to schedule any team training before the first team meeting (and after the orientation meeting). Ideally you will explain any training session to the team at the orientation meeting.

The First Team Meeting

As Table 2.1 depicts, all teams go through four stages. How long they spend in each stage is largely dependent on you. The team charter helps a lot in the forming stage by clarifying purpose, expectations, and roles. The first meeting is a great way to help as well, as it helps establish your credibility as the project facilitator. Many people will not have been exposed to a facilitated meeting and will quickly be surprised at how effective and efficient it can be. The steps that are facilitated in the first meeting are fun and nonthreatening and give the team hope that this project will be nothing like the committees or work groups they have been a part of in the past.

Here are some ideas of what to cover in the first meeting:

- **Explain the four stages of team development and how team members can expect to feel at each stage.** The purpose for doing this is to help the team members realize that the pain they are going to experience from time to time is natural and is not a sign of dysfunction. Having a common understanding of these four stages allows you as the facilitator to point out when the team is in one or the other and to ask for help in getting through it.

Table 2.1 Team stages.

Forming	Storming	Norming	Performing
• Uncertain	• Fighting	• Come together	• Good decisions
• Questioning	• Push back against the project	• Follow team rules	• Shared roles
• Role not clear	• Question roles	• Resolve issues together	• Appreciate each other
• Commitment not yet made	• Tense	• New relationships formed	• Good use of time
• Confusion—what do they want from me?	• Personality conflicts	• Can I help?	• Breakthrough ideas
• Is this project worth my energy (physical)?	• Why did I agree to do this?		• What's next? Bring it on!
	• Is this ever going to get better?		
	• Do I want to continue?		

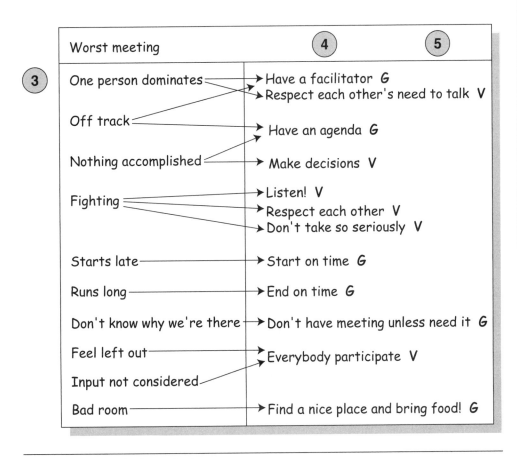

Figure 2.4   Ground rules and values.

■ **Establish team ground rules and values.** Using the *team ground rules and values* tool is another quick way to help the team get through the forming stage and also to smooth the waters during the storming stage. By brainstorming the attributes of horrible meetings and then problem solving them (Figure 2.4), the *ground rules and values* tool becomes a fun way to get the team drawn into facilitation; at the same time, it creates a shared agreement about how the team will function. The *ground rules and values* tool becomes effective for you as a facilitator when team dysfunction sets in. You can simply point to the team-created rules and values and ask the group if any are being violated. It is then up to the team to enforce these ground rules and decide how they are going to proceed.

■ **Develop a team mission statement.** While the team charter provides guidance on the direction of the team, it is helpful to have the team synthesize that charter in a one-sentence mission statement (Figure 2.5). You will be amazed at the discussion the *misson statement template* creates. Inevitably, the discussion causes the need for charter clarification from the sponsor. This is exactly what you want to happen. The team mission also serves as a rallying cry for the team. It is hard to regurgitate a two-page charter, but few teams will forget their one-sentence mission.

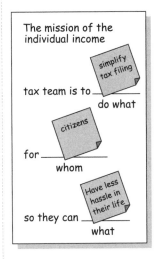

Figure 2.5   Mission statement template.

- **Assign team roles.** There are four critical roles to be filled on any team:[1]
  - **Facilitator.** There is no assigning; you are it. However, you can start to share the role as the team matures. The facilitator is in charge of the process the team will use while remaining neutral on the content. The facilitator acts as an advocate for the sponsor, the customer, each team member, and out-of-the-box thinking.
  - **Team spokesperson.** The team spokesperson is the primary contact with the team sponsor, informing the sponsor of any issues that need assistance and apprising him or her of the team's progress. The team spokesperson is also the group's primary contact if any problems are encountered. With the exception of these duties, the team spokesperson should be no different than any other team member. He or she does not have veto power or any other power over the ideas and recommendations of the team. During a team meeting it should be impossible to distinguish who the team spokesperson is. The team spokesperson does not run the meetings or decide what process the team will use; these are the domains of the facilitator. However, it has proven to be quite successful for the facilitator and team spokesperson to collaborate on meeting agendas and to work together when problems on the team arise.
  - **Recorder of meeting minutes/action items.** The recorder takes the meeting minutes. Meeting minutes do not need to be detailed, play-by-play accounts of all that is said in the meeting. Rather, they are brief statements of what was covered and any key decisions that are made. In addition, recorders keep a running record of action items that occur during the meetings, and they lead the review of action items at the beginning of each meeting to ensure they have been completed.
  - **Recorder of recommendations.** This person is responsible for keeping a running log of the recommendations suggested in the course of group discussions. Throughout the project there will be many ideas (some good, some not) or potential solutions that surface. The team should not act on them until it is time. However, we do not want to lose any ideas. The recorder of recommendations ensures that all ideas are documented so they can be evaluated in the later phases of the project.

  You can augment these roles with any other you choose. Teams often assign a timekeeper, someone to type flipcharts, and someone to handle logistics. These four roles outlined will likely be sufficient for a team, but you may choose to add new roles as necessary.

- **Determine a consistent time (and preferably place) to conduct team meetings.** I strongly recommend meeting for two and a half to three hours every week to maintain team momentum and to complete the project in an acceptable time frame. Many teams have found 10:00 A.M. to 2:00 P.M. a convenient option, as it allows for a working lunch if necessary. Not all meetings will last three hours, and there will be some weeks when the team does not meet at all; however, it is better to cancel a meeting than to scramble to set one up.

During a team meeting it should be impossible to distinguish who the team leader is.

Facilitation Skills

Facilitation is one of the foundational skills of a change agent. Without superior facilitation skills, change efforts struggle to get off the ground. If you ever have been in a facilitated meeting, you have experienced the difference it can make (see Table 2.2). In fact, most facilitators find it hard to sit through meetings that are not facilitated.

While facilitation is a critical skill of change agents, it is not the only one. I have met numerous outstanding facilitators who were not change agents. They were fantastic at managing group dynamics and leading a meeting but were unable to analyze a process or diagnose a performance issue. This book stresses a balanced change agent, with facilitation as one of the five bodies of knowledge.

The Role of the Facilitator

There are two popular uses of the term *facilitator,* and they involve two entirely different roles. The first popular description is what I call a *passive facilitator.* The passive facilitator observes the team, points out issues with group dynamics, and interjects when the team may be getting off track. This is a support rather than a leadership role. While there is a place for passive facilitators (especially with mature teams), this book is not targeted at that role. Rather, a change agent is usually an *active facilitator*—a blending of roles between a team leader and a facilitator.

The active facilitator (referred to simply as *facilitator* from this point forward) designs the process the team will use, leads the meetings using facilitation skills and change process tools, and helps manage the politics of the project. The facilitator is guiding the team—not leading it. The facilitator's job is to:

- **Manage the team process, not the content.** This is the distinction between a team leader and a facilitator. A team leader is someone with outstanding content knowledge and a familiarity with the politics and issues surrounding the team's work. This person is probably not skilled at running meetings or using disciplined change processes and appropriate tools. In short, he or she may not be a change agent. Although the facilitator does not need to be an expert about the content of the team's project, he or she should know enough to diagnose the issue, organize the project, and select the appropriate change process. Often, the team is better served if the facilitator is not familiar with the content. This allows the facilitator to ask "why do you do that?" and perhaps move the team outside the box. The facilitator works with the team spokesperson and leaders on the team to draft meeting agendas and resolve team issues, but the facilitator runs the actual meetings.

Table 2.2   Typical meetings.

Facilitated	Not
• Encourages discussion	• One person dictates
• Consensus	• Voting or no decision at all
• Quick	• Slow pace
• Focused	• Off track
• Tackle hard issues	• Ignore hard issues
• Fun	• Boring

*The facilitator
designs the process
the team will use,
leads the meetings
using facilitation
skills and change
process tools, and
helps manage the
politics of the project.*

- **Help the team ask the right questions and reach consensus on the right answers.** All team projects are a search for answers: How do we reduce errors? How can we do this faster? What does the customer want? Who is going to do what by when? The quality of those answers is dependent on the quality of the facilitation. By using the appropriate change process and its related tools, the facilitator ensures the team is using a systematic approach to find the answers. It is a constant battle to keep the team from jumping to solutions or addressing symptoms rather than causes. The change agent's most powerful weapon is the question; wield it with abandon.

- **Create a roadmap, and guide the team through the process as quickly and painlessly as possible.** This does not mean that the team should rush through its project; nor does it mean there will not be pain. However, the team is counting on you to make this process as smooth as possible. While people want to see improvements happen, there is only so much time and aggravation they are willing to endure. The facilitator is obligated to be organized, clear in his or her direction, and well prepared for all meetings. The skilled facilitator is always thinking two meetings ahead of the team.

- **Serve as the advocate for:**
  - **The customer,** making sure the team never forgets who the customer is and what they said they wanted
  - **The sponsor,** making sure the team stays in bounds and addresses issues that will lead to the desired outcomes in the sponsor's charter
  - **Each team member,** making sure that no one dominates meetings, that everyone has a chance to participate, and that all contributions are valued
  - **Out of the box thinking,** making sure the team comes up with great ideas by pushing them to go further than they would without you

It is important to note that as a facilitator you are not always welcome. The first few minutes of any facilitation with a new group can be quite scary. People that dominate meetings will not appreciate your presence. People that like to "just do it" will not appreciate the deliberate attempts to fully discuss issues and reach consensus. Know-it-alls will not appreciate looking at other options. However, they all get over it. The facilitator has to earn their respect and faith by dazzling them with their subtle skills.

Facilitation skills are acquired in much the same way as wisdom—through time and experience. The best way to become a great facilitator is to do lots of facilitation. Having said that, all facilitators must have the following critical skills:

Neutrality. Facilitators need to remain neutral. It is not your job to solve the problems, offer suggestions, or judge others' ideas. Your job is to facilitate the discussions and let the team make decisions. This is easier said then done. How neutral does a facilitator need to be? There are times when a team is off track or working on a bad idea and you are just dying to jump in. What do you do? Ingrid Bens (2000) offers three strategies for helping a team without compromising your neutrality:

1. **Ask questions.** Instead of giving the team your idea, ask it as a question. For example, instead of saying, "Maybe we should hire temporary employees to fill the gap," ask, "What would be the pros and cons of hiring temporary employees?" The team is still the one making the decision; you simply have given them another question to contemplate.

*While people want to
see improvements
happen, there is only
so much time and
aggravation they are
willing to endure.*

2. **Offer suggestions.** When offering your idea as a question does not work, you may need to offer it as a suggestion. I always start by asking the group, "Would it be okay for me to make a suggestion here?" I then pay very close attention to body language. If both body and voice say it is okay, I will offer a suggestion. However, it is still the team's role to decide what to do with that suggestion.

3. **Take off the facilitator's hat.** This is a method of last resort and should only be used in cases where the team is really in danger of making a serious mistake. Although this does not happen often, when it does, you have an obligation to the team and the sponsor to step in. Before stepping in, make it clear to the team that you are removing your facilitator hat and would like to talk to the group. Let them know that this is not your usual role and that you would prefer not to do it but that you feel something needs to be pointed out.

   For example, I was working with a team on what was supposed to have been a customer-satisfaction project. We went out and talked to customers, prioritized their expectations, and so on. But when it came time to come up with recommendations, the customers' needs were nowhere to be found. The team members ignored the customers' wishes and were working to make their own lives easier. After questioning ("What can we do to address the customer's expectations?") and suggesting ("Do you all remember what the customers said in the focus group?") failed, I had to step in—only because the sponsor and the charter were clear that this project was supposed to be about customer satisfaction and not internal concerns. I removed my facilitator hat and politely told the team, "You can continue down this path if you choose, but I want to advise you that the sponsor will not be pleased. If you will look at the charter, you will see his top priorities, none of which your recommendations address."

Listening (not like how you listen to your spouse but really listening). Listening for emotion, for real meaning, and for hidden cues. A great way to help your listening (and to demonstrate to the team that you are listening) is to paraphrase back what you have heard. For instance, if a team member goes on and on about an issue, you demonstrate you are listening and help the team to understand by saying, "If I understand correctly, what you are saying is . . . ," or, "Let me make sure I've got this; you are saying . . . ." This helps to clarify the issue and also allows the team member to correct any misunderstanding. Summarizing is akin to paraphrasing. Again, you condense what a participant has said into a summary statement (usually capturing it on a flipchart). Summarizing lets you check for clarity and also is a great way to get a team member to stop talking; your summary means that person is done!

Asking questions. This is the fine art of facilitation. You can spot a master facilitator right away because he or she will ask the perfect subtle question that will move a group to a place it never would have gotten to without it. This is the art—to move teams by asking simple, harmless questions. "What did the customers say?" "How does a fast-food restaurant do this?" "Why do you do that?" "What's the one thing preventing us from moving forward?" I believe that the ability to ask the right question is not dependent on facilitation skills so much as business knowledge and a deep understanding of the change processes. That is, if you know how to make change happen, you will know what questions to ask the group members to help them do the same.

This is the art of facilitation—to move teams by asking simple, harmless questions.

In God we trust, all others bring data.

—W. Edwards Deming

Left unchecked, the natural inertia of any team evolves to two people doing all the work, one person doing all the talking, and everybody else mentally checking out.

Challenge assumptions. This goes along with asking questions. One of the best questions you can ask is, "How do we know that?" When you see a team jumping to conclusions or making unproven assumptions, a gentle question can put on the brakes and make them think. Data is the best way to validate or disprove an assumption. As W. Edwards Deming said, "In God we trust; all others bring data." The skilled facilitator looks for places where assumptions are hurting the team's progress and challenges them with a question. (Note that you are not challenging the team member; rather, you are challenging an assumption. You must not make this confrontational. Another powerful question to ask is, "What assumptions are we making here?" This allows the other team members, instead of you, to challenge the assumptions.)

Cultivate participation. Left unchecked, the natural inertia of any team evolves to two people doing all the work, one person doing all the talking, and everybody else mentally checking out. It is the facilitator's job to stop this inertia by diligently cultivating participation at all times. Whether it is asking for people's thoughts ("Mary, what do you think about what Tom just said?") or delegating team tasks ("Greg, could you help us find participants for the focus group?"), it is your responsibility to keep people engaged from beginning to end. Everyone has something to offer; we just do not know when it will be. If they check out before their time, we have wasted their presence on the team. Another great way to cultivate participation is to "reflect" questions. For example, if a team member asks the facilitator, "What should be done about X?" the facilitator can turn to a different team member and say, "What do you think should be done about X?" The facilitator should try to answer very few questions, reflecting them instead to the team to maximize participation and to maintain neutrality.

Maintain team members' self-esteem. This goes hand in hand with cultivating participation. One of the drawbacks of participating is that sometimes you get shot. Even though team members are usually adults, they can often regress to elementary school behavior, whether it be taunting, ridiculing, ignoring, backstabbing, you name it. These behaviors cause people to withdraw, so the facilitator must work to preserve each member's self-esteem. This can be simple, like thanking somebody for his or her idea, or it can be tough, like a team member calling another a moron. There will be some team members who offer up, for lack of a better euphemism, dumb ideas. As soon as the ideas roll off their tongue, you are awestruck by the magnitude of the dumbness. And it is not just you; the whole team feels the same way. Yet, you have to maintain that person's self-esteem by not letting others criticize the idea and by offering the person opportunities to save face or redeem himself or herself. Maintaining self-esteem takes time; it is easier to try to keep the team moving than to stop and build somebody up. But you will pay in the end when there is no passion to implement the team's work. I have seen too many teams cross the finish line with one person left standing and seven battered psyches limping along behind. Take the time to care.

Keep the team on track. As mentioned previously, teams put their faith in you to make their project as efficient and painless as possible. When meetings get off track and conversations meander, team members are looking to you to stop it. Facilitators always walk a fine line between encouraging discussion and wasting time. The following are examples of questions you can ask to make sure a discussion is necessary: "Is this discussion going to help us figure out . . . ?" "While this is a great discussion, should we be having it now?" The team may come back and say, "Yes, we need to talk about this." That is great. However, if it is obvious that a discussion is way off topic, ask the group, "Would you mind if we table this discussion until a later time?" Then write the topic down in the parking lot (a special flipchart page reserved for this purpose) and come back to it at the appropriate time.

As a facilitator, here are some things to keep in mind:

Do not sit. When you are standing, you are the focal point of the meeting. When you sit, there is no focal point and discussions start to meander. Remember that the person with the pen (marker) has the power.

Do not ignore somebody. Even if the person drives you crazy, you have to continue to maintain his or her self-esteem. If this person simply talks way too much, talk to him or her after a meeting and politely say, "You've got a lot of great ideas and you are really contributing to the discussions. However, I think you might be contributing too much. It seems like the other team members don't talk as much because they figure you're going to have the answer. I want to make sure everyone contributes as much as you do. Would it be okay if for the next few meetings you wait until someone else talks before you contribute? That way we can start getting others more involved."

Do not judge ideas. When you judge one idea, you have crossed the line from facilitator to team member and you have compromised your neutrality. Even if it seems like no big deal at the time (because it was a really bad idea), team members will take notice and will be afraid that you will judge their ideas. All sorts of suspicions start to manifest themselves: Is he trying to make us do what he wants? Is he protecting Ted? Is there already an accepted solution and she's manipulating us to come up with it? Simply put, don't judge ideas—good or bad.

Do not offer solutions.

Do not get so wrapped up in a tool that you forget its purpose. The purpose of a tool is to help a team discuss and make decisions. Tools are there to assist teams in making decisions; they do not replace the team's decision making. For example, a facilitator was using a decision matrix to help a team select a software vendor for a major project. The team developed the criteria, weighted them, and then ranked each vendor against the criteria. When the scores were added up, a certain vendor won. However, the team did not want to use that vendor. Unfortunately, the facilitator said, "That is what the rankings show, so that's what we're going with." Instead, the facilitator should have recognized that the team was uncomfortable with the vendor and should have worked to uncover some latent criteria that were causing the dissonance. The tool still would have been helpful in triggering the discussion, uncovering the latent criteria, and challenging assumptions.

Do not give up. No matter how bad things get, never give up. Take a time out, cancel a couple of meetings until you can better see the project's future, or interview some people, but never quit. As mentioned previously, never sit down in a meeting. This is a sign to the team that you have relinquished control and anything goes.

Tools are not a substitute for rational thought.

Facilitation Phases

There are three phases to any facilitation:

- Before the meeting
- During the meeting
- After the meeting

Before the Meeting

As a change agent, you may be called on for two types of facilitation: a one-shot deal or an ongoing project. All of the following applies to both situations; however, some of the before-the-meeting items will not need to be addressed for each meeting of a team project.

Typical one-shot facilitations include tasks such as brainstorming a mission statement, leading a goal-setting session, helping a group make a decision, solving a conflict, and so on. Each of these essentially become mini-projects. That is, you have to do almost everything you would do for a full team project, including diagnosing the issue and the sponsor's expectations; organizing the meeting and its participants; planning the appropriate process and selecting the right tools; and managing ideas and ensuring these ideas are implemented, evaluated, and celebrated.

There are five steps to be completed before each facilitation:

1. **Diagnosis.** As a change agent, you likely will be asked to facilitate planning retreats, high-level meetings, parts of a conference, and so on. Usually, someone asks you to facilitate, and often that person will have a set idea in mind of what he or she wants you to do. For example, you might get a call asking you to facilitate a mission statement for a group. The first question you need to ask is "Why?" Why do they think they need a mission statement? I have been asked to facilitate numerous mission statements when what the sponsor really wanted was for two warring factions to get along better. (A mission statement rarely helps that.) Before each facilitation, you should diagnose the situation. You can use the same tools from chapter 1: the *Sponsor's Interview*, the *Diagnosis Worksheet*, an informal *Team Charter*, and so on. At the least, you should know the following:

   - The desired and undesired outcomes of the meeting
   - What they plan on doing next
   - Who should be involved
   - The urgency
   - The time frame
   - What they have already done to address the issue

   The last one is crucial. Be wary that whatever the sponsor is suggesting may have already been done last year, or the year before. For example, the sponsor might be new, but the staff is not, and they came up with a mission statement last year. In another situation, you might propose a strategic plan as the proper course of action only to discover that the group has a five-year strategic plan they are still using. The best way to avoid a painful injury in front of a large group is to do the proper diagnosis.

Once you have the situation diagnosed, you will want to pay special attention to who is invited to participate. The number of people will greatly affect the process and tools you can use. For example, a common situation you will encounter is that a sponsor wants you to fill two hours of a two-day retreat. The time frame and participants are already set. You then have to do a lot of work to understand the purpose of the retreat, what is being conducted before and after your part, the participant's backgrounds and level of cooperation (friend or foe). Although the ideal situation involves you selecting the process and tools first and then working with the sponsor to pick the participants, this rarely happens.

2. **Prepare the facilitator's agenda.** The facilitator's agenda is different than the meeting agenda. The facilitator's agenda is a minute-by-minute schedule of the meeting that you can use to stay focused and manage the clock. Before creating the agenda, you should have a clear idea of what process and tools you are going to use to achieve the meeting's purpose. For example, if the meeting is designed to develop a mission statement and to reach consensus on the major goals of the organization, you might create the facilitator's agenda shown in Figure 2.6.

You will be amazed how much you use this agenda during the meeting. When you get that deer-in-the-headlights look on your face, it is helpful to glance at a piece of paper and know what you are going to do next.

Facilitator's Agenda
10:00 Sponsor kicks meeting off.
10:05 Introductions.
• Name, title, what would you be doing if not here? What would you rather be doing?
10:15 Explain day's agenda and ask for questions.
10:20 Explain mission template.
10:25 Develop mission statement.
11:00 Break.
11:15 Finish mission statement if necessary.
11:30 Explain affinity diagram.
11:35 Generate affinity ideas.
11:45 Participants read all the ideas and go to lunch.
1:00 Review.
1:05 Sort ideas.
1:20 Develop goal statements.
1:45 Wrap-up and adjourn.

Figure 2.6 Facilitator's agenda.

3. **Prepare the room setup.** Well before the meeting takes place, you should have an idea of how you want the room set up. The process and tools you select as well as the number of participants will determine this. Figure 2.7 shows the ideal room setups for different types of meetings.

A few rules of thumb follow:

- Divide the room into teams at tables whenever possible.

- A table should have no fewer than five and no more than eight people. (Thus, if a meeting has six people, put them at one table. If the meeting has nineteen people, put them in two tables of six and one table of seven.)

- Divide and conquer. Try to find as many ways as possible to accomplish your agenda by using team participation. Try to give each team something separate to work on that they can then share with the group. For example, if the group brainstorms six goals, give three tables each two goals to brainstorm strategies. You never want to repeat the same process over and over again with the same group (like brainstorming strategies, or developing action plans for each strategy). An effective method is to complete the process once as a large group and then divide it out to the teams.

One thing you can always count on is that the room will never be set up to your specifications. Always arrive at least 30 minutes before you expect the participants to arrive. You will spend that time rearranging tables, hunting down missing equipment, panicking, and improvising.

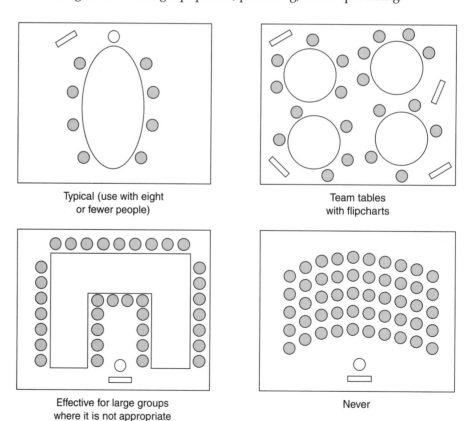

Typical (use with eight or fewer people)

Team tables with flipcharts

Effective for large groups where it is not appropriate to break into smaller teams

Never

Figure 2.7 Ideal room setups.

Toy company research has shown that creativity improves 70 percent when heads are raised 30 degrees.

4. **Prepare your materials.** The facilitator's best friend is his or her flipchart. I have developed a speech impediment; I cannot talk without a flipchart. Flipcharts are the most underused and most effective piece of office equipment around. A flipchart does the following:

- It creates a focal point for people's attention and the discussion.
- It makes ideas visual.
- It increases creativity. (People are 70 percent more creative when their head is up.)
- It records ideas so little note taking is necessary.
- It allows for group participation.

I can tell how effective a leadership team is by walking in their conference room. If there is a well-used flipchart, I know the team is pretty effective. If no flipchart is present, I can guess at the kinds of meetings they have and how decisions are made.

Each person will have his or her own style when writing on flipcharts. Some people are able to get very artistic, while others are lucky enough to not write downhill. The following are some general rules when writing on a flipchart:

- Write legibly.
- Write large.
- Use large markers. (I prefer scented markers.)
- Alternate colors for clarity or to add emphasis.
- Use dark colors (blue, black, or purple) for text, and save the reds for underlining.
- Spelling does not matter.

In addition to flipcharts, you will want to have a giant stash of stick-on notes of all sizes and colors as well as some permanent markers that are thicker than a ball-point pen but thinner than a marker. As you know, stick-on notes are the greatest invention known to man. As a facilitator, you will find unlimited uses for them. I use these notes extensively to capture ideas. The ideas then become portable for use in other tools, to give to a table to discuss, to discard, and so on.

You may also want to come equipped with the following:
- Masking tape
- Pens
- Stick-on flags
- Paper clips
- Note pads
- Transparencies and markers
- Stick-on name tags
- Aspirin
- Dry-erase markers

Facilitators have found it helpful to package all of the above into a bag or case so the items are always at their disposal. You may find yourself adding items over the years (bandages, anesthesia, crutches, and so on).

5. **Practice! Practice! Practice!** This goes for any meeting you are leading. Try to practice the tools you will be using with the team's real situation. For example, if you have to facilitate a mission statement, practice writing one for the organization. This should help you anticipate where the team might get stuck or where disagreement might occur. If you are leading a brainstorming session, practice different questions to see which might yield the best answers. By practicing the tools ahead of time, you get a better feel for how long they might take, how you can better divide them up to increase participation, or whether the tool is even appropriate for what you are doing. I have never had a meeting where the practice before did not change the agenda in some way.

During the Meeting

For a facilitator, a meeting can be a lot like conducting a symphony orchestra or a lot like working at a day care center. Which one you get depends on your level of preparation. While most of the battle is won before it has begun, there are some key things you should do during the meeting while you are executing your planned strategy.

1. **Start with introductions and an icebreaker.** Any time a new group comes together, they need to be introduced to each other. Try to go beyond the usual name and job title. I like to have the participants say what they would be doing if they were not in this meeting and what they would rather be doing if not at work at all. These two give some insight into what they do all day, their hobbies, and possibly some baggage they are bringing to the meeting.

   Icebreakers are a matter of personal preference. While some people love them, others think they are too touchy feely. If you choose to do one, consider the following:

   • Know your audience.
   • Keep it short (preferably under five minutes).
   • Make it relevant to the rest of the meeting.
   • Make sure it is politically correct (blonde jokes are not good icebreakers).

2. **Explain the meeting agenda.** The participants need to feel confident in the scope and direction of the meeting before they will let you lead them. You do not have to go through the facilitator's agenda; just give them the high points—the purpose, the activities, and next steps. Remember that at all times participants worry about three things:

   • What are we doing?
   • Why? (How will it help us accomplish our task?)
   • What is next?

   After explaining the agenda, ask the group if the agenda is acceptable. This step is crucial, for this is where you will find out that the group already has a mission statement, or that they already have a plan. Whenever I ask this question, I brace myself for whatever is coming. But you have to do it. You cannot lead people down a path they do not want to go down.

   As a facilitator, I never like to start the meeting. I prefer to have the person who invited me give me some kind of introduction and explain why I am there. This helps build your credibility with the group (unless the group does not like the person who invited you!).

At all times participants worry about three things:

■ *What are we doing?*

■ *Why? (How will it help us accomplish our task?)*

■ *What is next?*

3. **Manage the clock.** If you have a minute-by-minute facilitator's agenda, this becomes pretty easy. You should know where you are supposed to be by when. In addition, you should have already thought about what you will cut if you get behind and what you will add if you get done too early. As the meeting commences, some things will take more time and some will take less time than you anticipated. The facilitator's motto (taken from Clint Eastwood in *Heartbreak Ridge*) is *Improvise, Adapt, Overcome.* You will need to do all three.

Facilitators' Motto: Improvise, Adapt, Overcome

   Another motto that helps is "break often—leave early." If you can accomplish everything on the agenda and get people out early (not too early), they will love you. However, you cannot forget the importance of breaks. The mind can only absorb what the behind can endure. I try to let people take a break every hour or every 90 minutes at the worst. Smokers need at least seven minutes to smoke a cigarette, so breaks should be at least ten minutes. Break time is also your time to catch your breath, to rearrange the agenda, to check with people about the pace, to think about group dynamics, to change room temperature, and so on.

The mind can only absorb what the behind can endure.

4. **Constantly update the participants** on the three things they care about: What are we doing? Why are we doing it? What is next? Do this after each part of the agenda.

5. **Check the feeling in the room** regarding the process, the progress, and group dynamics. Ask for feedback on how things are going. Look for body language, including signs that things are going too slow (head in hands) or signs that the room is too cold (someone has gone to the car to get a stadium blanket). Work the room while people are engaged in an activity and listen to what is being said and how people are treating each other. Step in where appropriate.

6. **End the meeting by summarizing** what they have done, why it is important, and what will happen next with all the work they have done. Thank the group, and let them go. Another thing I like to do at the end of a meeting is to give out my phone number and tell them that if they come up with any more ideas while they are driving home or are in the shower to give me a call. Someone always does.

After the Meeting

The facilitator's job is seldom done after the meeting ends. There are usually some loose ends to tie up. It is advisable to check with the sponsor to see how the meeting went. Did it meet the sponsor's expectations? Was he or she pleased? You will probably need to type the flipcharts in a manner to be distributed to the participants. If the session was just one part of a series of sessions (like a team project), you will want to reevaluate your overall game plan and make any changes in strategy.

Managing Group Dynamics

One of the most challenging parts of facilitation (and being a change agent) is understanding people and their motivations. Facilitation is one part strategy and two parts psychology. The more you understand about people and human behavior, the better off you will be. There are many schools of behavioral psychology, and I cannot begin to do any of them justice here. They all have pros and cons. However, I have found one explanatory tool that has been most helpful for my change agent colleagues and me: the Myers-Briggs Type Indicator.

The Myers-Briggs Type Indicator categorizes people into 16 different personality types based on combinations of preferences. You will innately tend to be classified as follows:

Introverted or Extroverted

INtuitive or Sensing

Thinking or Feeling

Perceiving or Judging

The combination of these preferences determines your personality type, or how you tend to behave. For example, I am an Introverted INtuitive Thinking Judger, or an **INTJ** in "type" language. So what does that mean? I'll expose my inner workings and shortcomings to help explain.

Introversion vs. Extroversion

Introversion and *extroversion* describe how people interact with the world. They also describe where an individual gets his or her energy—internally or externally.

Extroverts thrive off of being around people. They get their energy from others. They are outgoing, expressive, and have little trouble talking to perfect strangers. Introverts get their energy from inside, through reflection. Being around a lot of other people, especially strangers, drains their energy. Cocktail parties are a nightmare for introverts.

It is important to note that there is no value judgment associated with the preferences. Extroverted is not better than introverted. However, if you are going to be a salesperson, extroversion would help. The Myers-Briggs types are not labels or judgments; they are simply a way to understand other people and especially yourself.

Sensing vs. Intuition

Sensing and *intuiting* refer to how people prefer to gather data. Sensors look to the external environment (empirical observations) and to experience when gathering information. Intuitives look inwardly to their mind and imagination.

People who are sensing tend to be "sensible." They are practical, they want facts, and they do not like change. They do not like to talk about hypotheticals or fantasies but want to stick to reality and experience. They are highly observant of things in their immediate environment. Sensors see the details rather than the big picture and lean toward precision. When asked what time it is, they will reply, for example, "4:03." Sensing parents want their child to go to college and major in something useful like accounting.

Intuitives think about things differently. They are the idea people—always thinking of a new way to do something. They are the innovators, and they make sensors crazy. Their heads are in the clouds, and they revel in imagery and metaphors. They see the big picture and get frustrated by the details. When asked what time it is, they will reply, for example, "around 4:00." Intuitive parents want their child to go to college to learn how to think and to experience new things. I have been asked repeatedly, "What makes a good change agent?" If the questioner understands the Myers-Briggs types, I will tell them that any letter combination is okay, but I prefer that it has an **N** in it. A change agent cannot be innately resistant to change, set in his or her ways, and overly practical.

Feeling vs. Thinking

Feeling and *thinking* describe how we make decisions. Feelers make choices based on how something feels. For example, in deciding whether to hire a new person, feelers will look to their feelings to help make the decision. How do I feel about this person? How will others in the work area feel? Thinkers make choices objectively; they think it through. For the same hiring decision, thinkers might evaluate the applicant against some set criteria, weigh their experience against the job criteria, and study the effects on salaries in the work area. Oftentimes feelers describe thinkers as "cold hearted," while thinkers will describe feelers as "touchy feely." As David Keirsey and Marilyn Bates (1984) describe in their excellent book *Please Understand Me*, "an **F** wife may insist that her **T** husband 'let his feelings show' while he might wish she 'would be logical for once!' " (Welcome to my house!)

Another key difference between thinkers and feelers is how they react in situations. Thinkers tend to stay calm and react in an objective manner. Feelers get more engaged and may end up taking on the situation as their own and investing a lot of emotion in it. In a meeting, a thinker is more concerned with being right than being liked. A feeler may be just the opposite. Each presents its own facilitation challenges.

Judging vs. Perceiving

Judging and *perceiving* describe how people prefer to orient their lives (Kroeger and Thuesen 1992). Judgers tend to be more structured and organized (Felix), while perceivers are more spontaneous and open (Oscar).

Judgers prefer to make decisions. They want closure, they tend to set deadlines and meet them, and they are organized. Judgers are constantly waiting on perceivers. Perceivers like to put off decisions until they have more information. They do not like closure and would prefer to keep options open. Perceivers are not fans of deadlines and are also playful. Perceivers just want to have fun. Their response to judgers is, "What's your hurry?" Judgers want to get the job done. They often describe perceivers as indecisive or wishy-washy, while perceivers may describe judgers as driven, pushy, and inflexible. Again, neither is better than the other; there are just differences.

Have you found yourself in these descriptions? If not, I would recommend the following references:

> David Keirsey and Marilyn Bates. *Please Understand Me: Character and Temperament Types*. Del Mar, CA. Gnosolgy Books. 1984.

> Otto Kroeger with Janet M. Thuesen. *Type Talk at Work: How the 16 Personality Types Determine Your Success on the Job*. New York: Dell Publishing. 1992.

Both of these resources include a test or quiz to help you determine your type and then provide detailed explanations of what each means.

In addition, www.keirsey.com contains an on-line test to determine your type. It is free and includes some great links to resources on understanding the personality types.

For personality-type novices and people with busy lives, it is hard to remember all the different letter combinations and what they mean. Similarly, looking at a new team of eight people, how can you know what type they are? (If only people would wear their type on a necklace, life would be so much easier.) Fortunately, there is a shortcut.

The sixteen personality types tend to group themselves into four main temperaments. These temperaments are described by David Keirsey and Marilyn Bates in *Please Understand Me* as two-letter combinations. A popular workshop created by Don Lowry[2] uses colors instead to describe each of these temperaments.

The Gold temperament *(SJ)*. Golds are the protectors of sacred institutions. They are stable, sensible, task-oriented individuals. They are the ones who are on time and want a detailed agenda. They are the ones that reject your expense account because you included tax in your tip calculation.

The Orange temperament *(SP)*. Oranges live by the motto "just do it!" They want action, they like to have fun, and they are risk takers. They are the ones who plan the office party and then sneak a keg of beer into the copy room.

The Green temperament *(NT)*. Greens love intelligence and knowledge. They like complex theories and value intellectual stimulation. Greens love to read. They are pretty much oblivious to other people's feelings. They despise errors and inefficiency. They are the ones who interject Stephen Hawking's theories on time into a staff meeting about punctuality.

The Blue temperament *(NF)*. Blues are all about people. They care how decisions affect people, and they want meaningful relationships with people. They want to talk. They are the ones who want the team to do a group hug.

Obviously, I am exaggerating and poking fun at the different temperaments. Again, each temperament is valuable. No one is better than the other. However, each has its strengths and weaknesses. Ideally, you would like your team to have a balance of each color, but that rarely happens. Table 2.3 depicts how to work with each of the temperaments on a team. As a facilitator, you should be able to quickly deduce each team member's type and act accordingly. You will need to plan your meetings and their activities to meet the needs of all four. For example, if you are planning a brainstorming meeting, the **oranges** *(SP)* are going to want to get up and move around, the **blues** *(NF)* are going to want to sit and talk, the **golds** *(SJ)* are going to be concerned with whether they are doing it right, and the **greens** *(NT)* are going to challenge the process. You need to accommodate them all. People ignorant of type theory tend to think all of the world should think and act like they do, and they plan activities and meetings to suit their preferences. That is, they project their personality type onto the group. For example, an **orange** facilitator might plan many hands-on, fun team activities, but if the team is full of introverted **greens,** she is in trouble. It is vital that a facilitator and change agent understand the people with whom they are working.

Once you understand people and yourself, you will start to change the way you communicate and the way you plan your facilitations. In addition to personality types, there are also some other types of people you will encounter along the way. Figure 2.8 represents a rogues gallery of the "problem" people you will get on any team.

Table 2.3 Facilitating personality types.

Personality	Facilitation Tips
Blue (NF) • Search for meaning and authenticity • Empathetic • See possibilities in institutions and people • Communicate appreciation, enthusiam, approval • Highly responsive to interpersonal transactions • Keep in close contact with staff • Highly personalized • Give and need strokes freely	• Give them opportunity to talk • Take time out of project to let people socialize and build relationships • Have them buddy up with others when working on a task • Discuss the "human" or "people" side of decisions
Green (NT) • Hunger for competency and knowledge • Work well with ideas and concepts • Intrigued and challenged by riddles • See systematic relationships • Focus on possibilities through nonpersonal analysis • Like to start projects but not good with follow through • Not always aware of other's feelings • Responsive to new ideas	• Delegate "system" or "conceptual" issues to them • Have them research issues, best practices, and possible solutions • Involve heavily in idea phase of projects; don't expect much during implementation • Be prepared to be challenged on the ideas, methods, and tools you present to the group • Reinforce the big picture and how what currently doing fits in • Help maintain the self-esteem of other team members
Gold (SJ) • Hunger for belonging and contributing • Prize harmony and service • Orderly, dependable, and realistic • Understand and conserve institutional values • Expect others to be realistic • Supply stability and structure • More likely to reward institutionally rather than personally (trophies, letters, etc.) • Can be critical of mistakes more easily than rewarding of expected duties	• Delegate "fact-finding" to them • Use them as devil's advocates in ideas • Will be wary of challenging rules and authority; find ways to reinforce that it is okay to question and change things • Will want approval/recognition from higher ups; find opportunities for that to happen • Excellent during implementation phase; not strong during idea phase • Pair them with greens during supporting ideas stage
Orange (SP) • Hunger for freedom and action • Deal with realistic problems • Flexible, open-minded • Willing to take risks • Highly negotiable • Can be perceived as indecisive • Challenged by "trouble spots" but not long term • Best at verbal planning and short-range projects	• Build activities into team's work; let them be active • Involve them in "coordination" activities (setting up focus groups, planning celebration event, etc.) • Use tools to help them make decisions, but allow oranges time to reflect and get comfortable with decision • Involve heavily in implementation; use them to help sell ideas • Make meetings fun

Source: Don Lowry is the creator of the True Colors® personality type methodology and associated training courses. The temperament letters were created by David Keirsey and Marilyn Bates (1984).

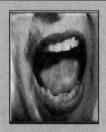

Blabber Mouth

M.O.

To talk all the time about "whatever"

How to Handle

- Review ground rules.
- Keep reminding the group members that they need to stay on track.
- Ask Blabber Mouth to hold any side discussions until after the meeting.
- Dedicate 5 minutes at beginning of each meeting for discussion and talking.
- (See Dominator.)

Brick Wall

M.O.

Won't budge . . . on anything

How to Handle

- Why will they not budge? Get to the root cause, and look for faulty assumptions (or they may be right).
- Ask what it would take to get them to change their mind. (It is usually a concern the team has not addressed.)
- See the team sponsor.

Buddha

M.O.

The group will not make decisions without this person's wisdom.

How to Handle

- Buddhas usually earn it. They have a lot of knowledge and expertise. They do not try to be the Buddha; they just are.
- Talk to Buddha off-line, and share your concern. Teach him or her how to reflect questions to the group to maximize participation.

Devil's Advocate

M.O.

Always raises the opposing viewpoint.

How to Handle

- Seeing the other point of view can be constructive unless it is meant to be destructive. If it persists, ask Devil's Advocates to identify what they like about the idea before they oppose it.

Dominator

M.O.

To dominate every discussion.

How to Handle

- Call on other people first.
- Use structured brainstorming.
- Meet with them off-line and politely tell them that you think they are contributing too much and that maybe they could help you get others to contribute. You still want them to talk, but give others a chance too.

Einstein

M.O.

Already has the whole thing figured out.

How to Handle

- They are usually wrong.
- Tell them to wait until the solution or idea phase before sharing "the answer." (Have them write it down in the meantime.)
- Let them give "the answer" and record it on a flipchart. Tell the team that we will see if this is the right answer once we get to the idea or solution phase.

Figure 2.8 Rogues gallery.

Best Friends

M.O.

Always talking to each other during the meeting

How to Handle

- Stand behind them.
- Ask a question of the person sitting next to them.
- Ask one of them a question.
- Do not let them sit together.
- Talk to them off-line about your concern.

Church Mouse

M.O.

Says nothing . . . ever

How to Handle

- Do you know why they do not talk? Off-line ask them. It is usually one of three things:

  a) They do not like the project and wish they did not have to be there.
  b) They have nothing to say.
  c) They do not feel safe to contribute.

- For a) and b) consider freeing up their future. For c) get to the root of the concern and solve it. (It is usually one of the other rogues.)

The Pack Mule

M.O.

Does all the work for the team—carries all the burden

How to Handle

- Ask them off-line to let others volunteer for tasks.
- Assign tasks to other people.

Needler

M.O.

Makes a sarcastic comment about everyone and everything

How to Handle

- How does the group feel? Are they okay with it? Is it hurtful or disruptive?
- Make it a ground rule not to criticize others and their ideas.
- Talk to them off-line and tell them that while you think they are funny, other people's feelings might get hurt. Ask if they could tone it down.

Senator

M.O.

Cannot make any decisions without talking to his or her "people" first. Thinks the team is a representative democracy.

How to Handle

- Make sure the Senators know what will be on the agenda ahead of time so they can get input *before* the meeting.
- Have the sponsor explain the team member's role better.
- See if there is someone else from the Senator's district who should be on the team with the Senator—so that person can decide.

2Cool4U

M.O.

Pop in and out of meetings
Answer every page and cell call
Miss meetings

How to Handle

- Review the team ground rules with 2Cool4U, and ask if he or she can commit to them.
- Have the sponsor communicate the importance of the project to 2Cool4U.
- Remove 2Cool4U from the team.

Figure 2.8 Continued.

Once you are able to manage individuals, you are left to manage their interaction as a team. Teams also have personalities—usually multiple. The skilled facilitator is able to manage the rogues gallery while accommodating the strengths and weaknesses of each personality type.

Endnote

1. Adapted from IMT's workshop, "Creating a Customer-Centered Culture."® Used with permission. (See Appendix A.)
2. Don Lowry is the creator of the True Colors® personality type methodology and associated training courses.

Team Charter

What do we want the team to accomplish?

Objectives

- Provide guidance and direction to the team.
- Clarify the desired results of the project.
- Define the scope of the project.
- Identify the right team members.
- Allocate the necessary resources (including time).

Prework

- Identified the project sponsor.
- Worked with the sponsor to determine who should help charter the project.
- Set up the chartering meeting.

Estimated Time

60 to 90 minutes

How to Introduce It

- Have the sponsor explain why the folks have been gathered, including a brief summary of why he or she thinks the project is necessary.
- Have the sponsor introduce you.
- Explain that the purpose of the meeting is to reach consensus on some critical issues before the project begins.
- Explain that the charter provides guidance and direction to the team so that they work on the right things and stay within defined boundaries.
- Explain the objectives of the charter.

Diagnosis
Organize the project
Change processes
  Customer satisfaction
  Process improvement
  Problem solving
  Planning
Managing ideas
Creating buy-in
Implementation
Evaluation
Celebration

TEAM CHARTER

Action Steps

1. Brainstorm the *current situation* by asking the group, "What is occurring right now that makes us want to work on this project?"

2. Brainstorm the *desired outcomes* of the project by asking the group, "A successful project will result in . . ."

3. Brainstorm the *undesired outcomes* of the project by asking the group, "A successful project will not result in . . ."

4. Prioritize the outcomes from steps two and three by multivoting. Give each participant three total votes to use across both lists combined.

5. Brainstorm the *scope* of the project by asking the group the following:

   ■ "What is the scope of the project?" (If working on a process, define the first and last steps of the process.)

   ■ "What are the boundaries of the project?"

   ■ "What things are off the table (not to be considered)?"

6. Brainstorm potential *team members* by asking the group the following:

   ■ "What functions should be represented on the team?"

   ■ "Who are some potential candidates to represent each function?" (Get at least two for each function.)

7. Brainstorm project *resources* by asking the group the following:

   ■ "How much time can team members devote to the project?"

   ■ "How much money can the team spend during the project?"

8. Brainstorm project *due dates* by asking the group the following:

   ■ "When should the team present final recommendations to the sponsor?"

   ■ "When should the project be completed (including implementation)?"

   ■ "When should the desired outcomes be achieved?"

TEAM CHARTER

Example

Individual Income Tax Team Charter
Sponsor: Stan

Current Situation
- Forms are too difficult
- Too many errors (us & customer)
- Process takes too long
- Too many people paying to have taxes done

Desired Outcomes
A successful project will result in . . .
- Increased customer satisfaction
- Time savings for citizens
- Reduced errors
- Reduced complexity
- Faster refunds and deposits

Undesired Outcomes
A successful project will not result in . . .
- More FTEs (employees)
- Layoffs
- Increased complexity
- More turf battles

Scope
- Everything from forms to refund check
- Don't let the law be a constraint; we can try to change it
- Think long-term and short-term
- May need to involve suppliers and partners

Team Members
Purchasing
Legal
Forms
Error correction
Field office
Customer service rep.

Resources
Up to 4 hours per week
See sponsor for financial needs

Due Dates
Recommendations: July
Implemented: January 1
Outcomes achieved: end of next tax season

When complete, type a charter for the sponsor to approve.

Checklist

❏ You have a firm understanding of what success for this project means.

❏ You have a good idea what system will be worked on and what change process is necessary.

❏ The charter defines the direction, *not the solution.*

❏ The scope of the project is appropriate (not too large, not too small).

❏ The scope is within the organization's control.

❏ Timelines are realistic.

❏ The right team member functions have been identified.

Mission Template

What is our purpose?

Objectives

Define the purpose or mission of the team.

Diagnosis

Organize the project

Change processes

   Customer satisfaction

   Process improvement

   Problem solving

   Planning

Managing ideas

Creating buy-in

Implementation

Evaluation

Celebration

How to Introduce It

- Explain that a mission statement is a document that serves as a shared purpose for the team. It is something they can keep coming back to if they feel they are getting off track.

- Show the team the mission statement template on the flipchart, explaining each of the blanks.

- Explain that it may take several iterations through each of the blanks before they get a statement with which they are comfortable.

- Warn them that this can go quickly or can take a while.

Estimated Time

10 to 50 minutes

MISSION TEMPLATE

Action Steps

1. Create the mission template on a flipchart.

2. Ask the group which blank they would like to fill in first.

3. Brainstorm possible answers for that blank. (You complete a stick-on note with each answer.)

4. Reach consensus on the answer.

5. Repeat steps two through four for each blank.

   Note: There may be considerable bouncing around between blanks; as one blank gets decided, it changes the answers in the other blanks. That is why it is advised you use stick-on notes.

6. Write the complete mission statement on a fresh flipchart page.

7. Do a gut check with the group by asking, *"Can you all live with this? Is there anybody with a strong objection?"*

Example

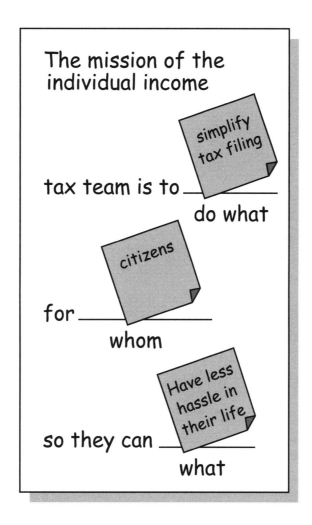

Checklist

❏ It is clear what the team is trying to achieve and who it is trying to satisfy.

❏ The team feels good about the statement.

❏ The statement is short, sweet, and inspiring.

❏ The statement does not contain a lot of run-on sentences or "ands."

❏ The team did not spend too much time wordsmithing.

Ground Rules

What rules and values will we live by to make our meetings effective?

Objectives

- Discuss the common elements that make for bad meetings.

- Develop ways to minimize or prevent them from happening.

- The team has created shared expectations of each other. Help the team see that this project will be like nothing else they have ever experienced.

Diagnosis

Organize the project

Change processes

Customer satisfaction

Process improvement

Problem solving

Planning

Managing ideas

Creating buy-in

Implementation

Evaluation

Celebration

How to Introduce It

Explain that we are going to spend a lot of time together in the coming weeks and that we would like that time to be productive and painless. We all have been part of bad meetings before and know how excruciating they can be. So before we get too far down the road, let's define the rules of engagement—how we are going to work together.

Estimated Time

5 to 10 minutes

GROUND RULES

Action Steps

1. Draw a line down the middle of a flipchart page.

2. Ask the group to think of the worst meetings they have ever attended.

3. On the left side of the page, brainstorm the attributes of a bad meeting by asking the group, "What are the characteristics of the worst meetings you have attended?"

4. Once the participants have exhausted their ideas, tell them that they must now develop a solution for each item they have listed.

5. Go one by one through each attribute of a bad meeting and ask, "How do we prevent this from happening at our meetings?" Write the answers down on the right side of the page, across from the attribute.

6. For each item on the right side of the page, identify whether it is a ground rule or value by placing a "G" or a "V" next to the item. Ground rules are things teams must do (start on time); values are things the group will aim to do (respect each others' opinions).

7. Ask the group if there are any other ground rules or values that the team should consider.

GROUND RULES

Example

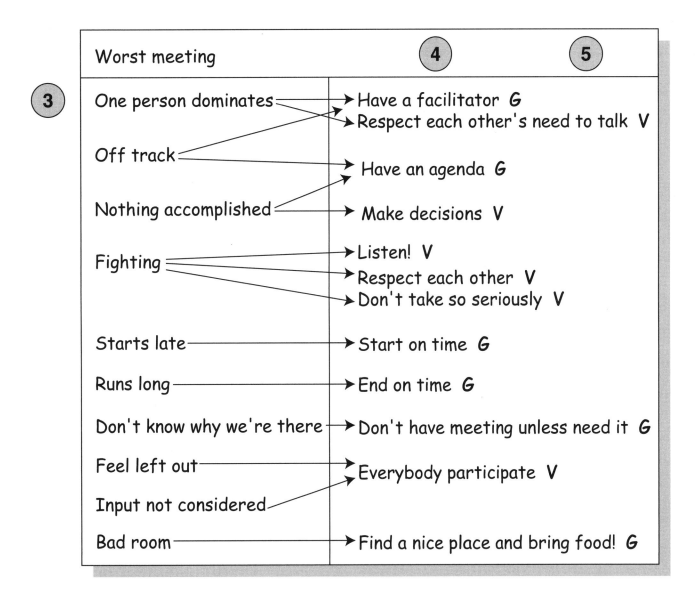

Worst meeting	④	⑤

③

One person dominates	→ Have a facilitator **G**
	→ Respect each other's need to talk **V**
Off track	→ Have an agenda **G**
Nothing accomplished	→ Make decisions **V**
Fighting	→ Listen! **V**
	→ Respect each other **V**
	→ Don't take so seriously **V**
Starts late	→ Start on time **G**
Runs long	→ End on time **G**
Don't know why we're there	→ Don't have meeting unless need it **G**
Feel left out	→ Everybody participate **V**
Input not considered	
Bad room	→ Find a nice place and bring food! **G**

Checklist

❑ The team had fun.

❑ The right stuff is on the list.

❑ The team members believe they can honor the rules and values.

Chapter Three

The Customer-Satisfaction Process[1]

The conventional wisdom about customer satisfaction has evolved over the years; it started with the industrial age definition: zero defects = customer satisfaction. Popular in the early days of the quality movement, organizations invested heavily in systems to capture, count, and eliminate defects. The assumption they were making was that if a product had zero defects, customers would be satisfied. Does this assumption hold? One only has to think of the AMC Pacer (the fishbowl on wheels) to see the fallacy in this assumption. Suppose the AMC Pacer had been defect free; the clutch never went out, the 8 track cassette player lasted forever, and the engine was totally reliable. Would you buy it? Clearly customer satisfaction is based on more than the technical quality of the product. Dr. Deming, the father of the quality movement, looked down on his creation and admonished this obsession with internally focused quality. He reminded his followers that quality is defined by the customer.

Eventually people caught on and recognized that if quality is defined by the customer, then they had better find out what the customer was complaining about. This brought forth the second popular definition of customer satisfaction: zero complaints = customer satisfaction. Again, organizations built elaborate systems to capture, count, and eliminate complaints, assuming that if no one were complaining, then customers must be satisfied. Is this assumption true? Is it possible you could be dissatisfied with a product and not complain? It is not only possible, but it is also the norm. Research conducted by the Technical Assistance Research Program (TARP) confirmed this. In their first study, the data showed that only 4 percent of unhappy customers complained directly to the organization. (A more recent study has seen that number rise to 20 percent.) What do the rest of the customers do? They leave, of course, and the organization never knows why.

There are many reasons why people do not complain: they have given up hope, they do not think anybody will do anything about it, they are not that emotionally vested in the product, and so on. The key point is, however, that if organizations are measuring customer satisfaction by counting complaints, they are fooling themselves. For every one complaint they do get, there are at least five they are not getting. And more importantly, when organizations measure customer complaints, all they are really capturing are customer *dissatisfiers*—that is, those things that dissatisfy the customer. What they are not capturing are the customer satisfiers. An organization could work to remove all of the things that dissatisfy customers and still not satisfy them. The absence of dissatisfaction does not equal satisfaction.

An organization could work to remove all of the things that dissatisfy customers and still not satisfy them. The absence of dissatisfaction does not equal satisfaction.

The management gurus will tell you that the key to building a long-term, meaningful relationship with your customers is to do a survey. Yet with the other area in your life where you are trying to create such a relationship (with your spouse) you do not survey. Why not? Because intuitively you know there is a better way.

This exact point was made by Frederick Herzberg regarding employee satisfaction. Take a minute and jot down the five things that bug you the most about your current job—the things that really aggravate you. (I am going to guess you put down things like computer problems, no parking, unrealistic deadlines, office politics, and so on.) Now, suppose all of those items were eliminated; they had been solved. Would you be satisfied? Would you skip into work saying, "Thank God it's Monday?" Not likely. What would make you do cartwheels coming into your office? I am sure your list would look quite different. With customers as well as employees, it is not enough to remove the items that cause dissatisfaction; we must also replace them with items that lead to satisfaction.

Most organizations are now trying to do more than merely capture customer complaints. This brings us to the current conventional wisdom about customer satisfaction: a good survey score = customer satisfaction. Surveys are absolutely everywhere. I recently stayed in a hotel room that had three separate surveys: one in the bedroom, one in the TV room, and one in the bathroom (you've got to hand it to them on that one; they had a captive audience). It seems that any organization that embraces the "get close to the customer" mantra immediately does a customer survey. So what is wrong with that? Let me ask you this: do you survey your spouse? Probably not. All the management gurus will tell you that the key to building a long-term, meaningful relationship with your customers is to do a survey. Yet with the other area in your life where you are trying to create such a relationship (with your spouse), you do not survey. Why not? Because you intuitively know that there is a better way.

My personal opinion is that customer surveys are generally suitable for wrapping fish.[2] I feel this way because surveys generally:

- Ask the wrong questions of
- The wrong people
- At the wrong time
- For the wrong reasons

Figure 3.1 shows a typical survey one might find in a hotel room. Is it possible that you could mark "satisfied" for all the questions listed and still not be satisfied? What is the number one outcome a business traveler would like from a hotel stay? It is probably a good night's sleep. (This is why it is important to segment your customers. A good night's sleep is unlikely to be a high priority for honeymooners.) You can have a clean room with friendly service, a nice remote control and fluffy pillows, but if housekeeping knocks at 4:00 A.M. to clean the room, you will not be satisfied.

While *good night's sleep* is the number one priority of business travelers, it is never asked on hotel surveys. Why not? This is no great mystery when you think of how most surveys get created. A team gets locked in a room and cannot get out until a survey is created. Usually there is not a customer in sight. At best, with these surveys, all we are discovering is how satisfied customers are with things we think they think are important. The right way to find out what customers want is to ask them, but not in a survey. Organizations can learn more from their customers in a 90-minute focus group or a 15-minute interview than they will ever find out in a decade of surveys. The customer-satisfaction process is designed to ensure the team asks customers the right questions.

	Excellent		Good		Poor
1. How would you rate our staff:					
Front desk	5	4	3	2	1
Housekeeping	5	4	3	2	1
Room service	5	4	3	2	1
Restaurant services	5	4	3	2	1
2. How would you rate our:					
Front desk services	5	4	3	2	1
Check-in efficiency	5	4	3	2	1
Check-out efficiency	5	4	3	2	1
3. How would you rate:					
Bathroom cleanliness	5	4	3	2	1
Bedroom cleanliness	5	4	3	2	1
Television	5	4	3	2	1
Heat/air conditioning	5	4	3	2	1
Lighting	5	4	3	2	1
4. Overall, how would you rate your stay?	5	4	3	2	1
5. What could we do to make your stay more pleasant next time?					

Figure 3.1   Hotel satisfaction survey.

With the hotel room survey, it is not too hard to ensure you are surveying the right people. But in many other cases, the situation can be far more difficult. If you are IBM, do you survey the person who buys the computer, the person who installs the computer, the person who uses the computer, or the person who fixes the computer? If you are a bank regulator, do you survey the bank, the legislature, or the citizens who use the banks?

The customer-satisfaction process helps the team figure out who the real customer is and how to balance competing customer priorities.

One of the big problems with surveys is that they are reactive. In the case of the hotel survey, I am already gone. There is little they can do to satisfy me. Total quality management became popular in manufacturing because it challenged a common practice—trying to inspect quality into a product. By the time defects made it to quality assurance, it was too late. While most organizations have learned this lesson on the shop floor, they are still applying the old logic to surveys. Quality cannot be surveyed into a product. Rather, organizations must take the steps to build quality into their products and services from the beginning. The right time to survey is after determining what customers want and after designing the product or service to meet those expectations.

In many cases, the reason for a survey being conducted is unclear (Figure 3.2). People just know they want to survey, and they set about doing it. Little thought is given to what will be done with the results. Any customer-inquiry method should be for the purpose of driving action. Sadly, most organizations with whom I have

At best, with these surveys, all we are discovering is how satisfied customers are with things we think they think are important.

- The wrong people are surveyed.
- The wrong questions are asked.
- The questions are asked the wrong way.
- The questions are asked at the wrong time.
- Satisfaction and dissatisfaction are assumed to have equal importance.
- Those who did not buy or use the product/service are not surveyed.
- Surveys are conducted for the wrong reasons.
- The results are generalized to groups not surveyed.
- Surveys are used as a substitute for better methods.
- The results do not direct improvement actions.

Figure 3.2   Common problems with surveys.

Source: Adapted from IMT's workshop, "Creating a Customer-Centered Culture."® Used with permission. (See appendix A.)

talked about surveys trumpet the score, with little to say about improvements they have made for the customer. A 95 percent satisfaction rating can be very deceiving:

- Did the survey ask the right questions?
- Did it ask the right people?
- Did you survey the people not using the product or service?
- Are you making a highly satisfactory slide rule (making perfect what should not be made at all)?

The customer-satisfaction process helps the team get out in front of the customers and proactively determine their expectations so the product or service can be designed for satisfaction.

The objective of the customer-satisfaction process is to enable the team to determine who their customers are, what they want, and how to proactively satisfy them. The customer-satisfaction process consists of seven steps:

1. Define work as a tangible product
2. Determine customers/roles
3. Segment customers into relevant groups
4. Determine customers' prioritized expectations
5. Measure the degree to which those expectations are achieved
6. (Re)design the product to meet customer expectations
7. Develop innovative new products that better achieve customer-desired outcomes

Define Work as a Tangible Product

When you think of industries that struggle with customer satisfaction, the following immediately come to mind:

- Government
- Health care
- Education

- Utilities
- Insurance companies

There are several factors these industries have in common that account for their poor levels of customer satisfaction:

- **Captive audience.** In each of these industries, customers have little choice. They are essentially monopolies. They do not have customers; they have hostages. Parents have little choice (currently) where to send their kids to school. Their insurance options are selected by their employer, and their health care options are selected by their insurance company. When customers have few choices, organizations do not have the natural incentive to improve.

- **Competing customer interests.** The issue of *who is the customer* is especially difficult in each of these industries. Government (especially regulatory agencies) struggles mightily with who they should be trying to satisfy—the legislature, the taxpayers, the people that use their service, the companies they regulate, and so on. Health care has to deal with the often competing interests of patients, insurance providers, and physicians. Education has to balance the needs of parents, students, employers, society at large, government at every level, and so on.

- **They do not make widgets.** Like most of today's economy (85 percent of the workforce), the people that work in these industries do not make widgets like cars, TVs, radios, and so on. Yet they have been trying to apply the quality methods of the industrial age to their knowledge and service work. It is my opinion that the biggest hurdle to improving customer satisfaction in these industries, or any nonmanufacturing organization for that matter, is the way work is defined.

Each of these factors (or excuses) can be overcome. The key is to recognize that everyone makes widgets.

No matter what industry you are in, you use the same model to get work done (see Figure 3.3). The model is intuitively obvious when applied to manufactured

The biggest hurdle to improving customer satisfaction in service industries is the way work is defined. We say, "We don't make widgets."

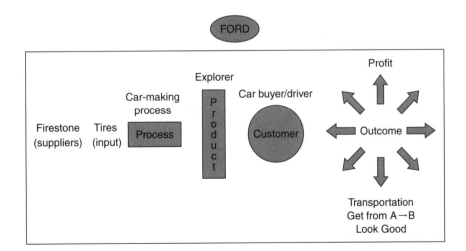

Figure 3.3 The system of work.

Source: Adapted from IMT's workshop, "Creating a Customer-Centered Culture."® Used with permission. (See appendix A.)

products. Manufacturing organizations manage the heck out of each of the interactions in the model. From supplier quality to lean manufacturing and cycle time reduction to quality function deployment (a sophisticated method of involving the voice of the customer in product design), sophisticated techniques are in place to maximize profit.

Let's take a nonmanufactured product and show that the model applies as well. Clearly, churches and automobile manufacturers are quite different, yet they use the same model to get work done (Figure 3.4). We could substitute any nonmanufactured product and the result would be the same. What is different, however, is that nonmanufacturing organizations rarely measure and improve the components of the model. Why not? The answer lies in the middle: the product. One of the most common excuses I hear when dealing with service organizations is that "this quality and customer-satisfaction stuff would be so easy if we made widgets." When people say they do not make widgets, they are really saying they do not know what their products are. Let's look at the implications if we remove the product from the model (Figure 3.5).

When the product is removed, two things happen:

- We lose the connection between *what* we do all day (the process or activity) and *who* we do it for (the customer). Customers do not care about process. Think about the last time you bought a car. Did you ask the salesperson whether the employees that built the car were in self-directed work teams? Did you ask about their employee suggestion system? No, you asked about the car.

- We lose the connection between *what* we do all day and *why* we are doing it (the outcome).

Sound familiar? The key, then, for nonmanufacturing organizations to begin to make real progress in customer satisfaction and performance improvement is to first find their widgets. They must think about their squishy service and knowledge work as tangible products. This is also the first step for a team working on a customer-satisfaction project.

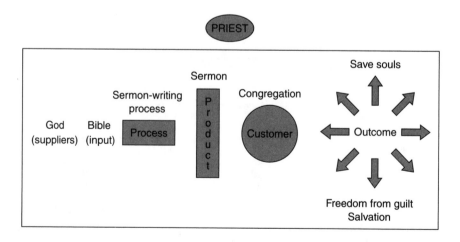

Figure 3.4 The system of work for a priest.

Source: Adapted from IMT's workshop, "Creating a Customer-Centered Culture."® Used with permission. (See appendix A.)

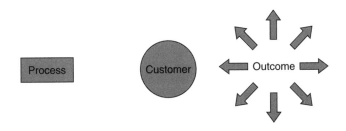

Figure 3.5 When we say we do not make widgets.

Source: Adapted from IMT's workshop, "Creating a Customer-Centered Culture."® Used with permission. (See appendix A.)

A product is something created by work, which can be given to someone else to achieve a desired outcome. It is:

- **A deliverable.** A product has to be something that can be given to someone else. *Knowledge* is not a product until it is packaged in some form (like an article or a workshop) and delivered to someone. This rule helps get from the squishy to the tangible. Ask the question, "What pops out at the end of your factory?" That is the deliverable.

- **A noun.** Verbs like training, coaching, processing, and selling are all activities. Customers do not care about our activities; they care about the thing we are going to give them that helps them achieve their desired outcome. The product is the bridge between activities and results. Defining work as nouns ensures we are not describing activities.

- **Countable.** Think of any widget. Now imagine a room full of them. You can because they are countable. You can count TVs, stereos, and cars. Now try to count the following: "foster collaboration among mutual partners to create windows of opportunity for clients." This is how so many people describe their product. If you cannot count them, you are still dealing in the land of the squishy.

- **Expressed as something that can be made plural with an "s."** Things like training, helping, and assisting all end in *-ing.* They are activities. The product is the tangible result of the activity, such as training courses, counseling sessions, technical support answers, and so on. Words like *satisfaction, assurance, security,* and *health* are also not products. They are the outcomes obtained by using a product. If you cannot make the word plural with an "s," you likely have described an activity or result.

A fifth rule is designed to ensure that the team is working on a specific product over which it has control. Oftentimes people will define the product too generally (like a plan or a policy). Which plan? Which policy? The more specific we are, the better we will be able to determine customers and their expectations. Another typical problem groups have when defining their products is that they define someone else's product. For example, if you were to ask the CEO of Ford what he produces, what do you think he will say? Cars. Yet I doubt he spends much time on the production line. He may produce strategic plans, speeches, sales contracts, or product recall announcements.

Another example of this took place in a workshop with OB-GYNs. When asked what their product was, what do you think they said? Babies. The rule of thumb is that if anybody else can claim the product as theirs, it is not yours. There are a couple of other people in the delivery room that would like to take credit for the baby. The OB-GYN's product was *deliveries*. (Any chance they will benchmark speed of delivery with Domino's pizza?)

Products occur at every level in the organization[3] (Figure 3.6). At the top, or the enterprise level, are the "final" products. For Motorola these would be pagers or cell phones. For the Immigration and Naturalization Service (INS) they would be green cards. For a hospital it would be an appendectomy. Products also occur at the functional and personal levels (Table 3.1). These products include items such as marketing plans, design documents, approved applications, performance appraisals, PC repairs, and so on. When the team is selecting its product for improvement, it is usually best to avoid the enterprise-level products. These products can be too large and too hard to change. (For example, we would not ask a team at Ford to work on the Mustang.) Rather, try to focus on products created earliest in the chain. Products that cross functions are always a good place to focus.

Once the team has identified its product, the process of defining the customers, determining their expectations, and measuring performance all become much easier

A word of caution: When the team describes the product it will be working on, try to obtain a physical sample of it. You want to actually touch and feel it if possible. For example, if they tell you the product is an "environmental permit," ask to see one. What you will quickly discover is that the product is actually several products. There likely will be seven different types of permits. The team will have to make a decision about which one to work on. A good rule is to focus on the biggest product first (the product with the most volume) and then apply the learnings to the others.

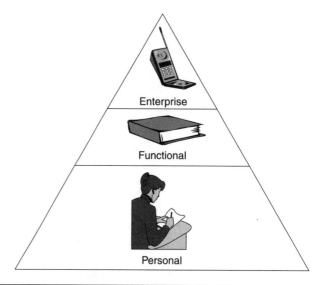

Figure 3.6 Levels of products.

Source: Adapted from IMT's workshop, "Creating a Customer-Centered Culture."® Used with permission. (See appendix A.)

Table 3.1 Sample products by function.

Function	Sample products	
Executive management	Policies Strategies	Plans Mission statements
Marketing	Brochures Ads Campaigns	Surveys Marketing plans
Personnel	Policies Procedures Processes	Programs Placements Perfomance reviews
Quality	Policies Processes	Audits Specifications
Training	Courses Manuals	Programs Needs assessments
Sales	Orders Presentations	Plans Needs assessments
MIS/data processing	Installations Reports	Applications (software) Systems
Shipping/receiving	Deliveries	Schedules
Accounting	Reports Audits	Balance sheets Entries
Purchasing	Approved purchase order Procedures	Authorized vendor lists
Engineering	Designs Layouts Procedures	Processes Specifications Instructions
Field service	Repairs Upgrades	Installations Diagnoses

Source: Adapted from IMT's workshop, "Creating a Customer-Centered Culture."® Used with permission. (See appendix A.)

SELF-TEST 1

Identify two products your organization creates.

Identify two products you personally create.

Define Customers Segmented by Role

As mentioned previously, the issue of who is the customer can be quite confusing, especially in government, health care, and education. However they are not the only ones. Take Xerox, for example. Who is its customer? The person who buys the copier? The person who installs the copier? The people who use the copier? The person who fixes the copier jams? If they are all customers, then who gets the top priority?

Similarly, think of a health insurance provider. Who is the customer of the insurance policy? The employer who pays for it, the employee, the employee's spouse or sick child, or the doctor?

Clearly, there is more to customer satisfaction than first meets the eye. There is an easy way to sort all this out. Simply, the customer is defined by the product. When the product changes, the customer changes. In addition, customers can play three distinct roles with the product:

- **End users** are individuals or groups who personally use the product to achieve a desired outcome. They are the folks we ostensibly had in mind when we designed the product. There are usually more end users than any other kind of customer.

- **Brokers** transfer the product to someone else who will use it. They may either act as an agent of the end user or the producer. As an agent of the end user, the broker makes the product more accessible, easier to use, or more appealing. As an agent of the producer, the broker *encourages* the end user to accept the product.

- **Fixers** transform, repair, or correct the product at any point in its life cycle for the benefit of the end users.

The automobile industry offers a classic example of what can happen when we do not clearly understand customer roles. During the energy crisis of the mid-1970s, Jimmy Carter asked the automakers to start building more fuel-efficient cars. He was acting as a broker for all of the car owners in the nation. (Had he asked them to build *him* a more fuel-efficient car, he would have been acting as an end user.) The automobile manufacturers, in turn, asked their customers, the people who bought the cars from them, whether this might be a good idea. The dealers (brokers) said, "Heck no, we want the big ones!" Why might they say this? Whose interests were they representing? In this case, you have a broker (Carter) talking to the producers (automakers) who then talked to the brokers (dealers). Who was talking to the end users? The Japanese. The rest of the story is history.

I experienced firsthand another example of what happens when an organization fails to differentiate customers by role. A state tax agency had tried to improve its tax forms every year for at least a decade. In some instances, they actually decided to talk to customers. When identifying their customers, they listed taxpayers, tax preparers, the IRS, and a few others. Since tax preparers were easier to find and were more likely to talk to them, the agency solicited only their input. Each year they talked to the tax professionals, the forms got more difficult. This is a classic case of competing interests. Taxpayers' number one expectation of tax forms is that they are "easy to complete." Tax professionals' number one expectation is that they are "hard to complete." Houston, we have a problem. (To show how absurd this gets, Congress is considering legislation to prevent the IRS from developing Internet filing for fear that it will hurt the tax professionals. Who is the customer here?)

The customer is defined by the product.

One only needs to look at the music industry to understand the impact of brokers[4] (Figure 3.7). What impact do all of these brokers have?

- **Cost.** A compact disc costs over $15. Why? All of the brokers need to make money. That is why the end user has to pay $15 for nine lousy songs and the one good song they actually wanted.

- **Speed.** How long does it take from the time an artist writes a song until the end user can hear it? Typically over two years.

- **Competing interests.** Whom does the artist try to satisfy? VH1 is full of has-been performers who tried to satisfy the record companies and radio stations and lost their fans. It is also full of artists who "followed their own vision" and lost their recording contract in the process.

- **Not knowing what the end user wants.** For artists to succeed, they have to appeal to the record company, the producer, radio stations, and record stores. In the process, it is easy to lose sight of the listeners, especially when you consider the two years it takes to get a record to market. By that time, listeners' fickle tastes have changed.

It is easy to see how powerful Napster and the digital music revolution has been. An artist can record a song on a home computer, post it to the Internet that night, and people all over the world can hear it for free. The end users are given unlimited options to find the kind of music that appeals to them, without relying on the brokers (radio stations and record companies) to tell them what is "good for them." Fans of Moravian hip-hop polka music can finally find what they have been looking for. End users always win in the long run.

Our objective is to satisfy all of the customers of a product, even though their needs are different. If the different customer groups have competing interests, then preference is given to the needs of the end users over the brokers.

Customers' roles only can be defined by their relationship to a specific product. Most fights over *who is the customer?* occur because of confusion over the product. It does little good to speak of customers in the abstract. When you hear someone saying, "My customers are so and so," ask them, "For which product?" and "What role are they playing with that product?" This will clear up any discrepancies. It is important to note customers can play more than one role with a product. For example, I might create a strategic plan for my unit (producer), give it to my staff to use (broker), and use it myself to plan my activities (end user).

Most fights over who is the customer? occur because of confusion over the product. It does little good to speak of customers in the abstract.

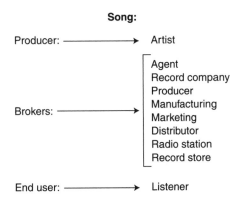

Figure 3.7   Impact of brokers.

The *customer roles matrix* (Figure 3.8) is a great tool to help the team identify the specific customers, segmented by their role, for its product.

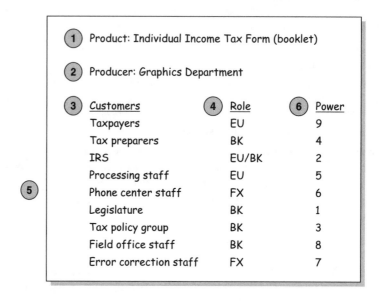

	Customers	Role	Power
	Taxpayers	EU	9
	Tax preparers	BK	4
	IRS	EU/BK	2
	Processing staff	EU	5
	Phone center staff	FX	6
	Legislature	BK	1
	Tax policy group	BK	3
	Field office staff	BK	8
	Error correction staff	FX	7

Figure 3.8   Customer roles matrix.

SELF-TEST 2

For one of the products you identified in the first self-test, complete the following roles:

Producer:

End user(s):

Brokers:

Fixers:

Who has the most power over the way the product is currently designed?

Who has the least?

Segment Customers into Relevant Groups

Not all end users are created equally. Inside each end-user group may be several separate and distinct groups with different expectations of the product (Figure 3.9). For example, men and women might both be lumped together in an end-user group called *car buyers*, but their expectations could be totally different. A car manufacturer would do well to consider breaking the end-user group down into males and females and talking to them separately. Similarly, the car manufacturer may want to consider age, geographic location, income, and so on when segmenting customers.

A classic example of what can go wrong when a team fails to segment involves a team working on a performance appraisal. The team identified *company employees* as the end users of the performance appraisal and proceeded to conduct focus groups. Unfortunately, the team included supervisors and employees in the same room together. What was the likelihood that the employees truly shared their expectations of the appraisal? The goal is to organize customers in such a way that will maximize the chance that they say what is on their mind while ensuring we do not miss any key end-user segments.

Let's use a lawn mower to illustrate this further. Suppose I am a lawn mower manufacturer and I would like to improve my lawn mower. The first step in the customer-satisfaction process is to define the product; in this case, it will be a push-mower model XJ2000. The next step is to determine the customers segmented by their role with the product. The end users might be called *mowers* or *teenagers*, while the brokers would consist of the retail chain that sells the mower and possibly the parent who purchases the mower for their child or spouse to use. Clearly, not all *mowers* are created equally. Step three of the process asks us to segment customers into relevant groups. What segments may best apply to mowers? Here are some possibilities:

- Geography
- Size of lawn
- Gender
- Weather
- Physical strength
- Income

You can quickly see that it is possible to segment customers in infinite ways. So how do you know how much to do? The rule of thumb is to consider only those segments that will have different expectations of the product. For example, does education level change expectations for a lawn mower? Probably not.

> *The goal is to organize customers in such a way that will maximize the chance they will say what is on their mind.*

Income tax form—single, married, income level

Life insurance policy—men, women, single, married, elderly, middle-aged, smokers

Loan application—first-time homebuyers, experienced buyers, income

Marketing plan—accounting management, manufacturing management, purchasing management

Performance appraisal—supervisors, professional staff, hourly workers, different divisions/units in the organization, HR staff

Physical exam—age, gender

Figure 3.9 Sample customer segments.

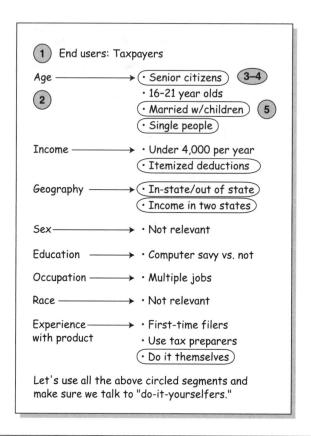

Figure 3.10 Customer-segmentation tool.

The *customer-segmentation tool* (Figure 3.10) is designed to help the team first consider all the possible ways to segment its customer groups and then select those that are the most relevant.

Once the team has identified the various segments within an end-user group, it has two options:

- Conduct separate focus groups for each segment (preferred).
- Ensure that each segment is represented in some way at a focus group.

The decision you make should be based on time, cost, and the impact of the decision on project outcomes. If the segmentation is critical, do separate focus groups.

For example, team members working on a performance appraisal might decide that they want to have different focus groups with hourly workers versus professional staff. However, they also want to ensure they have people from every function of the company. The team might consider having one focus group with hourly workers, including one worker from each function in the company. The other focus group would be professionals, with at least one representative from each function in the company. (Remember that focus groups should not exceed 15 people.)

Once the team members have decided which groups and segments they want to talk to, they will need to decide how many focus groups to have with each. The general rule is to conduct focus groups until you see a pattern. If you have only a few discreet sets of end users, then you probably will want to conduct two or three focus groups with each segment. However, if you have many different end-user groups, you may choose to do only one focus group with each. The patterns of expectations will start to emerge after many focus groups, with only the relative priorities being unique from group to group. There is little substitute for the team's gut feeling on this. If the team feels confident that it has ascertained the desires of the end users, it has done enough. If after talking with end users the team is not quite sure what is most important to whom, it will need to do more.

The team members should also consider whether they would like to conduct focus groups with brokers as well. Most teams have found this quite helpful, although they do not usually go to the degree of work as they do with the end users.

Determine Customers' Prioritized Expectations

There are three terms that are used interchangeably when discussing customer satisfaction:[5]

- Wants
- Expectations
- Needs

While used interchangeably, the three may mean entirely different things. Needs tend to be the smallest in scope, or the minimum, while wants are the broadest, or the optimum. What about expectations? Are expectations the same as wants? A popular slogan used now by nearly everyone says, "Our aim is to exceed your expectations." Is that a good thing? Consider the Department of Motor Vehicles (DMV). When you go there, do you expect to wait a long time? Now suppose when you entered the building there was a giant banner exclaiming, "Our aim is to exceed your expectations!" You would run screaming for your car. We can exceed someone's expectations and still not give them what they want. Expectations are based on past history. We expect to wait in line at the DMV, but we sure do not want to.

We can exceed customers' expectations and still not give them what they want.

I once had the misfortune of working on a project dealing with unemployment centers. At one urban location, citizens waited in line for six hours to be helped. I asked the manager if this might be a problem. The manager was adamant that this did not need to be improved because the customers "expected it." Ouch!

National Tire and Battery has a great slogan that makes this whole point: "National Tire and Battery—everything you want from a tire store and nothing you would expect."

Clearly, the focus of the team's efforts should first be on customer wants.

Customers care about three things (Table 3.2), regardless of the product:

- **Outcomes**—the results achieved by using the product
- **Attributes**—the characteristics of the product
- **Features**—how the outcomes and attributes come to life

Table 3.2 What customers care about.

	Hotel room	Strategic plan
Outcomes	Good night's sleep	Direction and priorities for the organization
Attributes	Safe, clean, quiet	Concise, well-supported, easy to follow
Features	Coffeemaker, mini-bar, iron	Executive summary, action plan, pretty pictures

Customers care most about outcomes, but as discussed previously, outcomes are rarely asked about and hardly ever measured.

As I demonstrated at the beginning of this section, we determine customers' expectations by talking to them and by asking them what they want—not by surveying them to find out how satisfied they are with what we think they think is important. The customer focus group technique is carefully structured to uncover all three things customers care about. The task of the team is to design the product for maximum customer satisfaction. In order to do this, the team needs to discover the customers' priorities for all three elements—outcomes, attributes, and features. Each element will be treated separately in the rest of the customer-satisfaction process. **Outcomes** will be used to drive new product innovation (see *innovation tool*), and **attributes** will be used to develop objective measures of satisfaction (see *voice-of-the customer tool*) and to brainstorm key product **features.**

Focus Groups

Customer focus groups work best with a group of six to twelve homogeneous customers. The format is very basic (think Phil Donahue or Oprah). The facilitator leads the customers through a series of brainstorms and discussions around specific questions:

1. **If you could change one thing about (product name), what would it be?** This question is asked primarily to allow the customers to vent before we get into the questions we need to ask to drive product design. Many customers come to focus groups with a lot they want to get off their chest. They may have complaints, suggestions, a story about a bad experience, or a great feature they want to add to the product. If we do not let them voice these things up front, they will try to answer every other question we ask with these items. Chances are the team will not do a lot with the responses from this question. That is by design. The goal of the project is not to identify all of the customer dissatisfiers; rather, we want to uncover what will satisfy the customers. That is the purpose of the other questions.

2. **A satisfying (product name) is one that is . . .** This question uncovers the desired attributes of the product. Answers will be descriptive words like *easy to use, fast, timely, safe, understandable,* and so on. There are two ways to facilitate this question. One is to simply ask it and write down participant responses. Another way involves using an *attribute wall*[6]—a large poster with every conceivable attribute of any product imaginable. With this tool, participants place sticky dots next to the attributes that most reflect their priorities. Teams have found this to be extremely helpful. Customers have difficulty thinking of the attributes they care about. The ones they brainstorm tend to be the obvious ones or the dissatisfiers. The *attribute wall* has over 200 possible attributes, which helps customers better articulate what they want or think of latent attributes they had not even considered before. (Do I want a strategic plan to be portable? Do I want a performance appraisal to be flexible?) Experience has shown the *attribute wall* to produce richer customer data.

Once the attributes have been identified and prioritized, the facilitator leads a discussion about each priority attribute. Essentially, you are trying to uncover the following:

- **The true meaning of the attribute.** Robin Lawton tells a great story of a focus group he conducted for an airline around the product of *in-flight meals*. One of the priority attributes identified was *just like home*. Well, what does that mean exactly? It could mean lots of things to lots of different people. The customer explained that *just like home* meant *served on round plates*. Had the team members not determined that, they would have chased their tails later.

- **What features could be designed into the product to make it more (attribute name)?** This question helps solicit only those features that relate to customer priorities. I may want a CD player, cup holder, and headlight on my lawn mower, but if *easy to start* is my top priority, then the features should be focused there (electric ignition).

3. **A satisfying (product name) is one that results in . . .** This question reveals the customers' desired outcomes of the product. Answers should describe the results they want to achieve by using the product. For example, the following might be desired outcomes of a cell phone:

   - More free time away from the office
   - Staying connected with important business
   - Personal safety

   The answers to the outcomes question should look nothing like the answers to the attribute question. Things *like easy to use, accurate, simple, fast, timely,* and so on are all attributes. If participants respond with answers like these, ask them the following: "Why do you want the product to be easy to use?" "Why do you want the product to be accurate?" You are trying to uncover their *purpose* for using the product. Some good probing questions include the following: "Why do you want this product?" "Why do you use this product?" "What are you hoping to achieve by using this product?" "Suppose this product did not exist; what would happen?"

   There may be some focus groups where you choose not to ask the outcomes question. That is, the outcome is so intuitively obvious that it is an insult to ask the customer. For example, "a satisfying table is one that results in . . . a place to put my stuff." Be careful, however; there are times when you might think the outcomes are obvious and the customers surprise you. It is the rare focus group where I have not asked the outcomes question.

   A great companion to the desired outcomes question is the undesired outcomes question. That is, *a satisfying (product name) is one that does not result in . . .* Here we learn what customers are hoping to avoid when using the product. Undesired outcomes are not merely the opposite of desired outcomes. They provide great insights into the drawbacks of the product that could be improved to increase customer satisfaction (see Table 3.3).

The sequence and inclusion of questions will differ if the product being discussed does not currently exist (see *focus group for new product* tool). Here the emphasis is heavy on outcomes, as you want to know very clearly what the product should do before you worry about how it does it.

Table 3.3 Sample undesired outcomes.

Product	Undesired outcomes
Unemployment check	Standing in line, feeling ashamed
Tire	Being stranded with a flat
Perfomance appraisal	Decreased motivation, increased animosity between management and employees

---

SELF-TEST 3

Brainstorm the desired attributes of your product from Self-Test 1 as if you were the end-user group identified in Self-Test 2.

A satisfying (product name) is one that is . . .

A typical focus group should last no more than 90 minutes. The *focus group tool* provides detailed instructions on how to lead one. At its most basic element, it is a series of *brainstorms* and *multivotes*. However, focus groups require strong facilitation. Every conceivable person, pitfall, and scenario outlined in the facilitation portion of this book can happen in a focus group. You get the dominant people, the storytellers, and the church mice. You get the killer phrases and arguments. Worst of all, sometimes you get nothing—just blank stares. Carefully review the facilitation portion of this book before leading a focus group, and be prepared!

Planning a Focus Group

A focus group can be quite a challenge to pull off, especially with customers external to the organization. Focus groups take careful planning and setup to ensure maximum effectiveness.

The first step is to identify the actual customers you want to invite. That is, if you are doing a focus group with senior citizens who complete their own taxes (an end-user segment), which senior citizens will you invite? How do you find them?

If your product is of importance to the end users, you will have a much higher probability of attendees agreeing to talk to you. For example, if you were a health insurer and wanted to conduct a focus group with senior citizens about a prescription drug benefit program, there is a good chance that if invited, they will come. However, if you are a manufacturer of commercial paint solvents and want to do a focus group with working mothers, you will have a hard time getting participants. In this case, you may need to do other forms of customer inquiry (phone interviews, personal interviews, and so on).

A great way to get focus group participants is to call on the aid of groups, associations, or organizations that may have a relationship with your target audience. These groups can usually supply a ready list of participants that meet your criteria. In a best-case scenario, they will cosponsor the focus group, provide a facility, and invite the participants. For example, Chambers of Commerce are great at organizing business owners for focus groups. Senior citizen homes are a great resource for that particular segment. Churches, civic groups, and trade associations all work well for this purpose. When you contact them, explain what you are doing and why, including how many participants you need and for how long. I have seen organizers of conferences devote an hour and a half of their program to focus groups I have requested. You will be amazed what happens when you try this. If all else fails, you are left with cold-calling random customers.

The responsibility for rounding up the focus group participants should fall on the team's shoulders. Once it is determined how the participants will be selected, there is a strict protocol, which ensures people actually show up. There is nothing more embarrassing than holding a focus group in a large room with lots of flipcharts and sack lunches and having two people show up. The following protocol was created to prevent this from happening (again):

- **Assign a coordinator for the focus group.** This person is the one you blame if no one shows up.

- **Determine a date, time, and place most convenient for the focus group.** Here are some tips:
  - The date of the focus group should be approximately three weeks from the day you will be inviting the members (for external customers). This maximizes the chance that the invitees will be available.
  - The time of the focus group should be what is most convenient for the participants. Many teams have had success conducting focus groups around lunch. For example, they will serve lunch from 12:00 P.M. to 12:30 P.M. and then conduct the focus group from 12:30 P.M. to 2:00 P.M. This provides the added benefit of slack time for people arriving late. Other times that work well include 10:30 A.M. to 12:30 P.M. with lunch, 11:00 A.M. to 1:00 P.M. with lunch, and 8:00 A.M. to 10:00 A.M. with coffee and donuts. Evening focus groups are usually harder to find participants for. However, it all depends on your product and your end users.
  - The focus group should be conducted at a place that is convenient for the participants. The team might have to do some traveling in order to conduct the focus groups. The place must be large enough to fit up to 20 people comfortably, must be conveniently located (that is, easy to find, suitable parking, and so on), and should be attractive.

- **Determine who will be responsible for calling the participants and by when.** In many cases, this will be the person assigned as coordinator for the focus group. However, there may be instances when the task needs to be divided up among team members. As a rule of thumb, when the team has many focus groups to complete, one person calls all of the participants for a single group. When the team has few focus groups, the list of participants can be divided up so everyone carries part of the load. The phone call is the first contact with participants to see if they will volunteer (Figure 3.11).

NAME: _____ Phone No: _____

The (ORGANIZATION NAME) is planning to conduct focus groups in (MONTH) to collect customer input on some of its key services. We want to talk to the people using the (PRODUCT) to learn what we can do to make (PRODUCT) easier to use and more timely for our customers. What we learn from talking with our customers will be developed into recommendations for improvements to (PRODUCT) that will be submitted to the (BIG KAHUNA). Your input and participation is vital.

The focus groups will:

    ✔ Consist of no more than 14 participants
    ✔ Last approximately one and one-half hours
    ✔ Include refreshments

Have you participated in a focus group before? (We may need to explain the process more if they have not participated in one. Most focus groups are relatively similar in format, so if they have participated before, they will have a good understanding of what to expect.)

A representative from the department will ask participants four or five questions about (PRODUCT), and everyone's responses will be collectively captured on a flipchart. We will use this information to look at ways to improve customer satisfaction with (PRODUCT).

Would you be willing to participate in a focus group at (LOCATION) on (DATE) to discuss the (PRODUCT)?

NO response:

    Thank you for your time. Please feel free to contact us at any time if you should have questions or comments about any (ORGANIZATION NAME) service.

YES response:

    Thank you for agreeing to participate. May I have your mailing address? We would like to send you a written invitation confirming the location, date, and time.

    NAME: _____

    STREET ADDRESS: _____

    CITY/STATE/ZIP: _____

Thank you for agreeing to participate. We look forward to seeing you (DATE).

Figure 3.11 Focus group telephone dialog.

- **Determine who will send the letter of invitation.** The letter of invitation (Figure 3.12) puts in writing the relevant information about the focus group (purpose, date, time, place, and so on). The letter should go out immediately after the calls are made. One nuance of any letter is whose signature should be on it. You want to use the signature of the person who will have the strongest impact on the invitees choosing to attend. If we refer to our state tax form example again, the letter could come from the Director of Revenue or even the Governor. We want to motivate invitees to become attendees by appealing to their desire to make a difference. The letter and signature should convey this.

- **Determine who will call the participants for confirmation.** These calls should take place approximately four days prior to the focus group so that you get a final head count (and remind the invitees of their commitment). Not everyone uses a Palm Pilot, so one more reminder will not hurt. If the head count is below five at this point, cancel the focus group and do phone interviews.

- **Assign responsibility for selecting and setting up the meeting room.** In most cases, this will be the coordinator. There are times, however, when someone else may be instrumental in finding a location for you. They need to ensure the room meets minimum specifications and is equipped with the appropriate materials.

Dear _____:

One of the (ORGANIZATION NAME)'s top priorities is looking at ways to improve customer satisfaction by reducing the burden of customers. We are interested in what our customers think and are seeking their input in improving key products such as the (NAME OF THE PRODUCT).

This letter is to confirm our invitation to you to participate in a focus group discussion sponsored by the (NAME OF TEAM) Team on (DATE) from (BEG. TIME) to (END TIME) at (NAME OF CO/BLDG) located at (ADDRESS). The purpose of the focus group discussion is to gather information from customers like you about the (NAME OF PRODUCT).

We welcome your ideas and suggestions for improving the (NAME OF PRODUCT). Refreshments of (DEPENDING ON TIME OF DAY—TYPE OF REFRESHMENT) will be provided.

Please contact (NAME OF FOCUS GROUP COORDINATOR) at (PHONE NUMBER) if you have any questions. We look forward to seeing you (DATE).

Sincerely,

Big Kahuna

Figure 3.12   Draft of letter of invitation.

While focus groups can be effective, there is no better way to learn about your customers than to observe them in their natural habitat using your product.

- **Assign responsibility for bringing the materials,** including the following:
  - Two flipcharts, colored flipchart markers, and masking tape
  - Name tags
  - Refreshments (coffee, soda, ice, lunch, cups, plates, napkins)
- **Determine who will play the roles of facilitator and observers.** There should be no more than two observers in the room during the focus group. The observers need to stay silent. It is not their job to rebut the customer's remarks. They can answer questions but only if asked by the facilitator. (Real-life horror story: I was conducting a focus group between a regulatory agency and the regulated industry. One of the industry people shared a concern, and from the back of the room, the observer shouted, "That's a bunch of bull #$@*!" Needless to say, the rest of the focus group did not go too well.)

While this protocol may seem like a lot of work, it is worth it. Be sure to have update meetings while these focus groups are being planned to ensure things are getting done. Unfortunately, this is one of those times when change agents must disguise themselves as baby-sitters.

While focus groups can be effective, there is no better way to learn about your customers than to observe them in their natural habitat using your product. There are some things that customers just cannot articulate. One of my favorite examples of this was a team working on income tax forms. Surprisingly, the internal staff did not think the forms were that difficult. (Of course, they are not difficult when you are a CPA or a tax attorney.) "If only the customers would read the instructions," they said repeatedly. As part of their team project, we scheduled a simulation where real taxpayers came in, and using some basic dummy information, attempted to complete a tax return. The team watched in horror as people struggled to get past line two. The participants were turning page after page, looking for information, asking for new forms because they messed up, and cursing under their breath. The simulation had to be halted early because the frustration level was so high in the room that we feared for the team's safety. The simulation not only clued the team into better ways to satisfy the customer, but it also shook up their assumptions and beliefs that everything was fine.

Perhaps one of the best marketing organizations in the world is Viacom's MTV. MTV continually reinvents itself to stay "cool" with teenagers. As teenagers' fickle taste change again and again, MTV seems to always be one step ahead. How? MTV continuously observes and interacts with its customers. They send researchers out to kids' homes to watch them watch MTV. While they are in their homes, they look in their closets and ask about their favorite clothes, favorite music, new things they are excited about, and so on. By staying close to their customers and observing their actions and preferences, MTV is able to not only keep up with changing customer expectations but to shape them as well.

Once the focus groups are complete, the information goes to separate places; outcomes are used for innovation (*innovation tool*), and attributes and features are used for product design (*voice-of-the-customer tool*).

Measure the Degree to Which the Customers' Expectations Are Achieved and (Re)design the Product to Meet Customers' Expectations

One of the things teams quickly discover after talking to customers is that most of their expectations are subjective perceptions. Things like *easy to use, timely, clear, concise,* and *simple* are all perceptions. One person's definition may be different than the other. So what is the team to do? The *voice-of-the-customer tool* is used to convert these *subjective* perception attributes into *objective* measures that can be used to:

- (Re)design the product
- Determine customer satisfaction in the future

The key part of this method is the measurement of customer priorities. In the case of the lawn mower (Table 3.4), if *easy to start* is the customer's number one priority, *number of pulls* is the measure, *less than or equal to one* is the target value, and *four pulls* is Toro's current performance, do they need to survey to find out how satisfied customers are? No! They need to fix the mower. These objective measures and targets are clear, specific ways of gauging customer satisfaction in real time.

Table 3.4 Voice of the customer for a lawn mower.

Attribute	Measure	Target	Feature
Easy to start	Number of pulls	0–1	Electric start
Safe	Number of severed toes	0	Kill switch, safeguard
Lightweight	Number of lbs.	<5	Titanium
Cheap	Number of dollars	<250	
Easy to maintain	Number of hours of maintenance per year	<1	Self-cleaning, self-sharpening blade

SELF-TEST 4

Complete the following voice-of-the-customer table for the attributes identified in Self-Test 3

Attribute	Measure	Target	Current perf.	Feature

The chapter on managing ideas shows how to come up with exciting ways to meet customer targets.

Develop Innovative New Products That Better Achieve Customers' Desired Outcomes

Innovation is the process of making a desired outcome easier to obtain.

Everything we have done up to this point is consistent with the traditional definition of quality or continuous improvement. That is, we have taken our product to the customer, determined their expectations, and added new features to better satisfy them. However, what impact might these new features have on the product's cost? Continuous improvement taken to its logical extreme produces overengineered products that hardly anyone can afford. (Consider, for example, the riding lawn mowers with headlights, cup holders, and stereos or the average laptop computer that has more features than anyone can figure out how to use.) While continuous improvement is necessary, it is not sufficient.

The opposite of continuous improvement is innovation (Figure 3.13). Rather than focusing inwardly on the product, innovation focuses outwardly on the outcome. *Innovation is the process of making a desired outcome easier to obtain.* Instead of adding features to the lawn mower, innovation asks, "What is the purpose of the lawn mower? And might there be a better way to achieve it than a lawn mower?" The desired outcomes of a lawn mower might include the following:

- A beautiful lawn
- More personal time
- Pride
- Peace with the neighbors

Customers don't buy products; they buy results.
—Peter Drucker

There are other ways to achieve these outcomes without purchasing a mower. One exciting innovation on the horizon is a genetically engineered grass seed that you plant once; it grows only two inches high and stays green year round. Interested? What are the odds the major lawn mower manufacturers will invent this grass seed? Their six sigma, best-in-class mowers, assembled by highly empowered, gain-sharing, self-directed work teams in lean manufacturing plants with b-to-b e-commerce hook ups to ISO 9000 registered global suppliers are irrelevant. It is entirely possible to make absolutely perfect that which should not be made at all.

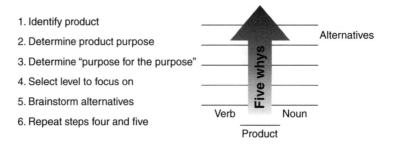

1. Identify product
2. Determine product purpose
3. Determine "purpose for the purpose"
4. Select level to focus on
5. Brainstorm alternatives
6. Repeat steps four and five

Alternatives

Five whys

Verb   Noun

Product

Figure 3.13   The continuous innovation process.

I mentioned before that customers do not care about process; they also do not care about products. Customers are only loyal to one thing: outcomes. How loyal have you been to Smith Corona? As Peter Drucker said, "Customers don't buy products; they buy results." We do not buy drills; we buy holes. We do not buy cars; we buy transportation. We do not buy cologne; we buy hope.[7]

The *innovation tool* is designed to help teams avoid "marketing myopia." It systematically nudges the team outside the box and helps them develop innovative alternatives to their existing product. Only when the team is absolutely sure it is making the right product should it worry about how to make it better, faster, and cheaper.

The customer-satisfaction process culminates with the following:

- New product ideas
- Ideas to close the gap between current performance and customer expectations
- Objective measures of customer satisfaction that can be used to evaluate the product's performance

Future Dead Products

Film
Glasses
Copiers
Pens
Billboards
Overheads
Stamps
TV Guide
Day planner
Lawn mowers
Tax forms
Keys
Yellow pages
Fax machines
Greeting cards

SELF-TEST 5

Complete the innovation tool using the product and end users from Self-Tests 1 and 2.

1. Identify product
2. Determine product purpose
3. Determine "purpose for the purpose"
4. Select level to focus on
5. Brainstorm alternatives
6. Repeat steps four and five

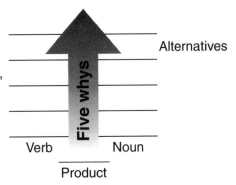

Endnotes

1. The customer-satisfaction process and the contents of this chapter are derived from the "Creating a Customer-Centered Culture method"® of IMT (a firm for which I was a partner). This material is used with IMT's permission. (See appendix A.) For more information on the topics of this chapter, please visit www.imtc3.com.

   Other materials used in this chapter reference chapters 1–5 from *Creating a Customer-Centered Culture*, Robin Lawton (Milwaukee, WI: ASQC Quality Press, 1993) and *Customer-Centered Improvement Tools for Teams*, Robin Lawton, 1995.

2. For more on this topic, see Ken Miller, "Are Your Surveys Generally Suitable For Wrapping Fish?" *Quality Progress* (December 1998): 47–51.

3. The concept of three levels of products was first introduced by Robin Lawton in *Creating a Customer-Centered Culture* (Milwaukee, WI: ASQC Quality Press, 1993). The idea about which products to address first is an integral part of IMT's workshop, "Creating a Customer-Centered Culture."®

4. The four impacts of brokers were first explained by Robin Lawton in IMT's workshop, "Creating a Customer-Centered Culture."® (See appendix A.)

5. The difference between wants, needs, and expectations was first articulated by Robin Lawton in IMT's workshop, "Creating a Customer-Centered Culture."® In addition, the "our aim is to exceed your expectations" anecdote is also a workshop example. (See appendix A.)

6. To obtain a copy of the attribute wall, visit www.changeagents.info

7. Courtesy of Mark Towers (personal communication).

Customer Roles Matrix

Who is the customer?

Objectives

- Identify all existing and potential customers for the product.

- Determine the roles each customer is playing with the product.

- Discover who currently has the power over the product's design.

- Help the team focus on the wants of the end users.

Prework

Have identified a specific product that is a noun, a deliverable, and can be made plural with an "s."

Estimated Time

20 to 40 minutes

How to Introduce It

Explain that the way we determine who the customer is in relationship to a specific product. Once we are clear about the product, we can determine who the customers are.

Explain that not all customers are the same. Customers play different roles with a product. Read the definitions of end users, brokers, and fixers.

Explain that the goal is to satisfy end users first then to worry about brokers.

Diagnosis

Organize the project

Change processes

Customer satisfaction

Process improvement

Problem solving

Planning

Managing ideas

Creating buy-in

Implementation

Evaluation

Celebration

CUSTOMER ROLES MATRIX

Action Steps

1. Write the name of the product on the top of a flipchart page.

2. Write the name of the product producer on the flipchart.

3. Brainstorm all current and potential customers of the product.

   ■ Ensure that the customers identified actually have a role with the product being discussed.

   ■ If necessary, trace all the hands the product touches from the time it leaves the producer's hands.

4. For each customer on the list, identify whether they are end users, brokers, or fixers.

5. If the team has not identified any fixers, brainstorm them now.

6. Rank the customer groups in terms of who has the most power over the way the product is designed, including producer. (If the product is a new product, this will not apply.)

7. Discuss the implications of the power rankings:

   ■ How much power do the end users have?

   ■ Who has the most power and why?

End user—The customer for whom the product is primarily intended. This customer will personally use the product to achieve a desired outcome.

Broker—A customer who acts as an agent of the end user and/or the producer. This person does not personally use the product. As an agent of the end user, the broker makes the product more accessible, easier to use, and more appealing. As an agent of the producer, the broker "encourages" the user to accept the product.

Fixer—Any customer who will have to make repairs, corrections, modifications, or adjustments to the product at any point in its life cycle for the benefit of the end user.

Example

(1) Product: Individual Income Tax Form (booklet)

(2) Producer: Graphics Department

(3) Customers	(4) Role	(6) Power
Taxpayers	EU	9
Tax preparers	BK	4
IRS	EU/BK	2
Processing staff	EU	5
Phone center staff	FX	6
Legislature	BK	1
Tax policy group	BK	3
Field office staff	BK	8
Error correction staff	FX	7

(5)

Checklist

❏ The end users defined are actual users of the product identified (they physically receive it and use it to achieve some desired outcome) and not some other product.

❏ The team has considered all of the end users (none are missing).

❏ The team has not mistakenly identified a broker as an end user.

❏ Product fixers have been identified.

Customer-Segmentation Matrix

Which customer groups do we want to talk to?

Objectives

- Better understand the different segments inside each end-user group.

- Identify the end-user segments that are likely to have different expectations of the product.

- Determine which customers to include in customer inquiry method (focus groups, interviews, and so on).

- Help the team focus on the wants of the end users.

Prework

Have completed the customer roles matrix.

Estimated Time

20 to 40 minutes

How to Introduce It

Explain that not all end-user groups are homogeneous; inside each end-user group are different segments.

Give an example (for example, not all end users of a car are the same; different segments might include age, gender, income level, occupation, and so on).

Explain that we are looking for the customer segments that might have different expectations of the product so that we can talk to them separately. We want to make sure that we know what each segment wants so we can decide how to tailor the product (customization) or whether we can get by with one size fits all.

Diagnosis

Organize the project

Change processes

Customer satisfaction

Process improvement

Problem solving

Planning

Managing ideas

Creating buy-in

Implementation

Evaluation

Celebration

CUSTOMER-SEGMENTATION MATRIX

Action Steps

For each end-user group identified using the customer roles tool:

1. Write the end-user group on the top of a flipchart page.

2. Recreate the sample page on a flipchart, with the customer-segmentation categories listed vertically down the side of the page. You may add additional categories.

3. Identify whether the possible segmentation categories are relevant by asking, "Is this category relevant to this customer group?"

   Remember that a segment is only relevant if the segment will have different expectations of the product.

4. If the category is relevant ask, "What are the different segments in this category that might have different expectations of the product?" Write these responses on the flipchart next to the segment category.

5. Once complete, circle the end-user segments you would like to consider for focus groups.

   When building focus groups, you have two options:

   ■ Conduct separate focus group with each end-user segment (preferred).

   ■ Ensure each segment is represented in one focus group (when time and money are short).

CUSTOMER-SEGMENTATION MATRIX

Example

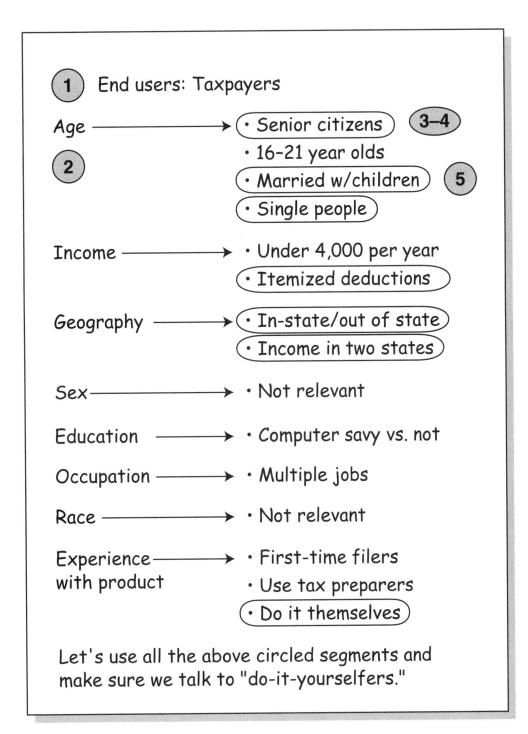

(1) End users: Taxpayers

Age ⟶ • Senior citizens   (3–4)

(2)   • 16–21 year olds
           • Married w/children   (5)
           • Single people

Income ⟶ • Under 4,000 per year
           • Itemized deductions

Geography ⟶ • In-state/out of state
             • Income in two states

Sex ⟶ • Not relevant

Education ⟶ • Computer savy vs. not

Occupation ⟶ • Multiple jobs

Race ⟶ • Not relevant

Experience ⟶ • First-time filers
with product   • Use tax preparers
               • Do it themselves

Let's use all the above circled segments and make sure we talk to "do-it-yourselfers."

Checklist

❑ The team has considered all the possible ways to segment the customers.

❑ The team has decided to focus on segments that are likely to have different expectations of the product.

❑ The team has not lumped together segments that are likely to have different expectations.

❑ The number of focus groups identified is manageable.

Focus Group Action Plan

Who will do what by when to make our focus group successful?

Objectives

- Define all the tasks necessary to set up the focus group.

- Delegate responsibility for completing them.

- Make sure that the focus group is successful.

Diagnosis

Organize the project

Change processes

Customer satisfaction

Process improvement

Problem solving

Planning

Managing ideas

Creating buy-in

Implementation

Evaluation

Celebration

Prework

Have completed the customer segmentation matrix and decided which focus groups will be conducted.

Estimated Time

10 minutes per focus group

How to Introduce It

Explain that there is nothing more embarrassing than showing up at a focus group and there are only two customers there.
Explain that there is a protocol we will be following and that if everybody does their part, we will have a successful focus group.

FOCUS GROUP ACTION PLAN

Action Steps

For each customer focus group identified using the customer-segmentation tool:

1. Appoint a coordinator responsible for the focus group.

2. Give the coordinator a copy of the focus group action plan* and ask him or her to fill in the blanks while you facilitate.

   Download a blank action plan at www.changeagents.info

3. Determine the date, time, and place most convenient for the focus group participants.

4. Brainstorm who should be invited to attend.

5. Assign responsibility for:

   ■ Calling the participants and a due date

   ■ Sending letter of invitation

   ■ Confirmation calls

   ■ Meeting room reservation and setup

   ■ Bringing the materials and refreshments

   ■ Team roles: facilitator and observers

6. Set a date for a progress check.

FOCUS GROUP ACTION PLAN

Example

① Focus Group: Married with Children
Coordinator: Mary
Date: 6/10
③ Time: 11:30 a.m.–1:30 p.m.
Place: Baptist Church

Filled in at progress check

④

Invitees	Who calls	By when	Coming Y/N	Who sends letter	By when	Sent?	Confirmation calls	When	Coming Y/N
Tom Norum	Joe	5/1	Y	Joe	5/4	Y	Joe	6/6	Y
Marty Hedges	Joe	5/1	Y	Joe	5/4	Y	Joe	6/6	N
Erica Moore	Joe	5/1	Y	Joe	5/4	Y	Joe	6/6	Y
Tammy MacAlpine	Greg	5/1	N	Joe	5/4	—	Greg	6/6	—
Ed Johnson	Joe	5/1	Y	Joe	5/4	Y	Joe	6/6	Y
Livia McLaughlin	Lesa	5/1	Y	Joe	5/4	Y	Lesa	6/6	Y
Joe Vaughn	Joe	5/1	Y	Joe	5/4	Y	Joe	6/6	Y

⑤
Room Reservation & Setup: Joe
Materials & Refreshments: Mary
Observers: Mike & Lisa
Facilitator: Mary

⑥ Progress Check: 5/12

Checklist

❏ There are specific dates for each task to be completed.

❏ The people responsible for carrying out the tasks are responsible individuals with the time to get them to done.

❏ The team members know how they are going to find the participants.

❏ The participants are a representative sample of the customer segment.

Focus Group

What do our customers want?

Objectives

■ Uncover customer's prioritized outcomes, attributes, and features of the product.

Prework

Have identified a specific product to focus on, have completed the customer roles matrix, and have completed the customer-segmentation matrix.

Have ensured participants will come by using the focus group action plan.

Estimated Time

90 to 120 minutes

How to Introduce It

Thank the participants for coming.

Explain why you are doing the focus group and what will be done with their responses. Link it to something that will make them feel like they are making a difference.

Explain the product you will be discussing, showing an example if at all possible. Ensure everyone is clear about the product you are discussing.

Explain that you will be asking a series of awkwardly worded questions to uncover their expectations of the product.

Go over the brainstorming ground rules.

Diagnosis

Organize the project

Change processes

Customer satisfaction

Process improvement

Problem solving

Planning

Managing ideas

Creating buy-in

Implementation

Evaluation

Celebration

FOCUS GROUP

Action Steps

1. Brainstorm* responses to the question:

   "If you could change one thing about (product name), what would it be?"

   *Recommend round-robin variation

2. Prioritize the list using multivoting.*

   *Recommend they call out votes to you

3. Introduce the concept of product attributes, and direct their attention to the *attribute wall*.*

   If you do not have an attribute wall, you will first need to brainstorm responses to the following question: "A satisfying product name is one that is . . ."

   *The attribute wall can be downloaded at www.changeagents.info

4. Using sticky-dot multivoting, have each participant vote for his or her five most important product attributes.

5. Tally the votes, and circle the apparent top priorities.

6. Do a gut check.

7. For *each top priority*:

   ■ Ask the group, "What does *attribute name* mean to you?"

   ■ Brainstorm product features by asking the group, "What do we need to do to the product to make it *attribute name*?"

8. (Optional, depending on product) Brainstorm* responses to the following question:

   "A satisfying (product name) is one that results in . . ."

   *Recommend round-robin variation

9. Close the meeting by summarizing the purpose of the focus group, what will happen next, and whom they can contact for more information. Thank them.

Example

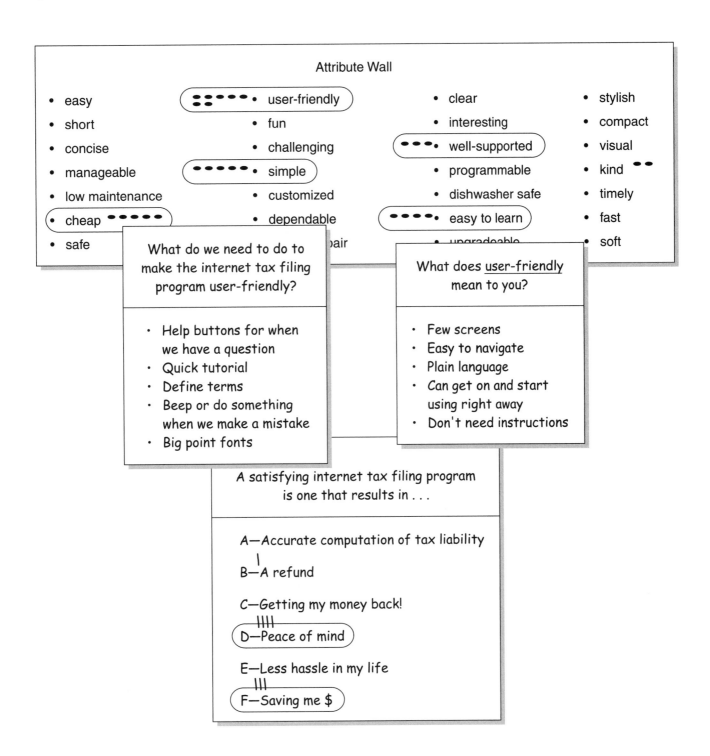

Attribute Wall

- easy
- short
- concise
- manageable
- low maintenance
- cheap ●●●●●
- safe

- user-friendly ●●●●●●●
- fun
- challenging
- simple ●●●●●●
- customized
- dependable
- ̶r̶e̶p̶a̶i̶r̶

- clear
- interesting
- well-supported ●●●●●
- programmable
- dishwasher safe
- easy to learn ●●●●●
- ̶u̶p̶g̶r̶a̶d̶e̶a̶b̶l̶e̶

- stylish
- compact
- visual
- kind ●●
- timely
- fast
- soft

What do we need to do to make the internet tax filing program user-friendly?

- Help buttons for when we have a question
- Quick tutorial
- Define terms
- Beep or do something when we make a mistake
- Big point fonts

What does <u>user-friendly</u> mean to you?

- Few screens
- Easy to navigate
- Plain language
- Can get on and start using right away
- Don't need instructions

A satisfying internet tax filing program is one that results in . . .

A—Accurate computation of tax liability
|
B—A refund

C—Getting my money back!
||||
D—Peace of mind

E—Less hassle in my life
|||
F—Saving me $

Checklist

❑ It is very clear what their priority outcomes, attributes, and features are.

❑ There were few mix-ups (such as talking about attributes when you were looking for outcomes).

❑ The customers were giving their expectations of the correct product.

❑ The responses were written in the voice of the customer (we captured what they said, not what we wanted them to say).

❑ You are clear about what each expectation identified means.

❑ The participants had fun and were comfortable saying what was on their mind.

Focus Group New Product

What do our customers want?

Objectives

Uncover customer's prioritized outcomes, attributes, and features of the product.

Prework

Have identified a specific product to focus on, have completed the customer roles matrix, and have completed the customer-segmentation matrix.

Have ensured participants will come by using the focus group action plan and have arranged the room properly.

Estimated Time

90 to 120 minutes

How to Introduce It

Thank the participants for coming.

Explain why you are doing the focus group and what will be done with their responses. Link it to something that will make them feel like they are making a difference.

Explain the product you will be discussing, showing an example if at all possible. Ensure that everyone is clear about the product you are discussing.

Explain that you will be asking a series of awkwardly worded questions to uncover their expectations of the product.

Go over the brainstorming ground rules.

Diagnosis

Organize the project

Change processes

Customer satisfaction

Process improvement

Problem solving

Planning

Managing ideas

Creating buy-in

Implementation

Evaluation

Celebration

FOCUS GROUP NEW PRODUCT

Action Steps

1. Brainstorm* responses to the question:

   "A satisfying (product name) is one that results in . . ."

   *Recommend round-robin variation

2. Brainstorm responses to the question:

   "A satisfying (product name) is one that does not result in . . ."

3. Combine the two lists and multivote.*

   *Recommend they call out votes to you

4. Tally the votes, and circle the apparent top priorities.

5. Introduce the concept of product attributes, and direct their attention to the *attribute wall*.*

   If you do not have an attribute wall, you will first need to brainstorm responses to the following question: "A satisfying *product name* is one that is . . ."

   *The attribute wall can be downloaded at www.changeagents.info

6. Using sticky-dot multivoting, have each participant vote for his or her five most important product attributes.

7. Tally the votes, and circle the apparent top priorities.

8. Do a gut check.

9. For *each top priority:*

   ■ Ask the group, "What does *attribute name mean* to you?"

   ■ Brainstorm product features by asking the group, "What do we need to do to the product to make it *attribute name*?"

10. Close the meeting by summarizing the purpose of the focus group, what will happen next, and whom they can contact for more information. Thank them.

FOCUS GROUP NEW PRODUCT

Example

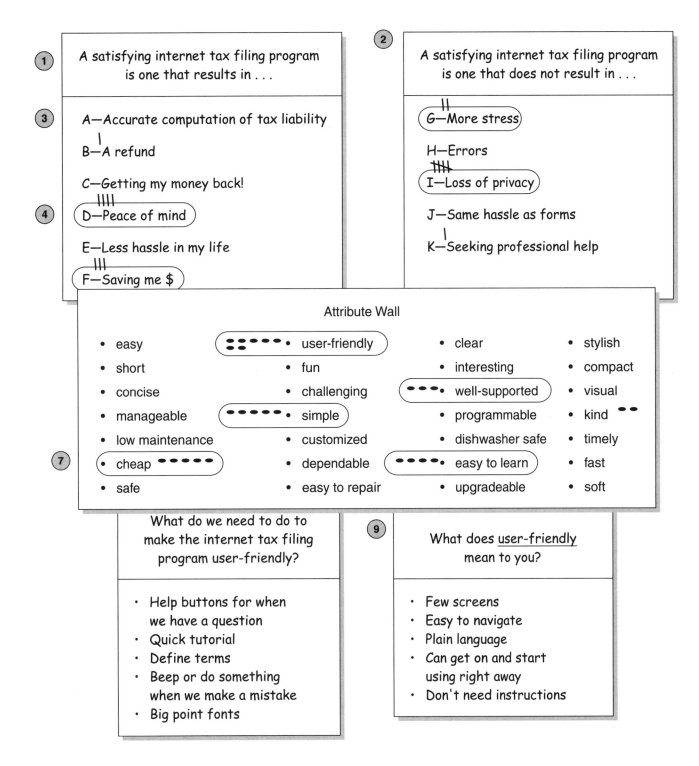

(1) A satisfying internet tax filing program is one that results in . . .

(3) A—Accurate computation of tax liability
B—A refund
C—Getting my money back!
(4) D—Peace of mind ||||
E—Less hassle in my life
F—Saving me $ |||

(2) A satisfying internet tax filing program is one that does not result in . . .

G—More stress ||
H—Errors ||||
I—Loss of privacy
J—Same hassle as forms
K—Seeking professional help

Attribute Wall

- easy
- short
- concise
- manageable
- low maintenance
- cheap
- safe
- user-friendly
- fun
- challenging
- simple
- customized
- dependable
- easy to repair
- clear
- interesting
- well-supported
- programmable
- dishwasher safe
- easy to learn
- upgradeable
- stylish
- compact
- visual
- kind
- timely
- fast
- soft

(7)

What do we need to do to make the internet tax filing program user-friendly?

- Help buttons for when we have a question
- Quick tutorial
- Define terms
- Beep or do something when we make a mistake
- Big point fonts

(9) **What does <u>user-friendly</u> mean to you?**

- Few screens
- Easy to navigate
- Plain language
- Can get on and start using right away
- Don't need instructions

Checklist

❏ It is very clear what their priority outcomes, attributes, and features are.

❏ There were few mix-ups (such as talking about attributes when you were looking for outcomes).

❏ The customers were giving their expectations of the correct product.

❏ The responses were written in the voice of the customer (we captured what they said, not what we wanted them to say).

❏ You are clear about what each expectation identified means.

❏ The participants had fun and were comfortable saying what was on their mind.

Voice of the Customer

How will we measure customer satisfaction?
What criteria will we use when (re)designing the product?

Objectives

Turn subjective customer expectations into objective measures of satisfaction that can be used for product design and real-time evaluation of customer satisfaction.

Prework

Have completed a customer-inquiry method (focus groups, interviews, and so on) that derives customers' priority attributes.

Estimated Time

5 minutes per attribute

How to Introduce It

Explain that many of the end user's priority attributes are subjective and squishy (read some of them).

Explain that if we are to be able to do anything with them, we need to turn them into something objective. (The definition of *objective* is that you and I can agree on exactly what it means.) For example, *fast* is subjective. *The number of minutes to complete the order* is objective.

Explain that once we have converted the subjective attributes into objective measures, we will use them for design criteria and as a way to measure customer satisfaction on an ongoing basis. (Use the lawn mower example. *Easy to start* can be measured by the number of pulls, with *zero to one* as the target. We want to identify ways to make the mower start in *zero to one* pulls.)

Action Steps

For each focus group conducted:

1. Write one of the priority attributes on the top of a flipchart.

2. Brainstorm possible ways to measure that attribute by asking the following:

   "The number of *what* would tell us this product is or is not (*attribute*)?"

   Remember, measures must start with either "number" or "percent."

3. Prioritize the best measures (the vital few).

4. Set a goal for each priority measure.

   ■ The goals, where possible, should be from the customer's point of view. (For example, how many minutes does the customer want to wait in line?)

   ■ Goals can be a single number or a range (for example, 25 percent, or less than 5 minutes).

5. Repeat steps one through four for each priority attribute.

6. Brainstorm ways to meet each of the numerical goals. Use the customers' suggestions from the focus groups as guides.

Examples of potential measures for an instruction booklet when the end users have said they want it "easy to understand" are as follows:

Number of clarifying questions asked by customers	goal = 0
Percentage of users who ask clarifying questions	goal = 0
Number of seconds to find an answer in the booklet	goal = <10 seconds

Example

(1) Easy to complete

(2) # minutes to complete (4) < 30 min.

% do it themselves 100%

% correct 100%

calls for assistance 0

lines to complete < 10

~~# requests of duplicate form~~

(3) ~~% of taxpayers that did own~~ ~~last year~~ and now use ~~preparer~~

Checklist

❏ The team has found an objective way to measure each subjective attribute.

❏ The measures are actual measures (number or percentage).

❏ The measures are not all reactive problems; that is, they can only be measured after the fact when something goes wrong (like number of grievances or number of complaints). Some are proactive measures of satisfaction (like the number of pages on the form or the number of days to complete an order).

❏ The goals are the ideal goals from the customers' view point (that is, if you asked them what the goal should be, this is how they would answer).

Innovation Tool*

Are we making the right product?

Objectives

- Decide what business we should be in.
- Come up with innovative new products that could better achieve customer- and producer-desired outcomes.
- Develop alternatives to the existing product that could better achieve customer- and producer-desired outcomes.
- Identify ways to improve the existing product to better achieve customer outcomes.

Estimated Time

20 to 40 minutes

How to Introduce It

Explain that continuously improving existing products is not enough to ensure long-term survival. (For example, the slide rule, typewriters, and film have been replaced by new products from different companies.)

Explain that it is important that we think of innovative alternative products that could better achieve customer-desired outcomes.

Explain that we are not trying to build a better mousetrap, but we are trying to find new ways to not have mice.

Explain that this exercise is going to push them outside of the box. They may not be comfortable out there, but it is a critical step in the process.

Encourage them to be creative. Reinforce the rules of brainstorming. Explain that at the end of the exercise they may decide that they are currently making the right product, but at least that decision will be made by choice and not by default.

*This tool is a conglomeration of several tools by GOAL/QPC, Ralston Consulting, and IMT.

Diagnosis

Organize the project

Change processes

Customer satisfaction

Process improvement

Problem solving

Planning

Managing ideas

Creating buy-in

Implementation

Evaluation

Celebration

Action Steps

1. On the bottom of a flipchart, write the name of the product.

2. Brainstorm the primary purpose/outcome of the product on a stick-on note.

   ■ The purpose should contain a verb and a noun (for example, the purpose of a home loan is to *buy a house*).

   ■ Use the desired outcomes from customer focus groups as guides.

3. Brainstorm the next purpose level by asking, "Why do we want to (verb and noun from the previous purpose)?" (That is, "Why do we want to buy a house?") Place the stick-on note above the previous note on the flipchart.

4. Repeat step three until it gets ridiculous.

5. Ask the group which purpose/outcome level they would like to use for brainstorming new product ideas.

6. Brainstorm alternatives* to the existing product that can better achieve the selected purpose/outcome by asking, "What could we do instead of a (product name) to better achieve this purpose?"

   Alternatives are not improvements to the existing product; they are fundamentally new products.

7. Repeat steps five and six for the next highest purpose/outcome level.

Example

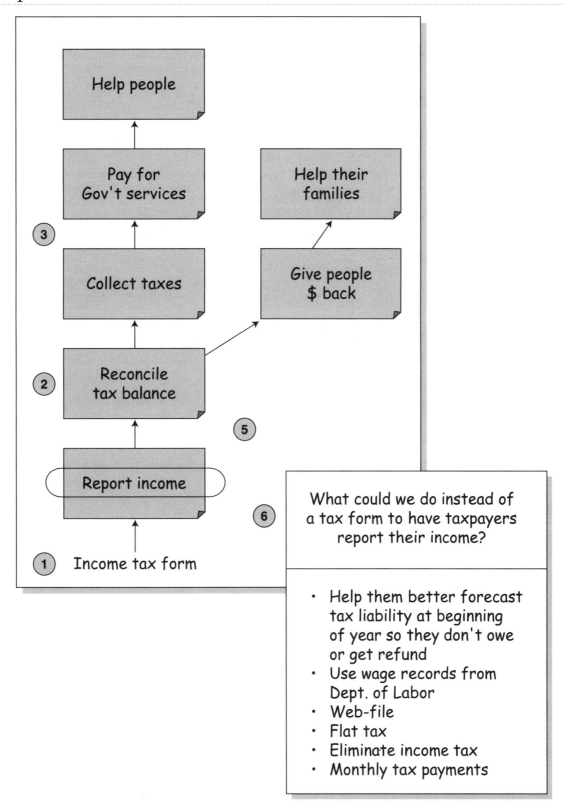

Checklist

❏ The team's focus was not too narrow (they got outside the box).

❏ The team came up with at least 10 interesting alternative products.

❏ The alternatives are focused on the customer-desired outcomes.

❏ The alternatives are totally different products, not just different versions of the same product. (For example, a training manual placed on a CD is still a training manual; the CD-ROM is not an alternative product.)

Chapter Four

Process-Improvement Process

Better, faster, cheaper . . .

Many organizations have some form of process-improvement process in place. Interestingly, however, they tend to be targeted at the wrong objective. Most process-improvement models stress the use of statistical process control and control charting techniques. This results in the absurd notion that the primary objective is to limit variation within a process. Consider the Department of Motor Vehicles (DMV) office once again. Conventional process improvement techniques would ask you to do the following:

- Establish a baseline performance level (let's say people waiting in line for 90 minutes).

- Create a control chart (Figure 4.1) so you could track the variance above or below the 90 minutes.

- Only when the process got out of control (people waiting in line 120 minutes) would you act, using problem-solving techniques to identify the cause of the increased delay.

What do you get by employing these methods? You get a very stable process (90 minutes in line) that is nowhere near customer expectations (less than 15 minutes). On the bright side, at least it is consistently bad.

Rather than focusing on *stability*, the process-improvement process focuses on *time*. The objective is to cut as much time from the process as possible.

How many times have you found yourself asking, "Why does this take so long?" Processes take so long and get so complex because they evolve over time. Gradually, what was once a very simple task becomes a 75-step nightmare as the following takes place:

- The organizational structure changes
- Mistakes happen (which create *protective* steps)
- Turnover increases
- Micromanagers enter the picture
- Computer systems are modified/added

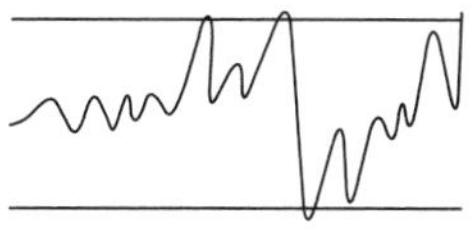

Figure 4.1 Control chart.

- Legislation is passed
- Auditors introduce more "controls"
- The boss says so
- Legal counsel wants to "minimize risks" (but not minimize the risk of losing the customer)

There are any number of events that turn a walk in the park into a walk through the maze from *The Shining*. Why don't these processes get better? After all, we have had teams, total quality management (TQM), quality circles, strategic planning, performance management, employee suggestion systems, and so on. The reason most processes do not improve is that there is rarely one person in charge of the entire process. Most substantial processes cut across the organization, dipping into any number of functional silos. Most improvement efforts are done vertically, down hierarchical lines, where every unit does what is best for the unit (Figure 4.2). Similarly, every employee is encouraged to do his or her best job. The culmination of everybody doing a good job and maximizing his or her performance is an incredibly cumbersome process.

Successful process improvement typically involves cross-functional products. It is the very nature of these processes that creates so much opportunity. The following are inherent in most cross-functional processes:

- Lots of handoffs
- Lost time sitting in in-baskets
- Numerous sign-offs and approvals
- Sequential processing (B cannot be done before A)
- Specialized functions (of which there are never enough people)
- Bottlenecks
- Lots of checking and rechecking
- Numerous contact people with whom the customer must deal

These processes are ripe for improvement. The improvement objective I like to set for any process that has not been through a major overhaul is an 80 percent reduction in cycle time on the first try. Skeptical? I never have seen a team not meet the 80 percent goal once they try. Here is why: Research has shown that between 95 percent and 99.95 percent of any process is waste.[1] That is, work is actually occurring in only .05 percent to 5 percent of the elapsed time of a process. The rest of the

The improvement objective I like to set for any process that has not been through a major overhaul is an 80 percent reduction in cycle time on the first try.

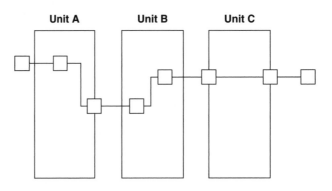

Figure 4.2 Processes and silos.

time is lost in handoffs, in-baskets, batches, and backlog. The team's challenge is twofold: get the elapsed time as close as possible to the work time, and eliminate as much work time as possible.

The process-improvement process uses unique and innovative analysis tools to help teams:

- Cut cycle time (by 80 percent)
- Reduce errors
- Reduce complexity
- Reduce cost
- Increase customer satisfaction

The process consists of four steps:

1. Observe the process
2. Flowchart the process
3. Measure process performance
4. Improve the process

Observe the Process

Processes are better seen than described. There is something about seeing the layout and meeting the people that really brings the opportunity to life. Observing the process firsthand also helps you spot problem areas you may not discover any other way. For example, team members were on a process walk-through when they observed a small closet filled to the top with boxes. One team member asked an employee what the purpose of the boxes was. The employee said he did not know but that they were going to need a bigger closet soon. It turned out that the boxes were filled with rejected customer transactions that nobody was working. The "missing" transactions languished in the closet for years.

The following strategies will make a process walk-through productive:

- Have a tour guide who is knowledgeable and unafraid.
- Let the folks working in the process know what is going on beforehand. Anytime employees see a group of people with clipboards watching them work, they get nervous and assume the worst.
- Observe the process in the order in which it happens. (Pretend you are one of the forms or inputs.) Try to first see the process as if everything went smoothly, then go back and visit the defect routes.
- Do not forget the customer's part of the process!
- Ask some very simple questions to uncover the opportunities:

Elapsed time	"How long does this step take?"
Work time	"How long would this step take you to do if you could just sit down and do one with no interruptions?"
Bottlenecks	"Why is that big pile there?"
Error points	"Where do the most errors occur?"
Rework	"Where do we do rework (fix errors)?"
Batches	"What are we waiting for here?"

And most importantly, **"Why do you do that?"**

Work time—*Time during a process when actual work is happening*

Elapsed time—*The total time in the process (work time plus any time spent on handoffs, waiting, batches, and so on)[2]*

When finished with the walk-through, the team should have a clear mental picture of the process and its players. Team members should also be giggling at all of the opportunity they have just discovered. It is helpful to assign somebody to capture the elapsed and work time for the whole process. At each process step, ask about both. When the walk-through is over, this person adds them all up. Further giggling occurs when the team sees that 95 percent of the process is waste.

A very helpful tip for observing and flowcharting a process is the *principle of one.* You will quickly discover that steps in a process often happen in batches. Step B cannot begin until step A has completed a batch of 50 forms. These batches make it very hard to determine work time. To avoid this, use the principle of one—flowchart the process and ask people questions as if the process only produced **one widget.** (Suppose you only had one form to process; how long would it take?) The team will quickly see how much work in the process exists to serve the batches (counting the widgets in the batch, recording the count, verifying the count, and so on).

Flowchart the Process

There are many different types of flowcharts, each with its own utility. Two common flowcharts are as follows:

> **Micro**—Low-level flowchart (Figure 4.3), good for seeing all the decisions and variations in a process
>
> **Macro**—High-level flowchart (Figure 4.4), good for big picture view

The *macro flowchart* is good to use when scoping a project. The *micro flowchart* is helpful when you really need to see the nitty-gritty. In between these two is a very powerful tool developed by Robin Lawton called the *FACT sheet* (**F**unction **AC**tivity **T**ime). The *FACT sheet* elegantly captures the following:

- The players in the process
- The tasks in the process
- Work time and elapsed time for each task
- Handoffs
- The total work time and elapsed time for the entire process (that is, the size of the opportunity)

The *FACT sheet* is the simplest way I have ever seen to truly understand a process and to surface the opportunities. The areas for improvement become obvious:

- Areas that have the longest elapsed time
- Areas with the biggest gap between elapsed time and work time
- Areas with a lot of work time
- Areas with large gaps between best-case and worst-case elapsed time

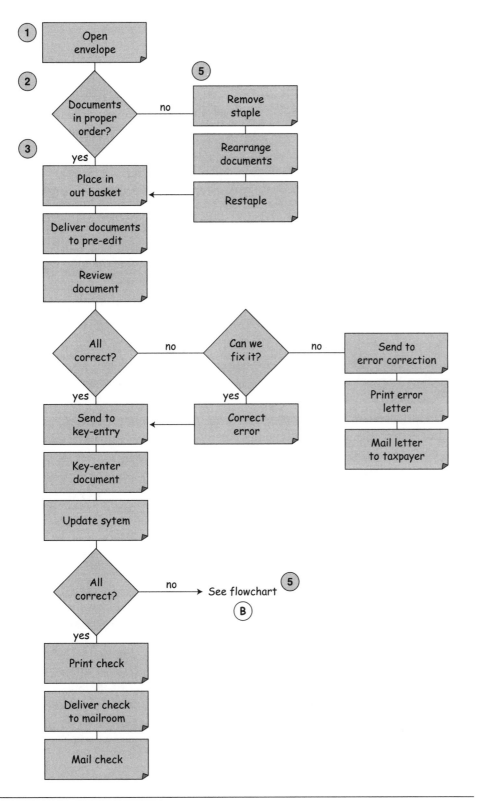

Figure 4.3   Micro flowchart.

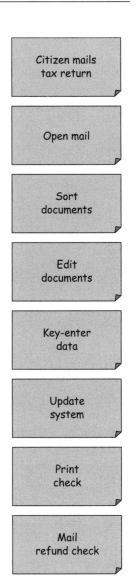

Figure 4.4   Macro flowchart.

The *FACT sheet* is easier to create using flipchart paper and stick-on notes. Cover a wall (or several walls) with flipchart paper or butcher's paper. Using stick-on notes, capture the tasks performed by each player. Keep the following helpful hints in mind:

- Remember the principle of one.
- Do not forget the customer's process.
- Flowchart the best-case/most typical scenario (without all the reject and decision routes). The *FACT sheet* does not work well with multiple paths. If the process has multiple paths, each path will need its own *FACT sheet*.
- Tasks should include a verb and a noun (complete form, get approval, call customer).
- Do not record tasks like *give to Mary*. The *give to* is obvious by the fact that the next task is performed by a separate player. Also, do not record *hold, wait*, and so on. These will be factored into the time estimates.
- Tasks processed in parallel should be in the same column.
- If someone does several things in a row, do not create separate steps for each.

Once all the steps have been laid out, record three measures of time on each stick-on note (Figure 4.5):

- In the upper-left corner, record the **work time** (how much actual work time it would take to do one without wait times, interruptions, batches, and so on).
- In the upper-right corner, record:
  - **Elapsed time for the *best-case* scenario.** This is not necessarily the same as work time. Often the actual best-case scenario may still be significantly longer than the work time.
  - **Elapsed time for the *worst-case* scenario.** This does not mean a hurricane hitting or an outbreak of the Ebola virus. Rather, when things go bad (when all the variations happen), how long does it take? For example, it may only take two minutes to look up a customer's account on a computer, but worst case is that the record is not in the system and a manual paper search has to be ordered. These searches take three days, and they do not work weekends.

Calculate the final values for total work time and total elapsed time—best and worst case. Do the math (elapsed time/work time), and see if there is 80 percent room for improvement. The *micro flowchart* can be used later to analyze specific parts of the *FACT sheet* if necessary (see Figure 4.6).

Another useful flowchart is the product flowchart. The product flowchart allows you to see the chain of deliverables produced in a process, their associated producers, and end users. This flowchart helps identify all of the customers in a process. The team can use this information (and the customer-satisfaction process) to ensure each product meets its customers' expectations. Additionally, one of the quickest ways to simplify or streamline a process is to eliminate a product inside the process. If a product can be made obsolete (such as an application form), then all of the process steps associated with it go away as well (editing the application, entering into the computer, verifying the accuracy, and so on).

```
4H   30D-120D
Find new
lease space
```

Figure 4.5 Sample task.

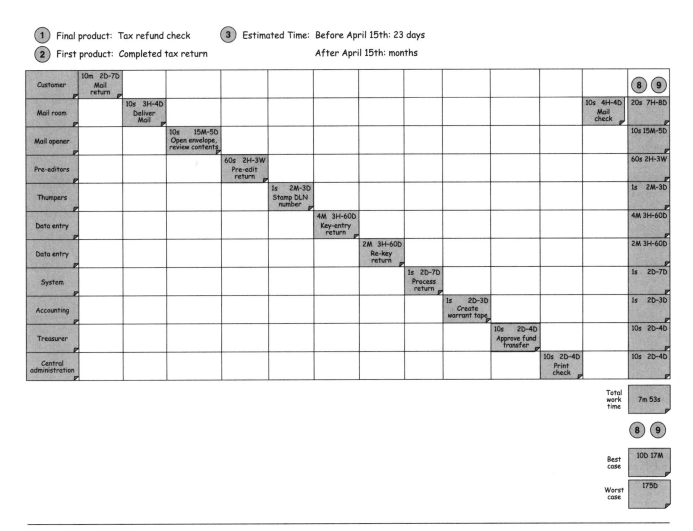

Figure 4.6 FACT sheet.

Measure Process Performance[2]

When analyzing a process it is helpful to know the following:

- **Volume.** Determine how many widgets are produced, preferably with trend data. The data are helpful for spotting issues. For example, if the team is working on an internal product like *PC repairs*, an increase in volume is not a good thing. By collecting the data, the team can then analyze why there is an increase and what impact it is having on the organization.

- **Cost to produce.** The cost to produce includes all of the costs that can be attributed to making the product. For example, if the product is a *Customer-Satisfaction Workshop*, the costs would include the costs of materials, renting a room, refreshments, travel costs, and most importantly, the cost to design and deliver the course. Remember, time is money. If an individual spends 10 hours developing a course, then the cost is 10 times that person's hourly wage. A good rule of thumb regarding what to include in *cost to produce* is to include only those costs that would go away if we stopped making this product. For example, if we stopped doing the Customer-Satisfaction Workshop, would the Training Manager go away?

- **Customer cost.** This is a measure of the customer's cost to own or use the product. Rarely is this captured by organizations, and rarely will you find a measure better able to spur innovation. To calculate the customer cost, you need to measure all the costs the typical customer incurs buying, using, and owning the product. For example, we all know that the cost to own or use a car is more than the sticker price; there is the cost of gasoline, oil changes, tire changes, routine maintenance, insurance, and so on. All of these factors contribute to the overall cost to own or use. However, there is also the cost of time. If my car has trouble, I have to take it to the repair shop. It might take me an hour to go there and deal with the staff and another hour to go there and pick it up when it is finished. Those two hours are cost!

- **Cycle time (elapsed time).** Cycle time is simply how long it takes to produce one product from start to finish.

- **Yield.** Yield is a process measure that tells us how much we "get" for our effort. It is traditionally used to show how many products are produced correctly the first time. For example, the yield for a mortgage application could be how many applications are submitted correctly, with no need for rework. If 80 out of 100 are correct, then the yield is 80 percent. In addition, the bank could also measure the yield of how many applications are approved. If 90 out of 100 are approved, the yield for this step is 90 percent. However, the yield for the whole process would only be 72 percent. (Of the 80 percent that make it through the first step, only 90 percent will make it through the second; 90 percent of the 80 percent = 72 percent.) The yield of an entire process can never be higher than the lowest yield inside of it (Figure 4.7).

The team members should look for all of the places in the process where they can measure yield. For example, a sales organization could measure how many leads are generated by promotional events, how many leads become prospects, and how many prospects become buyers. At the minimum, the team needs to know what percentage of the products is produced correctly the first time. That is, how many make it from the beginning of the process to the end with no rework or correction steps?

In addition, the team should measure the cost of low yield. That is, what does each error cost the organization? How much is spent to fix mistakes? For example, what is the cost to a bank when a mortgage application is denied? The team could show that it costs the organization $200 to process an application from start to finish. So each denied application costs $200. This could spur the teams to think of innovative solutions to cheaply prescreen applicants before they submit an application.

The team members should be able to pull these data from existing reports. If not, they may have to collect data themselves. In either case, use the *data-collection action plan* to guide their activity.

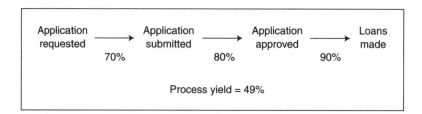

Figure 4.7 Process yield.

Improve the Process

There are two schools of thought regarding improving an existing process. One school says to carefully analyze all of the details of the process and find the opportunities for improvement. The other school says to start with a blank slate; throw everything out and start from scratch. Again, the best method is somewhere in the middle. While we do not want to get bogged down or paralyzed by analysis, we do want to make strategic decisions about process improvement. (I have seen too many "reengineering" projects where the team naively assumed all that "other stuff" in the process could be discarded. That "other stuff" usually kills the project. The devil *is* in the details.)

The *process-analysis checklist* is a great tool for finding the opportunities inside the *FACT sheet*.

The following example illustrates some key principles for making radical process improvements. The *FACT sheet* shown in Figure 4.8 illustrates the process for producing income tax refund checks (a process on which we all depend). Notice the

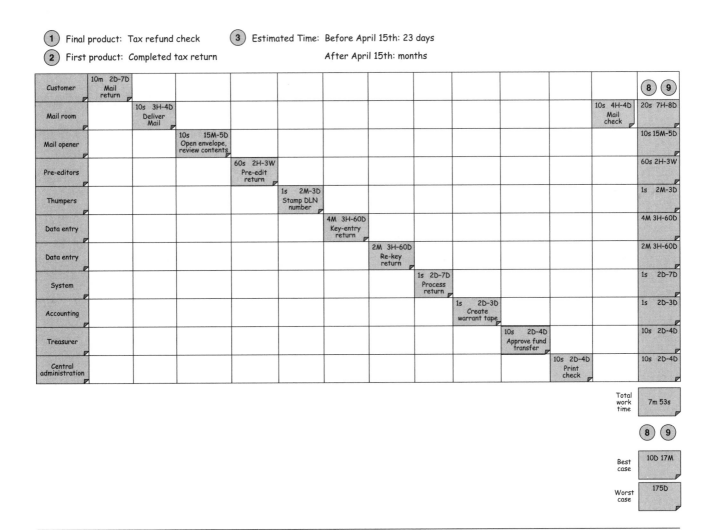

Figure 4.8   Income tax refund FACT sheet.

major discrepancies between work time and elapsed time. Simply put, it takes 3 minutes to do one tax return from start to finish with no interruptions, wait times, or backlog. However, it really took 23 days to produce a check from start to finish. How does 3 minutes become 23 days?

In the real world, few processes produce just one widget. Similarly, you can imagine the volume of tax returns that are received around April 15th. With large volumes, the goals quite often shift from *speed* to *control*. The operating questions are, "How do we keep from losing stuff?" "How do we manage the chaos?"

What causes chaos in a process? Handoffs. Any time there is a handoff, there is the sense that something may get lost. In fact, what does happen is that we do lose something. And somebody gets yelled at, so we create a procedure. That procedure says, "Count everything you get, and count everything you pass on, and record them." This creates a lot of extra work (not 22 days worth, but some). Before long, someone says, "It sure would be easier if, rather than recording each one, I could wait every hundred or so." This gives birth to Rosemary's baby—*the batch*.

Batch processing is the enemy of speed.

Batch processing is the enemy of speed. With a batch, we are saying that the progress of one widget is dependant on 99 other widgets. Widget A does not get anywhere until 99 of his friends are ready. Consider getting your family ready for church on Sunday. If you only had to take care of yourself, you would probably get there on time. But instead, you have to wait until every kid has been dressed, fed, hair combed, and loaded in the car. This is a batch. Your family arrives at church in a batch. Why do we batch the family? So no one gets lost.

The tax refund process was ripe with batches. How do you know where they are? Look for the major gaps between work time and elapsed time. If something only takes one second to do but languishes for three days, there is a good chance it is part of a larger batch. Here is how batches affected the tax refund process:

Toters and fetchers showed up at 9:00 and 3:00 to transport the tax returns from pre-edit to key-entry. This is two giant batches. If a tax refund was edited by 9:01, it could not move on in the process until 3:00. See how this robs time?

Behind most process problems is a policy decision (and the policy decisions reveal our values). Because of limited processing capacity in the mainframe computer, a policy decision had been made years ago that tax returns with checks attached to them (people owed taxes) would be processed nightly. Tax returns where the citizen was owed a refund would be processed on the weekend. What did this policy reveal about the values of the organization? What impact did this policy have on the speed of tax refunds?

No matter how hard individuals worked to do their job, if the refund return was not entered into the system by Friday at noon, it was not going to be processed until eight days later! The team members investigated the policy and, much to their surprise, they found out that the citizens' checks were being deposited daily, regardless of when the returns were entered into the system. The urgency of processing those returns nightly was gone, because the money was already in the bank. Refunds were time-sensitive and were not processed until the weekends. This little discovery eradicated a big batch and cut one to seven days of cycle time just like that.

If batches are Rosemary's baby, backlog is the devil himself.

Where else is there a large discrepancy between work time and elapsed time in the refund process of Figure 4.8? Clearly there is a problem in key-entry. It only takes a couple of minutes to data enter a return, yet it was taking one to two weeks for the process. Why? Backlog. If batches are Rosemary's baby, backlog is the devil himself. How do we get in a backlog situation? We get there through another B word—*bottlenecks*.

Every process has a bottleneck—a part of the process that is slower than all of the other parts, the area that cannot keep up, the place where inventory piles up, or the weakest link in the chain. Every process has a bottleneck; the trick is to find it. There are two ways:

1. Observe the process and look for piles.

2. Look at statistics. (Refer to Table 4.1.) For each of the functions, it identifies how many returns they can complete in a day. Suppose 25,000 tax returns came in a day. *Determine how many employees you would need in each function to keep up.* (All 25,000 need to be processed in a day.) Table 4.1 shows how many employees were actually in each unit. Clearly, there was a bottleneck in key-entry.

What is life like for workers in the bottleneck? Sticking with our theme, it is hell. They are constantly supervised; they usually have quotas, discipline, pressure, and high turnover. The operating management philosophy is MUSH! We need to recognize that the people are not the problem; it is the process!

A critical principle of process improvement is to fix the bottleneck first. It does little good to make improvements in front of the bottleneck. For example, referring to Table 4.1, suppose the mail openers found a way to double their output. How many more tax returns would be processed each day? Zero. Everything must be done to accelerate performance in the bottleneck.

Our friends in the tax refund process had to find a way to get more people doing key-entry. Their solution was to convert all of the non-value-added jobs into key-entry jobs. Which steps in the process were not adding value? (In other words, the task was not essential to process a return and to produce a refund check.) Essentially, all the tasks except key-entry were non-value-added. Consider the following example:

- The **toters and fetchers** were unnecessary if we could eliminate handoffs (no need to deliver paper all around the unit).

- The **thumpers** existed to stamp a batch control number on each return. If batches were eliminated, the thumping could also be eliminated.

- The **BAMS entry person** was there to enter the batch control numbers into the computer. Yet another slave to the batch.

- The **pre-edit folks** existed to keep the people in the bottleneck from thinking. Their job was to correct as many mistakes as they could so key-entry people did not waste their time. The same was true with the mail openers. They existed to make sure that the tax returns were in the right order for the key-entry people.

The team's solution was to consolidate all of the jobs into one. That is, a single employee would open the tax return, look for mistakes, and enter it into the

What is life like for workers in the bottleneck? Sticking with our theme— it is hell. They are constantly supervised, and they usually have quotas, discipline, pressure, and high turnover.

Table 4.1 Returns completed per day.

	Produce daily	# FTE	Total produced
Opener	300	75	25,000
Editor	400	60	25,000
Thumper	1,700	15	25,000
Key-entry 1	100	75	7,500
Key-entry 2	100	75	7,500

computer—no batches, no handoffs, no backlog. Each tax return could be finished in three minutes. By eliminating all of the other jobs, they had enough people to do key-entry and even saved some money (through attrition). This is the key to process improvement: **eliminate, consolidate, and then automate**[2]—in that order. Too often organizations rush to automate their process without ever changing the actual work. A friend of mine refers to that as "paving cow paths." Another state spent $75 million dollars to automate its tax return process. That state can now produce tax refunds in three weeks. The team I am describing can produce tax refunds in three days and saved money!

You will notice that in this entire example, we changed the structure of the work but not how the work was done. Nothing was compromised for the sake of speed. And most importantly, employees were not asked to work harder or faster. The gain is in the structure of the process. Our first goal in process improvement is to get elapsed time as close as possible to work time. Once that is accomplished, we move on to our second goal: eliminate as much work time as possible.

Unfortunately, most improvement efforts get these two goals backwards. That is, they start by trying to reduce the amount of time it takes to do each task. Again, these gains are irrelevant if there are bottlenecks and batches. Once the process structure is changed, then you can reap the rewards of individual task savings. In the case of the tax refund process, elapsed time went from 23 to 3 days. (Without major changes at organizations outside of their own, they would not be able to go any faster.) However, there was still only three minutes of work being done on each tax return. The team members shifted their goal to cutting out as much of the three minutes as they could. Based on the enormous amount of volume they were dealing with, calculation showed that each second of work time they saved would be one less temporary employee they needed to hire during tax season. What a compelling case for change! The team worked diligently to simplify the key-entry screens and to remove any cumbersome activities from the work. The team shaved over a minute off of the work time, saving over 60 positions. Imagine, faster speed at less cost (and better quality—error rates dropped by over 20 percent).

As I mentioned at the beginning of this chapter, the process-improvement process focuses first on time. Only after we have eliminated as much time (and work) as possible, do we start to work on the variation in the process. That is, the goal becomes as follows: how do we ensure that as many widgets as possible follow the straight path (no errors, no exception routes, no rework)? The problem-solving process is an excellent resource for finding and eliminating the causes of the process problems.

As you can imagine, the process changes recommended by the team were not easy. They were challenging the basic conventions of the core process of the organization. The solution was not just rearranging boxes on a chart, but surfacing and challenging the assumptions and values of the organization.

To successfully implement their new process design involved far more than rearranging chairs and writing procedures. The organization had to change the way it measured and rewarded people. The old system was based on quotas for each task. So every function in the process was rewarded for throwing their work over the wall as fast as possible (so it could pile up in front of the bottleneck). The new system switched to team goals consisting of the number of days to process refunds and the percentage of returns each day that were processed.

In addition, the organization had to change the way it was structured. (A key point I have hammered repeatedly—change the system first, then change the structure.) Under the old system, each step in the process was in a different organizational silo. No one had the authority or responsibility for the whole system. Under the new system, the structure was changed to put the entire process in one unit under one manager who had both the responsibility and the authority to ensure it ran smoothly.

This case study illustrates the key principles of process improvement:

- Every process must have a goal.
- In any process, 95 percent to 99.95 percent of the time is waste.
- It is possible to see 80 percent improvement at less cost.
- Change the structure of the process before changing the work.
- Watch out for the three Bs—batches, backlog, and bottlenecks.
- Eliminate, consolidate, then automate.
- Behind every process problem is a policy decision.
- Process design reflects the values of the organization.

Coupled with the *FACT sheet,* the *process-analysis checklist* can help you achieve the same extraordinary results for any process you set out to improve.

Endnotes

1. Adapted from IMT's workshop, "Creating a Customer-Centered Culture."® Used with permission. (See Appendix A.) The statistics are based on George Stalk and Thomas Hout. *Competing Against Time: New Time-Based Competition Is Reshaping Global Markets.* New York: The Free Press. 1990.

2. Adapted from chapter 6 of *Creating a Customer-Centered Culture* by Robin Lawton (Milwaukee, WI: ASQC Quality Press, 1993). The definitions appear as value-added time and cycle time in Lawton's work.

FACT Sheet

How long does the process take?
What percentage of the process time is opportunity?

Objectives

Help the team understand the whole process.

■ Help the team identify opportunities for time reduction.

■ Help the team determine where in the process to focus first improvement efforts.

Prework

Have observed the process from start to finish.

Estimated Time

2 to 3 hours

How to Introduce It

Explain that we want to get a clear picture of each of the steps and players in the process.

Explain that we want to identify how long the process takes and how much of that time actual work is occurring.

Define *elapsed time* and *work time*.

Explain that 95 percent to 99.95 percent of the time in most processes is waste (lost time due to handoffs, batches, approvals, and so on) and that our goal is to get the total process time as close to the total work time as possible. After that, we will try to cut as much work time out as possible.

Diagnosis

Organize the project

Change processes

    Customer satisfaction

**Process
improvement**

    Problem solving

    Planning

Managing ideas

Creating buy-in

Implementation

Evaluation

Celebration

Action Steps

1. On a flipchart, write the name of the final product the customer receives, which is the purpose of this process.

2. Write the name of the product/deliverable that is created first in this process. (Steps one and two define the scope.)

3. Estimate the usual amount of time the process takes to go from beginning to end.

4. On a stick-on note, identify the first activity in the process. The activity should contain a verb and a noun (for example, request product information). Place the stick-on note at the top of the left-hand side of the workspace.

5. Identify the organizational function or person that performs the activity. Write the name on a stick-on note, and place it to the left of the activity.

6. Repeat steps four and five for each activity in the process, sequencing the stick-on notes in the order in which they occur. The far left-hand column will be the players in the process. Only activities that occur simultaneously (in parallel) should be shown in the same column.

7. Record three units of time on each activities' stick-on note:

    a. In the upper-left corner, identify the actual *work time* to complete the activity, excluding any delays and waiting time. (How long would it take you to do one if you could just sit down and do it?)

    b. In the upper-right corner, identify the *best-case and worst-case elapsed time*. Best case is how long the activity will take if everything goes well (may or may not equal elapsed time). Worst case does not mean a hurricane or outbreak of the Ebola virus; rather, it refers to how long the activity takes when things go wrong.

8. Add up all of the work time for the activities in each row, and record them at the end of the row. Add up the row totals to get the total work time for the process.

9. Add up all of the elapsed time for the activities in each row (one total for best case and one for worst), and record them at the end of the row. Add up the row totals to get the elapsed time for the process. For any activities done in parallel, only count the longest activity in the row totals.

10. The difference between elapsed time and work time represents the size of the opportunity. The goal is to first get elapsed time as close as possible to work time and then to reduce work time.

Example

① Final product: Tax refund check

② First product: *Completed tax return*

③ Estimated Time: Before April 15th: 23 days

After April 15th: months

										⑧ ⑨
Customer	10m 2D-7D Mail return									20s 7H-8D
Mail room	10s 3H-4D Deliver Mail								10s 4H-4D Mail check	10s 15M-5D
Mail opener		10s 15M-5D Open envelope, review contents								60s 2H-3W
Pre-editors			60s 2H-3W Pre-edit return							1s 2M-3D
Thumpers				1s 2M-3D Stamp DLN number						4M 3H-60D
Data entry					4M 3H-60D Key-entry return					2M 3H-60D
Data entry						2M 3H-60D Re-key return				1s 2D-7D
System							1s 2D-7D Process return	1s 2D-3D Create warrant tape		1s 2D-3D
Accounting										10s 2D-4D
Treasurer								10s 2D-4D Approve fund transfer	10s 2D-4D Print check	10s 2D-4D
Central administration										

Total work time: 7m 53s

⑧ ⑨

Best case: 10D 17M

Worst case: 175D

127

Checklist

❏ The process was mapped as if there were only one widget being produced.

❏ The total work time is less than 5 percent of the total elapsed time. (If it is more than the work time, estimates are probably wrong.)

❏ Some real opportunities for time savings are readily apparent.

❏ The customers' tasks are part of the FACT sheet.

❏ Total time calculations include the customers' time.

Macro Flowchart

What are the major steps that occur in the process?

Objectives

- Understand the scope of the process and the major players (functions).

- See the major steps in the process.

Estimated Time

10 minutes

How to Introduce It

Explain that before we dive into the trees, we would like to see the forest.

Explain that the macro flowchart will help define the beginning and end of the process and will help determine who needs to be involved in improving it.

Action Steps

1. On a stick-on note, identify the last step in the process (when the process is complete). Place this stick-on note at the bottom of a flipchart page.

2. Identify the first step in the process (what starts the process). Place this stick-on note at the top of the flipchart page.

3. Identify the six major steps that happen in between the first and last step (using stick-on notes allows for easy editing).

   Note: There may only be four major steps, or possibly seven. The key is, it is not twelve. This is a high-level flowchart, so we are looking for the big picture.

MACRO FLOWCHART

Example

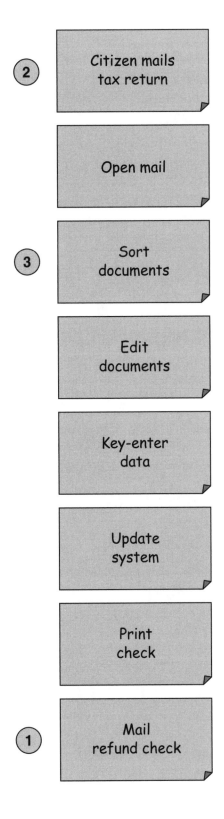

Checklist

❑ It is clear where the process begins and ends.

❑ It is clear what functions will need to be represented on a process-improvement team.

Micro Flowchart

What are all the major steps that occur in the process?

Objectives

- Understand everything that happens in the process, including decisions, decision routes, defect routes, exceptions, and so on.

- Uncover specific problem areas inside the process.

Prework

Have completed the macro flowchart or *FACT sheet* and have identified where in the process to drill down to the micro level.

Estimated Time

30 minutes to an hour, depending on the scope

How to Introduce It

Explain that with the micro flowchart we want to really drill down and see everything that occurs in the process so we can find where we have specific problems.

Explain that it is entirely likely we will have to do some problem solving to fix parts of the process.

Explain that it may take a while, but that their patience and attention to detail will be much appreciated.

Diagnosis

Organize the project

Change processes

  Customer satisfaction

  Process improvement

  Problem solving

  Planning

Managing ideas

Creating buy-in

Implementation

Evaluation

Celebration

MICRO FLOWCHART

Action Steps

1. On a stick-on note, identify the first step in the process (when the process starts). Place this stick-on note at the top of a flipchart page close to the left edge.

2. Identify the next step in the process. If the next step is an action, place the stick-on note as a rectangle below the previous note. If the step is a decision, place the stick-on note as a diamond.

3. Whenever a decision node appears, continue flowcharting the best-case scenario. We will go back and add the variations and alternate routes last. For example, if a decision node asks, "Is the application correct?" continue flowcharting the *yes* route. When finished, the micro flowchart should show vertically the smoothest route from beginning to end.

4. Continue step two until the best-case scenario is complete.

5. Go back to each decision node and flowchart the deviations off the main path. There should be plenty of room to the right of the main path. If more space is needed, make a note linking to another flipchart page.

MICRO FLOWCHART

Example

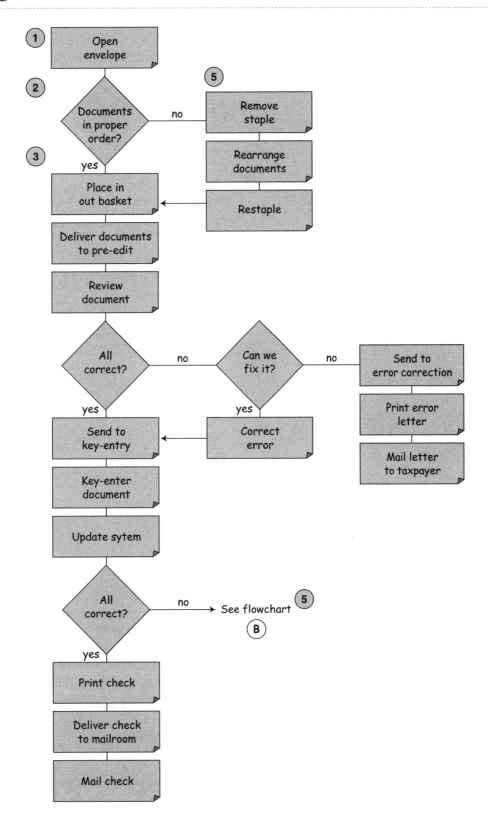

Checklist

❏ The flowchart has uncovered all of the exceptions and alternate routes in the process.

❏ The flowchart has identified where decisions in the process are made and what happens given each decision.

❏ The team has a pretty clear idea where some opportunities for improvement are.

❏ You can actually follow the process.

Product Flowchart

What are all the products produced in the process?

Objectives

- Uncover the flow of products (deliverables) in the process.

- Identify products that may be unnecessary (and, therefore, eliminate all of the steps that go into making that product).

- Identify products that may be causes of poor process performance or customer dissatisfaction.

- Identify the "internal" customers in the process to ensure that they are getting the products they want.

- Determine the quality of the source products (policies, procedures, and plans) that guide the process.

Estimated Time

45 to 60 minutes

How to Introduce It

Explain that inside each process is a flow of products—a chain of deliverables. Explain what a product is.

Explain that each product has its own set of customers and that we want to ensure that the needs of these customers are met.

Explain that the possible causes of poor process performance can be the products produced inside the process.

Explain that quite often, it is the products produced earliest in the chain (for example, the customer order, the application form, and the design specification) that have the biggest impact on the quality of the final product.

Diagnosis

Organize the project

Change processes

Customer satisfaction

Process improvement

Problem solving

Planning

Managing ideas

Creating buy-in

Implementation

Evaluation

Celebration

PRODUCT FLOWCHART

Action Steps

1. Write the name of the **target product** (the one the team is working on) on a stick-on note, and center it at the bottom of a flipchart page.

2. Write the name of the **first product** produced in the process (for example, an application form, an order form, and so on) on a stick-on note, and center it at the top of the flipchart page.

3. Identify the remaining products produced in the process. Write these products on stick-on notes, and sequence them vertically in the order in which they occur.

4. To the left of each product, identify its **producer.**

5. To the right of each product, identify the **end users.**

6. Discuss which products are troublesome, unnecessary, a source of customer dissatisfaction, and so on. Focus on eliminating products and improving those that remain. A general principle is that products produced earliest in the chain are the easiest to change and have the biggest impact on the success of the final product. For example, an airline reservation is the first product produced before a flight occurs. How well the reservationist determines the customers' needs may greatly affect the flier's satisfaction with the flight.

7. Consider identifying and discussing the **source products** (policies, rules, plans, and so on) that guide the process. Are they sufficient? Are they adversely affecting the process? Are they nonexistent (there is no guidance for the process)?

PRODUCT FLOWCHART

Example

Producer	Product	End user(s)
Graphics department	(2) Tax form and booklet	Taxpayers
(4) Taxpayer or CPA	Completed tax form	Data entry (5) Staff Auditors
Taxpayer	(3) Check (if owe taxes)	Bank
Tax information system	Customer record	Customer service reps Billing staff Error correction staff Auditors
Accounting staff	Accounting warrant request	Treasurer's staff
Accounting staff	Ledger entry	Central budget staff
Mail room	Envelope	Central administration Mailers Taxpayers
Central administration	(1) Tax refund check	Taxpayer Bank

Source Products
1. Tax code
2. Processing procedures manual

Checklist

❏ The team has accurately identified products (nouns, deliverables, can be made plural with an "s").

❏ It is clear who produces and uses each of the products in the chain.

❏ The team has targeted some of the products for improvement or elimination.

❏ The source products provide sufficient guidance for the process.

Process-Analysis Checklist

What are the opportunities for improvement inside the process?

Objectives

- Identify all the possible places in the process where improvements can be made.

- Identify which improvements should be made first.

- Identify which improvements will have the biggest impact on process performance.

- Help the team see opportunities they otherwise would have missed.

Prework

Have completed the *FACT sheet*.

Estimated Time

60 to 90 minutes

How to Introduce It

Explain that now that they have flowcharted the process, it is time to uncover all the opportunities for improvement.

Explain that once they identify the areas for opportunity, we may need to do some research and think of possible solutions. We may need to involve others who are not on the team to help research, to come up with ideas, or to bounce ideas off of.

Diagnosis

Organize the project

Change processes

    Customer satisfaction

    Process improvement

    Problem solving

    Planning

Managing ideas

Creating buy-in

Implementation

Evaluation

Celebration

PROCESS-ANALYSIS CHECKLIST

Action Steps

Functions

- Can the number of functions (departments, work units, or individuals) be reduced? (If so, consider using their talents to provide additional services for which you have not had resources.)

- Which movements between functions could be eliminated or the distance/time decreased?

Activities

- Which activities offer the greatest potential for improvements?

- Which steps are unnecessary and could be eliminated?

- Will changing the sequence of the steps result in greater efficiency?

Time

- Which activities consume the most elapsed time?

- Which activities consume the most work time?

- Which activities show the greatest discrepancy between work time and elapsed time?

- Based on the previous three answers, which activities should be improved first for greatest reduction in elapsed and work time?

- How can time be saved on critical path activities? (The critical path is the series of tasks that must be completed as scheduled to produce the final product. Time saved on noncritical path activity is a mirage. It has no effect on elapsed time.)

- Which activities could be done in parallel to reduce elapsed time?

Batch Processing

- Where does batch processing occur?

- What is its impact on elapsed time?

- Can reducing batch size improve elapsed time?

Inspections

- Where does inspection by third parties occur?

- Why are inspections done? What is the inspector's real reason for needing to see the product or information about it?

- How else could the need be addressed?

- Can the inspections be made unnecessary?

PROCESS-ANALYSIS CHECKLIST

Yield

- At what points (activities) should yield be checked?
- Measure and chart actual yield.
- How can yield be increased?

Variation

- Where does variability occur in the process (that is, something that necessitates exception processing or special handling)?

Rework

- Where do rework or correction cycles occur? How can they be eliminated or reduced?
- Where do errors occur in the process? How can they be reduced?
- What can be done earlier in the process to eliminate rework?

Cost

- Which activities represent the greatest cost?
- How can cost be reduced?

Complexity

- Where does the process seem unnecessarily complex?
- How can it be simplified?

Customer Contact

- Where are customers given an "I don't know" answer?
- Where can responsiveness to customers be improved?
- Where can "friendliness" of customer contact be improved?
- Where can information be given to customers to shape their expectations?
- How can the number and duration of contact points be reduced?

Checklist

❏ The team has identified numerous opportunities for improvement.

❏ The opportunities, if improved, will lead to at least an 80 percent reduction in process time.

❏ The team is not stuck in the "We have to do it that way!" mode.

❏ It is pretty clear how the process could be restructured to improve speed and to reduce complexity.

Chapter Five

Problem-Solving Process

Elementary my dear Watson, elementary . . .

Problem solving is the grandfather of performance improvement. Most early quality and continuous-improvement initiatives stressed problem solving and went to extraordinary lengths to teach all employees the methods and tools to solve problems in their work area. The investment in training far outweighed the returns to the bottom line. When people said total quality management (TQM) failed, it was actually problem solving that failed, often for the following reasons:

Random optimization. It was entirely possible to fix a problem in one area that either had no impact on overall performance or negatively impacted performance in another area.

Didn't involve the customer. Most problem-solving exercises centered around improving internal problems. In the rare instance when these efforts did focus on customers, it was usually to figure out how to eliminate customer dissatisfiers. Again, as discussed in chapter 3, it is entirely possible to eliminate all things that dissatisfy customers and still not satisfy them.

World hunger. The problem-solving tools and methods are effective for identifying and removing discrete, quantifiable problems. They are not effective for developing the strategy of the organization or "improving morale."

Reactive. Problem solving is reactive by its very nature. Organizations that actively embraced problem solving as their change method of choice were perpetuating their own problems. Change efforts should be focused on proactively improving systems and preventing problems. If you ever have seen the carnival game *Whack a Mole,* you have a pretty good idea of what problem-driven organizations look like.

Overreliance on tools, not the thinking behind problem solving. Problem solving is detective work. It involves looking for clues, interviewing witnesses, tracking down culprits, and so on. Tools are not a replacement for rational thought. It is entirely possible to solve a problem without using a seven-step process or building a histogram.

The problem-solving process is not a strategic tool. It does not replace the customer-satisfaction process, process improvement, or planning; it supplements them. It should only be used to solve discreet problems where the root cause is unknown. Consider a detective. You only call in a detective when you really do not know who committed the crime.

The problem-solving process is quite effective at preventing a common team foible: jumping to solutions. Our Western culture rewards problem solvers. People are paid to solve things. That will be the team's inclination throughout problem solving. As I have stressed many times, however, the solution is not the solution because the problem is not the problem. The problem-solving process uses five steps to help the team come up with the best solution to solve the real problem:

1. Define the problem
2. Verify the problem
3. Write the problem statement
4. Look for the root cause
5. Develop the solution

Define the Problem

The problem-solving process (Figure 5.1) can often start out a little vague. Teams will often set out to determine the following:

- How to reduce turnover
- How to eliminate rejects
- How to reduce abandoned phone calls (customers that give up on hold)

These are all problems, yes, but they are not specific enough to solve at this point. The *problem-solving template* (Figure 5.2) is a good resource to determine whether you have a broad issue or a specific problem.

Until you know the facts, you do not know the problem. If you can fill in the *problem-solving template* at this point, you may skip to the step, looking for the root cause. However, I would encourage you to try the next step, as it may further refine the problem statement.

Verify the Problem

Once we have an issue, such as *reduce rejected applications*, we need to collect some data to better understand the issue. Here we are trying to move from a vague issue to a specific problem statement.

We are trying to uncover the nature of the problem, or the following:

Who?

What?

When?

Where?

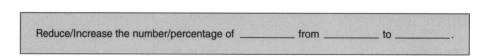

The solution is not the solution because the problem is not the problem.

Define the problem

↓

Verify the problem

↓

Write the problem statement

↓

Look for the root cause

↓

Develop the solution

Figure 5.1   Problem-solving process.

Figure 5.2   Problem-solving template.

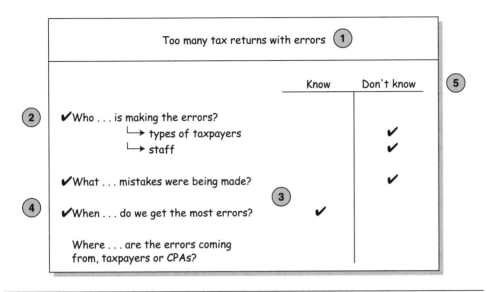

Figure 5.3   Know/don't know tool.

The *know/don't know* tool (Figure 5.3) is a great way to understand the problem and all of its dimensions.

Once the team members have thought of everything they would like to know about the problem, they then will set out to gather the data necessary to analyze the problem.

Data gathering consists of three parts:

- Collecting
- Displaying
- Analyzing

Collecting Data

Team members can use the *data-collection action plan* (Figure 5.4) to guide their efforts. The *data-collection action plan* was created to minimize the common problems that happen when teams try to gather information by:

Composing a clear research question. This way the team is seeking an answer and not just collecting data.

Clarifying all terms. This helps to ensure the team is comparing apples to apples. Practically any word can mean different things to different people. For example, a team was collecting data on rejected applications. One team member collected data on applications rejected by hand, while another team member thought rejects included those kicked out by the computer. The word *reject* was not clearly defined.

Building the chart before collecting the data. This prevents the team from collecting data that cannot be analyzed. Quite often a team member will bring in lots of data but no one can figure out what it all means. By building the chart first, the team member knows specifically what he or she is seeking. It also forces the team to think of things like scope and timeframes for the data before too much time is wasted.

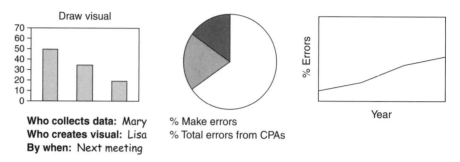

How many customers make mistakes?

Definitions: Mistakes—A tax return that has to be
sent back to the taxpayer for correction.
Customers—Can be taxpayers or
their accountants. (Break it out for each.)

Draw visual

Who collects data: Mary
Who creates visual: Lisa
By when: Next meeting

% Make errors
% Total errors from CPAs

This data will help us decide: Whether errors are significant and if CPAs make
significant errors.

Figure 5.4   Data-collection action plan.

For the items the team members already know (they have the data), they can
skip collection and move right to displaying and analyzing the data.

Displaying Data

There are numerous tools that exist for displaying and analyzing data. With many,
you can lose the forest for the trees. That is, team members get so wrapped up in
how to build a chart that they forget its primary purpose—to help find an answer.
To simplify things, I stress the use of three data-displaying tools (Figure 5.5):

Bar charts. Bar charts are best used to make comparisons (for example, this
year's budget compared to last year's or Unit A's errors compared to Unit
B's errors).

Trend charts. Trend charts are best used to see trends over time (such as
volume of customer calls each month or average turnaround time each
day). You can also use trend charts to compare the trends of two variables
over time (for example, Unit A's budget growth compared to Unit B's).

Pie charts. Pie charts are best used to show proportions (such as Unit A's share
of the organization's budget or the percentage of errors from repeat
customers).

It will be useful later if the team identifies the source of the data on the bottom
of the chart.

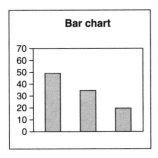
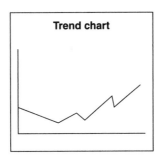
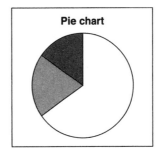

Figure 5.5 Data-displaying charts.

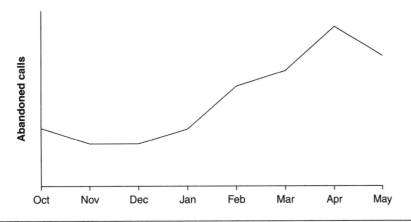

Figure 5.6 Trend chart.

Any team member can create these three simple charts. They can use pencil and paper, Microsoft Excel, or whatever. Rather than having the team members bring in reams of data, have them bring only information—the charts. The team can look at the charts to do their analysis.

Analyze Data

The charts and graphs should help the team figure out the who, what, when, where, why, and how. For example, the trend chart shown in Figure 5.6 shows that the problem did not start until February. What happened in February? This will help lead you to the root cause.

Analysis can be an iterative process; as the team members dig deeper and deeper, they will want more data. Just continue the same steps: collecting, displaying, and analyzing the data.

Reduce/Increase the number/percentage of _____ from _____ to _____ .

Figure 5.7 Problem-solving template.

Write the Problem Statement

Once the team members fully understand the scope and nature of the problem, they are ready to create the formal problem statement. The problem statement focuses the remaining steps of the problem-solving process.

Hopefully, through analysis, the team has determined what is not the problem, where the problem is not occurring, and so on. The problem statement crystallizes this analysis into a simple statement (Figure 5.7).

If the team members cannot complete this statement, they have not done enough analysis. If the team needs more than one problem statement, that is okay. However, each problem will be handled separately.

Look for the Root Cause

The root cause of the problem often becomes apparent during the data-collection phase. For example, Figure 5.6 revealed a sharp increase in abandoned calls starting in February. The team will probably be able to determine the root cause for that rather quickly (for example, a new phone menu was installed that confused customers).

When the root cause is not obvious, the team will need to brainstorm. (However, I always feel more confident in a root cause uncovered through data.) Here are a couple of effective ways to brainstorm the root cause:

Reverse the findings of the *know/don't know tool*. That is, if we know where the problem is happening, where is it not happening? What could account for the difference? If we know when the problem started happening, what is different between then and before it started happening? This is detective work using deductive reasoning.

Construct a fishbone diagram or *root cause chart*. One of the oldest quality tools around is called a fishbone diagram. I prefer the Western version called the *root cause chart* (Figure 5.8). The *root cause chart* works as follows:

1. The problem statement is written at the top of a flipchart.

2. The team uses stick-on notes to brainstorm all possible causes of the problem.

3. The team organizes the notes into logical groupings with a heading (for example, training issues, equipment issues, policies, and so on).

4. The team selects the most likely cause(s). These causes will need to be verified. Any cause identified using the root cause chart should stand up to the *know/don't know tool*. For example, the new phone menu could not be the cause of increased abandoned calls if it was also used with phone lines where the abandoned rate did not increase.

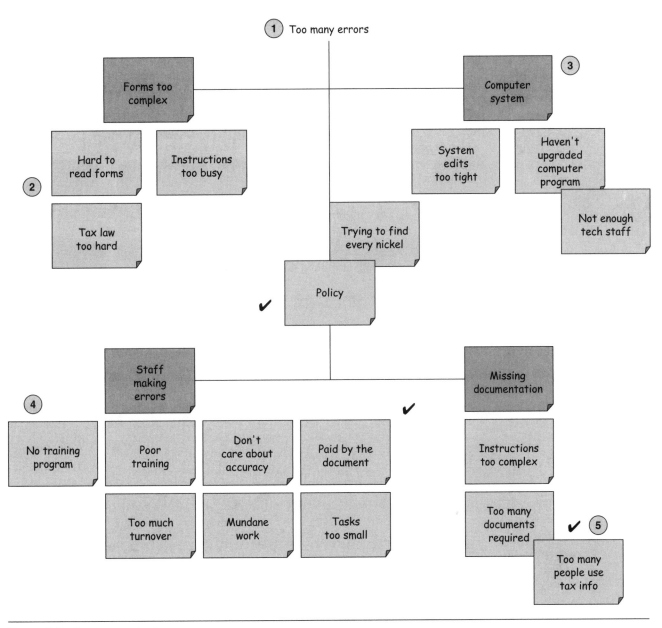

Figure 5.8   Root cause chart.

Ask five whys. This method helps the team get to the real root. If the team members feel they know why the problem is happening, ask them, "Why is *that* happening?" When they answer that, ask again, and again, and again. By asking why five times, you get past the easy, surface answers and find the hidden causes (see Figure 5.9).

Develop the Solution

Once the team members have identified the root cause, they will generate solutions that remove the root. The solution-generation process is described in chapter 7, Managing Ideas.

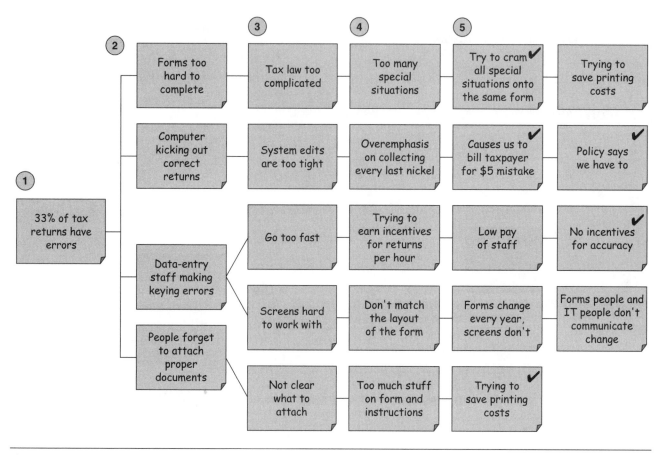

Figure 5.9 Five whys.

Know/Don't Know

What information do we need to gather to better understand the problem?

Objectives

- Identify the information the team wants to know to better understand the problem.

- Identify whether the information currently exists or needs to be researched.

Prework

Have identified an issue/problem to work on.

Estimated Time

30 minutes

How to Introduce It

Explain that before we can solve a problem, we need to get to its root cause. Without data, it is often hard to find the root cause. This exercise will help us uncover what we know about the problem and what we need to find out.

Diagnosis
Organize the project
Change processes
Customer satisfaction
Process improvement
Problem solving
Planning
Managing ideas
Creating buy-in
Implementation
Evaluation
Celebration

Action Steps

1. Write the problem/effect/issue at the top of a flipchart page.

2. Down the left side of the flipchart, write the following items:

   Who, What, When, and Where

3. Ask the team to try and come up with research questions for each of the items. (For example, "Who is resigning?" or "Where is the highest turnover?")

4. After all of the research questions have been developed, prioritize the ones in which the group is most interested.

5. For each of the prioritized research questions, indicate whether the team currently knows the answer or does not know and needs to do some research.

6. Have the team members complete a *data-collection action plan* for answers they do not know.

An effective way to find the cause of a problem is to reverse the findings of the know/don't know tool. That is, "What is different about where (when, who, and so on) the problem is *not occurring*, and *how might that be the cause?*"

Example

	Too many tax returns with errors ①		
		Know	Don't know ⑤
② ✔Who . . . is making the errors?			
└→ types of taxpayers			✔
└→ staff			✔
✔What . . . mistakes were being made?			✔
④ ✔When . . . do we get the most errors? ③		✔	
Where . . . are the errors coming from, taxpayers or CPAs?			

Checklist

❑ The research questions identified by the team are sufficient to understand the problem.

❑ The research questions are specific enough that the team knows what data it is seeking.

❑ It will be possible to collect the necessary data to understand the problem in a reasonable amount of time.

Five Whys

Why is the problem really occurring?

Objectives

■ Uncover the real root cause of the problem.

Prework

Have completed the problem-statement template.

Estimated Time

30 to 45 minutes

Diagnosis

Organize the project

Change processes

Customer satisfaction

Process improvement

Problem solving

Planning

Managing ideas

Creating buy-in

Implementation

Evaluation

Celebration

How to Introduce It

Explain that many times the solution is not the solution because the problem is not the problem.

Explain that this exercise will help the team get to the bottom of the problem and will ensure that their solutions eradicate the problem and not just treat the symptoms.

FIVE WHYS

Action Steps

1. Write the problem/effect/issue at the far left side of a flipchart page, halfway down.

2. Ask the team why this problem occurs. Write each of these possible causes on a stick-on note, and place the notes vertically to the right of the problem statement.

3. Each of the causes now becomes a problem statement. For each cause ask, "Why is this occurring?" and/or "How does it cause the problem?" Write each of these responses on stick-on notes, and place them vertically to the right of the cause.

4. Repeat step three until there are at least five columns (that is, you have asked why five times) or until the team feels it has reached the fundamental cause(s).

5. Place a checkmark on the causes the group wants to pursue further.

FIVE WHYS

Example

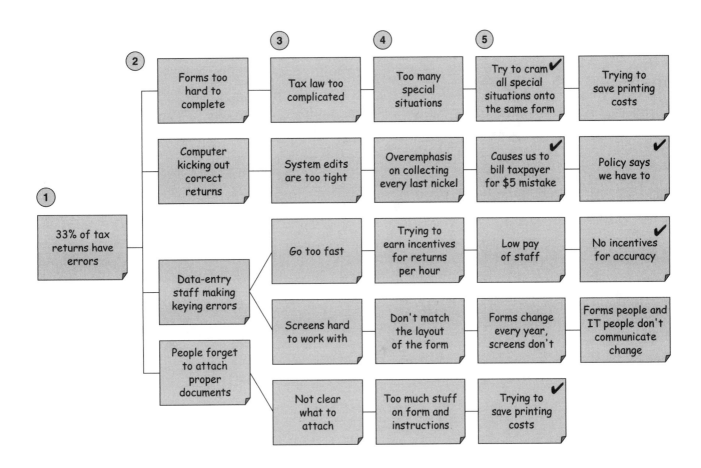

Checklist

❏ The team asked why five times.

❏ The team feels like it has gotten to the root of the problem.

❏ The root of the problem is not something vague like "poor training."

Root Cause Chart

What is the root cause of our problem?

Objectives

- Uncover the root cause of the problem.

- Systematically eliminate what is not the root cause.

Prework

Have completed the problem statement template

Estimated Time

30 to 45 minutes

Diagnosis

Organize the project

Change processes

Customer satisfaction

Process improvement

Problem solving

Planning

Managing ideas

Creating buy-in

Implementation

Evaluation

Celebration

How to Introduce It

Explain that the solution is not the solution because the problem is not the problem.

Explain that we want to get to the root of the problem and not just treat the symptoms.

Explain that once the team members think they have found the root cause, they may need to do some research to verify it.

ROOT CAUSE CHART

Action Steps

1. Write the problem/effect/issue at the top of a flipchart page.

2. Using stick-on notes, brainstorm all possible causes of the problem.

3. Organize the notes into logical groupings with headers (for example, training issues, policies, equipment, and so on).

4. Looking at the ideas/causes under each heading, probe to determine the "cause for the cause." For example, if possible causes of phone calls are customer errors, then ask, "Why are customers making errors?" Place these additional ideas on stick-on notes, and attach them to the original cause.

5. The team selects the most likely cause(s).

An effective way to find the cause of a problem is to reverse the findings of the *know/don't know tool.* **That is, "What is different about where (when, who, and so on) the problem is** *not* **occurring, and how might that be the cause?"**

Example

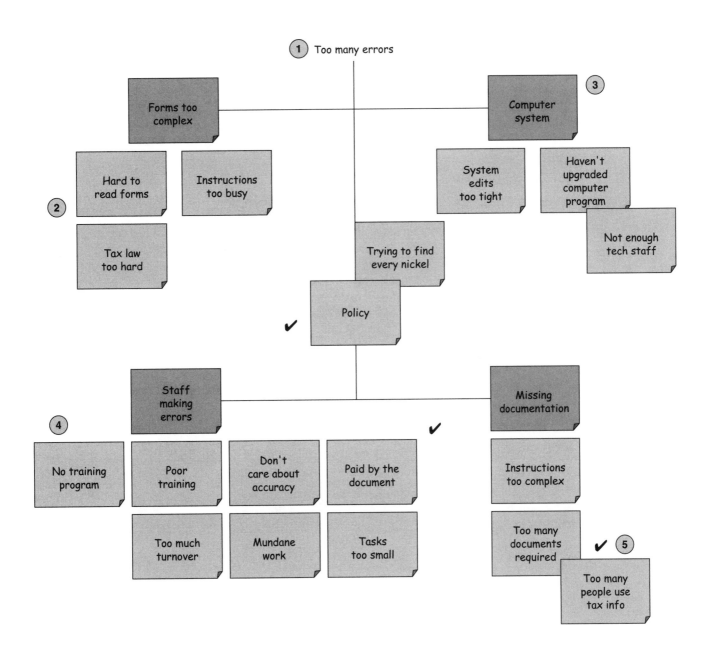

Checklist

❏ The team has uncovered the root cause.

❏ The root cause can be verified.

❏ The root cause is not vague (like "poor training").

❏ The root cause stands up to the logic of reversing the know/don't know tool (for example, if the root cause identified is also in place in another unit that is not having the problem, then it is not the root cause).

Data-Collection Plan

Who will do what by when to collect the data we need?

Objectives

- Help the team clarify what information they want before they spend time researching.

- Help the team get clear on what they plan on doing with the data once they have it.

- Ensure the data are collected in a valid and timely manner.

Estimated Time

15 minutes

Diagnosis

Organize the project

Change processes

Customer satisfaction

Process improvement

Problem solving

Planning

Managing ideas

Creating buy-in

Implementation

Evaluation

Celebration

How to Introduce It

Explain that before we spend time chasing our tails, it is best to be really clear about what we want to know before we set out to collect data.

Explain that the best way to figure out what data we need to collect is to draw the charts first; we can then see specifically what we need.

DATA-COLLECTION PLAN

Action Steps

The data-collection plan can be brainstormed on a flipchart or completed by a team member using the template.* In either case, it consists of the following steps:

1. Define the research question the team would like answered. (For example, "Why are we rejecting applications?" or "How much are we spending on rework?")

2. Specifically define each term in the research question. (For example, "What counts as a rejected application?" or "What is meant by rework?")

3. Select how the data should be displayed visually, using one of the following:

   Bar chart—Used to show comparisons or to show the frequency of a category (such as most frequently asked questions)

   Trend chart—Used to show a trend over time (such as average phone calls per month)

   Pie chart—Used to show proportions (such as sources of the phone calls)

4. For a bar chart or trend chart, label each axis. For a trend chart, determine the appropriate time period (scope) to document.

5. Determine the following:
   - Who will collect the data
   - Who will create the visual
   - By when

6. Complete the following statement: "These data will help us decide . . . "

Note: After complete, each visual should have a footnote at the bottom documenting the data source and the methodology used to compile it. For example, if the measure is the percentage of budget spent on overhead, the methods used to calculate overhead should be delineated.

*Blank data-collection plans can be downloaded at www.changeagents.info

Example

How many customers make mistakes?

Definitions: Mistakes—A tax return that has to be sent back to the taxpayer for correction. Customers—Can be taxpayers or their accountants. (Break it out for each.)

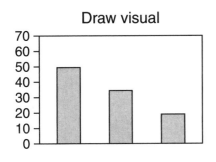

Draw visual

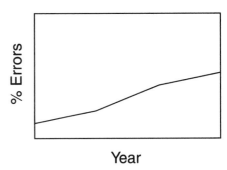

Who collects data: Mary
Who creates visual: Lisa
By when: Next meeting

% Make errors
% Total errors from CPAs

This data will help us decide: Whether errors are significant and if CPAs make significant errors.

Checklist

❏ It is clear what question the team is trying to answer.

❏ The team knows what specific data they will be seeking.

❏ All of the terms have been specifically defined.

Chapter Six

Planning Process

The planning process is a critical arrow for any change agent to have in his or her quiver. Planning can take many forms and is used in many different situations. Some of the more typical situations where the planning process is used are as follows:

- Starting a new initiative
- Two groups coming together to collaborate
- Goal setting for a work unit
- Setting priorities for the year

In short, any time an organization approaches you to help them set goals and figure out how to achieve them, you can use the planning process.

There are as many versions of planning models as there are planners. That is, everybody has his or her own nuance on planning. Each person throws in an extra step here or changes a term there, but in their essence, all planning models basically are the same. The following three key questions are at their core:

What do we want to accomplish?

What do we need to do to accomplish it?

Who will do what by when to make it happen?

Planning should be about answering these questions in the manner that best fits the situation. One size rarely fits all. Similarly, planning should not be a word-smithing exercise. I have seen organizations spend more time defining terms, training on the definitions, and editing their plans for correctness than they do on actually answering the three planning questions.

What Do We Want to Accomplish?

While this question appears self-explanatory, a lot goes into it. For one thing, nobody can agree on what to call the answers to this question. Are they goals? Objectives? Outcomes? I do not get wrapped around the axle on terminology (in fact, I prefer not to use terms at all—I just ask the planning questions). However, there are distinct differences between the terms. Goals and objectives can be somewhat interchangeable, but outcomes are an entirely different ball game.[1] Which term is appropriate depends on the type of plan you are preparing, your organization's preferences, and where in the organization the group falls. At the top of the organization, they are thinking about broad outcomes; at the bottom, they are likely developing some specific objectives. For the rest of this chapter, I will use the word *goal*; know that you can substitute whichever term you choose.

To best answer this question, there are four things you need to do ahead of time:

1. **Determine the exact wording of the planning question.** There are any number of ways to ask this question:
   - What results do we want to achieve in the next three years?
   - In light of the issues we have discussed, what do we want to accomplish?
   - What are all the things we have to do to be successful in the next three years?
   - A successful (organization name) will result in . . . .

   Each nuance or word change can fundamentally change the discussion and the output. Think hard about your audience and what they are trying to accomplish, and practice several different planning questions until you think you have the exact wording to yield the results you want.

2. **Select the appropriate time horizon.** The length of the planning horizon will impact how "big" people think. A five-year plan will have very broad goals and will be more visionary, while a one-year plan will be much more specific and action-oriented. Check with the sponsor to see what horizon he or she has in mind (and then check to make sure it is logical).

3. **Select the appropriate brainstorming method.** Consult chapter 7, Managing Ideas, for an in-depth discussion on the different brainstorming methods. The method you choose will depend on the following:
   - The size of the group
   - The amount of time available
   - The group's comfort and familiarity with each other
   - The group's past experience with planning and planning tools

   I have found the *affinity diagram* to be the best tool for this purpose. It integrates the disparate ideas of many people into a small set of shared goals. Each individual can see how his or her ideas fit into the big picture—there are no losers. In addition, it tends to elevate the group's focus. The individual ideas of the group members are often too specific or too tactical. The grouping and categorizing of these individual ideas creates broader goals with which to work. However, the affinity diagram does not work well with groups smaller than 10. For small groups or when time is short, consider freewheel brainstorming.

4. **Select the appropriate prioritization method.** The method you choose to prioritize the goals will depend heavily on the purpose of the plan and the degree to which the group members agree with each other. If the group members are comfortable with each other (or if time is short), I prefer to multivote. It is fast, and everybody gets a chance to lobby and discuss. If the group members are not very familiar with each other or they have strong, differing priorities, I will use some structured prioritization tools such as the following:

   Gap chart—Shows which goals have the most room for improvement (Figure 6.1)

   Relationship diagram—Shows which goals impact the others (Figure 6.2)

   Prioritization matrix—Shows which goals are more important than the others (Figure 6.3)

   For example, I have had the good fortune (sort of) on a number of occasions to facilitate planning sessions for leaders of opposing political parties. These folks are paid to disagree with each other. In these instances, I

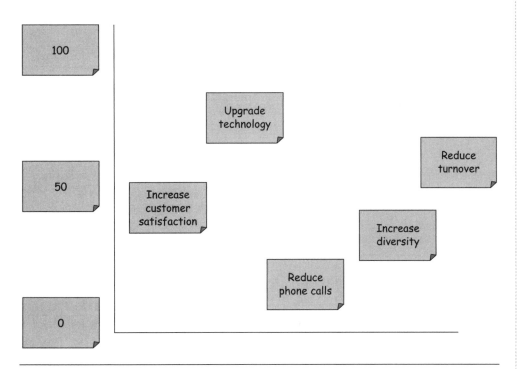

Figure 6.1 Gap chart.

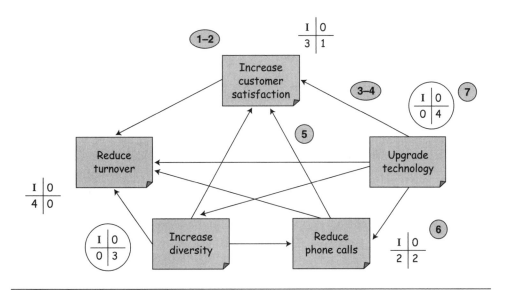

Figure 6.2 Relationship diagram.

used structured, anonymous brainstorming (affinity diagram) and all three of the prioritization tools listed previously.

A great way to use the three prioritization tools is to divide the group into three teams. Have each team use one of the prioritization tools on the goals the group has developed. When complete, each group shares the top few goals that popped out of their tool. The goals that pop out of all three tools (or at least two of them) become the top priorities.

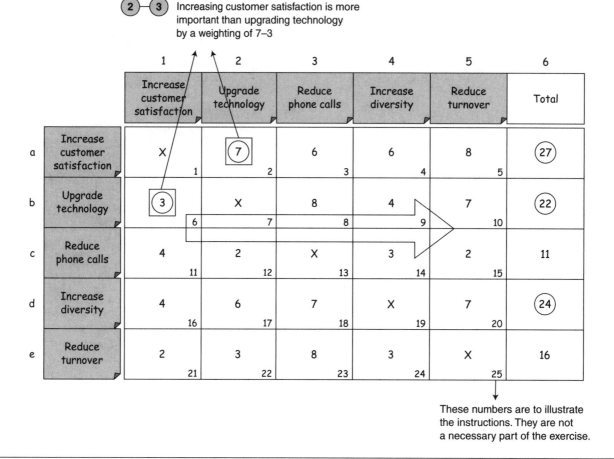

Figure 6.3 Prioritization matrix.

What Do We Need to Do to Achieve Them?

Commonly referred to as strategies, the answers to this question are the new things the organization must implement to achieve its goals. If you can think of the planning questions as a sandwich, the answers to this question are the meat in the middle of the sandwich. These answers are not broad directional statements (like goals), nor are they specific tactics (like "install the new software on all the PCs"). They are right in between.

To develop the answers to this question, you will follow similar steps as before:

- Determine the exact wording of the brainstorming question.
- Select the appropriate brainstorming method.
- Select the appropriate prioritization method.

My advice is to not use the same tools you used before. If you used an *affinity diagram* to develop the goals, do not use it again to develop the strategies (the participants will become violent. Similarly, if you used a *prioritization matrix* before, do not do it again here.

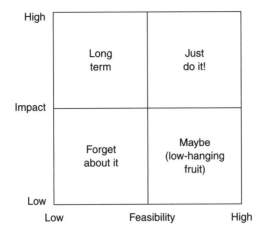

Figure 6.4   Idea filter.

The best prioritization tool I have found to use at this phase is the *idea filter* from chapter 7. The *idea filter* (Figure 6.4) sorts the ideas into four quadrants based on their impact and feasibility. Using this tool, low-impact or impossible strategies get weeded out, allowing the organization to concentrate its efforts on the strategies that will make a difference.

Who Will Do What By When to Make It Happen?

This question is actually an *action plan* (Figure 6.5). Once the priority strategies have been determined, it is time to make sure they actually get implemented. Strategies, by their very nature, are somewhat vague. Consider the following, for example:

- Build new partnerships.
- Determine how to reduce inventory.
- Expand our customer base.
- Better use the internet.

You cannot very well hand these to someone and say, "Go do it." The action-plan tool turns vague strategies into very specific deliverables to which we can attach a name and a due date.

Certain complex items on the *action plan* may require a plan of their own. For the particularly complex ones, where time is an issue and the sequence of tasks is critical, use the *project plan* from chapter 9, Implementation.

Referring to the DNA of change (Figure 6.6), planning is only part of the puzzle. Without the review sessions, the plans tend to become shelf-ware or doorstops. Review sessions should occur at regular intervals and should focus on success measures and action plan progress.

The diagram shown in Figure 6.7 can help you determine which tools, if any, to use in your planning process.

Action	Deliverable	Responsible	Due Date	Resources
Redesign 1040 booklet	New 1040 booklet printed	Tom	7/1	–
Create new short form	New short form printed	Mary	7/1	Rebid print contract
Develop Internet filing	First person files on-line	Joe	1/3/next year	Web staff (2 new hires) hardware
Offer free tax assistance in field offices	First customer uses service	Greg	1/3/next year	30 PCs
Redesign refund process	First tax refund goes out	Lesa	1/3/next year	Training We help with hiring New software New PCs
Change performance measures to include customer-satisfaction measures	New performance report	Mike	10/15	Facilitation support
Identify sources of phone calls and reduce them	Call study report with strategies	Dave	8/15	Possible new phone software

3 Review Date: 10/1

Figure 6.5   Action plan.

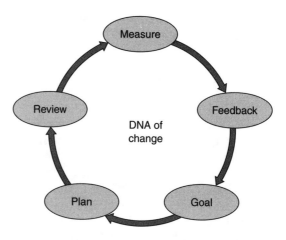

Figure 6.6   DNA of change.

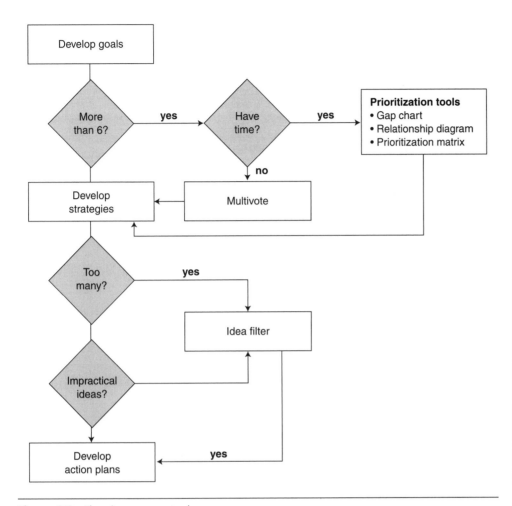

Figure 6.7 Planning process tools.

Supplemental Questions

The planning process just described is the basic, stripped-down version. It is also based on the assumption that the plan will be brainstormed as a group. This is not always the case. Strategic planning (one type of planning) is far more effective if it is driven by data. Referring again to the DNA of change, the measures and feedback (current performance) should drive the goals and the plan. Analysis should drive every stage of the strategic-planning process.

What follows is the fully loaded planning process with all the bells and whistles. You will again notice that it is driven by questions. These questions can be answered by a group during brainstorming or through research and careful analysis, whatever best fits your organization's needs.

The Big Planning Process

- What is our purpose/mission?
- What results are we here to achieve?
- How would we know we achieved them? *(What things could we count that would tell us we achieved them?)*
- What are the potential obstacles/opportunities that could greatly impact our ability to achieve those results?
- What do we want to accomplish in the next three years?
- How would we know we accomplished them? *(What things could we count that would tell us we accomplished them?)*
- What must we do to achieve them?
- Who will do what by when to make it happen?

Facilitator's Agenda: Strategic Planning Retreat

25 Participants

8:30-8:45   Sponsor kicks off the process.

8:45-9:00   Introductions. (What would you be doing today if not here? What would you rather be doing?)

9:00-9:10   Overview of the day's agenda and process.

9:10-9:45   Mission Statement (Mission Statement Template).

9:45-10:00   Break.

10:00-10:30   Strengths, Weaknesses, Opportunities and Threats (SWOT) Analysis.

Divide into four tables, and have each table work on one of the following questions:

1) *What is working well?* 2) *What is not working so well?* 3) *What* opportunities *will present themselves in the next three years that we should take advantage of?* 4) *What* threats/challenges *will present themselves in the next three years that we need to be prepared for?*

Pick someone at each table to scribe (person with the oldest car not on blocks in the yard).

10:30-10:45   Report out (have group pick a spokesperson).

10:45-11:00   Develop goals using *affinity diagram.* Planning question: *In light of the issues identified, what do we want to accomplish in the next three years?* (Everybody come up with at least five ideas.)

11:00-11:15   Break (each person needs to read all of the stick-on notes on the wall during break).

11:15-11:45   Complete *affinity diagram* (divide up the categories for each table to generate the headers).

11:45-11:50   Gut check.

11:50-12:30   Lunch (create three copies of each goal on stick-on notes).

12:30-12:35   Recap—what's next.

12:35-1:00   Prioritize goals. (Consolidate into three tables. Give each table a set of goals and one of the following prioritization tools: *prioritization matrix, relationship diagram, gap chart.*)

1:00-1:10	Report out.
1:10-2:00	Develop strategies. (Divide up the priority goals among the three tables. Let people move to the table with the strategies they want to work on, and have each table freewheel brainstorm around the following question: *"What are all the things we need to do to achieve this goal?"* Have the scribe record each idea on a stick-on note, and stick it to a flipchart.)
2:00-2:15	Break (prepare idea filter work space).
2:15-2:25	Report out.
2:25-3:00	The group at each table does an *idea filter* for its strategies.
3:00-3:15	I share the final strategies that have survived the idea filter, do a recap, and do a gut check.
3:15-3:45	I facilitate an action plan for the strategies using the *action-plan tool.*
3:45-4:00	Sponsor wraps up.

Endnote

1. Outcomes are the end result of our activities. They are usually the broadest things we plan for in that they are the definitions of success for the organization.

Affinity Diagram

What do we want to accomplish?

Objectives

- Brainstorm answers to a specific question.

- Organize the brainstormed responses into categories.

- Let the team see the affinity between their ideas.

- Develop broad, shared goals out of specific ideas (from specific to general).

- Develop great ideas/goals without people dominating the process.

Diagnosis
Organize the project
Change processes
  Customer satisfaction
  Process improvement
  Problem solving
  Planning
Managing ideas
Creating buy-in
Implementation
Evaluation
Celebration

Estimated Time

45 to 60 minutes

How to Introduce It

Explain that we want to come up with some shared goals.

Explain that we are going to take the individual ideas of everyone and look for the consistent themes among them.

Explain that this will take a little while but will produce great results.

Pass out stick-on notes and fine point markers (not pens).

AFFINITY DIAGRAM

Action Steps

1. Write the brainstorming question on a flipchart page.

2. Instruct all participants to come up with as many ideas as they can (you may give them a quota or time limit) to answer the question.

   - Each idea must be written on a separate stick-on note.

   - Each idea must contain at least four words.

   - Ensure the participants use a marker, not a pen, and write legibly.

3. When the participants are finished writing, have them place their ideas on the wall in random order.

4. Have each participant read every idea on the wall.

5. Have the group silently sort the ideas into like categories.

   - Two ideas that seem to go together (similar, same theme) should be stuck together.

   - As more and more ideas are organized together, long chains of stick-on notes should appear.

6. When all of the ideas are sorted, there should be four to eight categories. Identify a header for each category:

   - Read each idea in the category.

   - Ask the group the general theme to which the ideas point.

   - Ask the group to come up with words (at least a verb and a noun) that capture the gist of the theme. Write this statement on a different colored stick-on note, and place it atop the category.

7. Find a home for any "orphan ideas."

Example

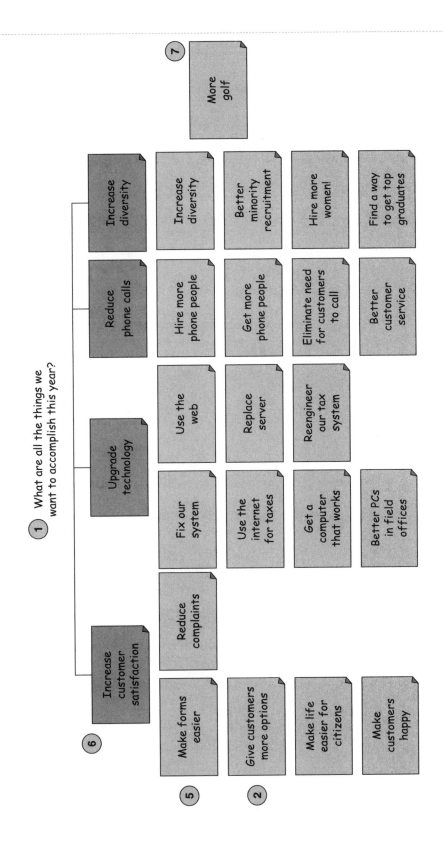

Checklist

❏ The ideas have been grouped into four to eight categories (maybe a few more).

❏ The header cards have been written with at least a verb and a noun.

❏ The team feels good about the goals identified.

Gap Chart

Which goals have the most room for improvement?

Objectives

■ Identify which goals have the biggest room for improvement (the largest gap between current and desired performance).

Prework

Have developed a list of goals

Estimated Time

10 to 15 minutes

Diagnosis
Organize the project
Change processes
Customer satisfaction
Process improvement
Problem solving
Planning
Managing ideas
Creating buy-in
Implementation
Evaluation
Celebration

How to Introduce It

Explain that when prioritizing a list of goals, it is often best to work on those that have the most room for improvement.

Explain that this tool will help them visually see the gap between actual and desired performance.

Explain that in the absence of real data, this may be a subjective analysis.

GAP CHART

Action Steps

1. Write each goal on a stick-on note.

2. Arrange the goals horizontally on the bottom of a flipchart page.

3. On the left side of the flipchart page, create a scale from 0 to 100 (*0* is bad, *100* is great, and *50* is okay but needs improvement).

4. For each goal ask the team the following question:

   "On a scale of 1 to 100, how well are we currently doing on this goal?"

5. Line up the stick-on note with its corresponding score.

6. The goals with the lowest score (the biggest gap between actual and desired performance) are the ones on which to focus.

GAP CHART

Example

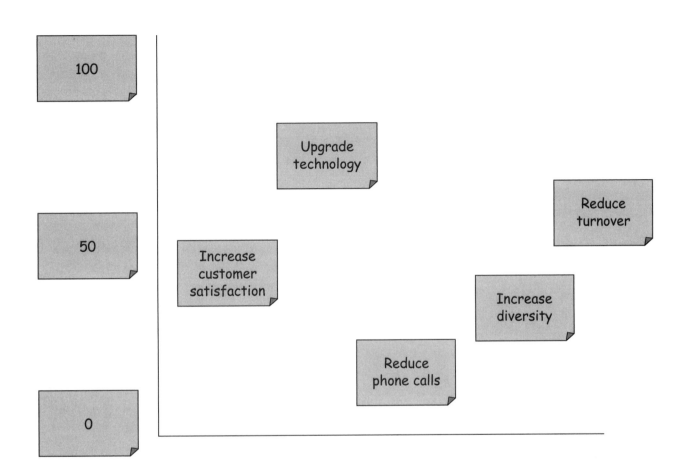

Checklist

❏ A few goals have surfaced as the greatest opportunities for improvement.

Relationship Diagram

Which goals have the biggest impact on the other goals?
(Which goals drive the other goals?)

Objectives

- Identify the "drivers" in a set of goals (those goals that if achieved would impact the achievement of the other goals).

- Focus improvement attention on the causal factors rather than the effects.

Prework

The team has generated a narrow list of goals using brainstorming.

Write each goal on an individual stick-on note.

Arrange the goals on a flipchart in a circle.

Estimated Time

20 minutes

How to Introduce It

Explain that we want to work first on the goals that if achieved would have an impact on the other goals.

Demonstrate how the process works using the first goal.

Explain that the tool starts out slowly but really picks up after the first few goals.

Explain that in the absence of real data, this may be a subjective analysis.

Diagnosis

Organize the project

Change processes

Customer satisfaction

Process improvement

Problem solving

Planning

Managing ideas

Creating buy-in

Implementation

Evaluation

Celebration

RELATIONSHIP DIAGRAM

Action Steps

Previous brainstorming and prioritization should have led to a manageable (six to eight) set of goals/issues.

1. Write each goal down on a stick-on note.

2. Arrange the goals in a circle on a flipchart page.

3. Starting with the first and second goal, ask the following:

   "Does *A* cause *B*, or does *B* cause *A*?"

   For example, does teen pregnancy cause school dropouts, or does dropping out of school cause teen pregnancy? Yes, many times this tool is a question of the chicken and the egg.

4. Draw an arrow reflecting the relationship. If *B* causes *A*, then the arrow should originate from *B* and point to *A*. (No ties are allowed!)

5. Determine the relationship between the first goal and all of the others. When complete, advance to the second goal and determine its relationship with all of the other goals. (Note that the relationship to the first goal has already been determined. The tool picks up speed as it goes along.) Continue around the circle.

6. For each goal, calculate how many arrows point in and how many point out. Write these numbers above the goal.

7. Circle the goals with the most out arrows. These are the drivers, or the goals to focus on that will lead to success in the other goals.

Example

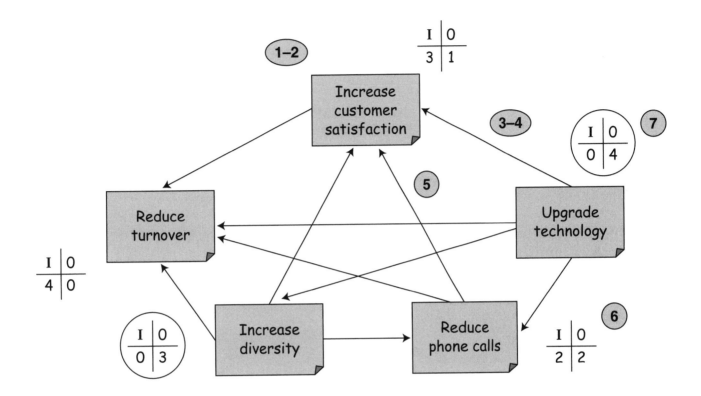

Checklist

❏ A few key drivers have been identified.

Prioritization Matrix

Which goals are the most important?

Objectives

- Identify the goals that are most critical.

- Surface the assumptions people are making about each goal.

- Create consensus using an objective tool.

Prework

Write each goal on two separate stick-on notes.

Create the matrix on the sample page.

Estimated Time

15 minutes to 1 hour, depending on the number of goals to be prioritized and the length of debate about each

How to Introduce It

Explain to the group that, while all of the goals are good, we want to focus on those that are most important.

Explain the process to be used:

- Compare each goal against each other (use two goals for an example).

- Decide (1) which is more important, and (2) how much more important it is.

- The goals with the highest scores relative to the others will be the top priorities.

Diagnosis

Organize the project

Change processes

Customer satisfaction

Process improvement

Problem solving

Planning

Managing ideas

Creating buy-in

Implementation

Evaluation

Celebration

PRIORITIZATION MATRIX

Action Steps

Previous brainstorming and prioritization should have led to a manageable (six to eight) set of goals/options.

1. Explain the rules to the group.

2. Comparing the first stick-on note on the side of the matrix (*a*) with the second note on the top of the page (2), ask the following:

   - Is (*a*) more important than (2), or is (2) more important than (*a*)? For example, is increasing customer satisfaction more important than upgrading technology or vice versa?

   - If you could only spend $10 on these two items, how would you divide up the money ($7 and $3, $6 and $4)? (You cannot do $5 and $5.)

3. Place the value that (*a*) receives in box (2). Place the value that (2) receives in box (6).

4. Repeat steps two and three, comparing (*a*) with the rest of the notes on the top of the page.

5. Repeat steps two and three for (*b*) through (*e*).

6. Total the scores for each row.

7. Circle the goals/options with the highest scores; these are the top priorities.

PRIORITIZATION MATRIX

Example

2—3 Increasing customer satisfaction is more important than upgrading technology by a weighting of 7–3

		1 Increase customer satisfaction	2 Upgrade technology	3 Reduce phone calls	4 Increase diversity	5 Reduce turnover	6 Total
a	Increase customer satisfaction	X 1	(7) 2	6 3	6 4	8 5	(27)
b	Upgrade technology	(3) 6	X 7	8 8	4 9	7 10	(22)
c	Reduce phone calls	4 11	2 12	X 13	3 14	2 15	11
d	Increase diversity	4 16	6 17	7 18	X 19	7 20	(24)
e	Reduce turnover	2 21	3 22	8 23	3 24	X 25	16

These numbers are to illustrate the instructions. They are not a necessary part of the exercise.

Checklist

❑ Some goals clearly stand out as most important.

❑ The group agrees with the prioritization.

❑ Nobody feels like a "loser."

Action Plan

Who will do what by when to implement the strategies?

Objectives

- Ensure that the strategies actually get implemented.

- Help the group understand what it will take to implement the strategies.

Prework

The group has developed strategies to achieve its goals.

Estimated Time

20 to 30 minutes

How to Introduce It

Explain that we are going to put in writing all the things we need to do to implement the strategies.

Explain that action plans usually only work if:

- Specific deliverables are identified
- One person is responsible for the deliverable (others can help, but we want one person we can tap on the shoulder when time is slipping)
- A specific due date is identified

Diagnosis
Organize the project
Change processes
   Customer satisfaction
   Process improvement
   Problem solving
   Planning
Managing ideas
Creating buy-in
Implementation
Evaluation
Celebration

ACTION PLAN

Action Steps

1. Identify the actions necessary to successfully implement the strategy.

2. For each action identify the following:

   ■ The deliverable (how we know when the action is complete—for example, if the action is *generate sales leads*, the deliverable would be *leads list printed*)

   ■ The person responsible for the deliverable

   Tip: When everyone is responsible, no one is. You are better off assigning responsibility to one person.

   ■ The date when the deliverable is due

   ■ Any resources needed to produce the deliverable

3. Set a date to review action-plan progress.

ACTION PLAN

Example

Income Tax Team Action Plan

Action	Deliverable	Responsible	Due Date	Resources
Redesign 1040 booklet	New 1040 booklet printed	Tom	7/1	–
Create new short form	New short form printed	Mary	7/1	Rebid print contract
Develop Internet filing	First person files on-line	Joe	1/3/next year	Web staff (2 new hires) hardware
Offer free tax assistance in field offices	First customer uses service	Greg	1/3/next year	30 PCs
Redesign refund process	First tax refund goes out	Lesa	1/3/next year	Training We help with hiring New software New PCs
Change performance measures to include customer-satisfaction measures	New performance report	Mike	10/15	Facilitation support
Identify sources of phone calls and reduce them	Call study report with strategies	Dave	8/15	Possible new phone software

3 Review Date: 10/1

Checklist

❏ There are clear deliverables for each action. (It is clear to see how we will know if each step is done.)

❏ The due dates are realistic. (Not so far away that people will die before they are done and not so soon that people will die trying to implement them).

Chapter Seven

Managing Ideas

So what's the big idea here?

To most creative people, the concept of "managing" ideas is not a welcome one. How can you manage what is supposed to be such an act of inspiration? Working with ideas is about much more than just brainstorming. There are four steps in the process of managing ideas:

1. **Generate the ideas.** This is where the creativity takes place. Teams generate as many ideas as possible to satisfy customers, to improve a process, to solve a problem, or to meet a goal.

2. **Evaluate the ideas.** In this step, the team sorts the good (high impact, feasible) from the bad. Note that by separating generation from evaluation, you will get more and perhaps better ideas.

3. **Support the ideas.** This is where the team researches the benefits and downsides of the ideas. The aim is twofold: first, the team members ensure that they can build a compelling case to sell the good ideas; second, the team members proactively think of all of the obstacles or possible objections to the ideas so they can find solutions.

4. **Choose the ideas.** Finally, after all of the thinking, evaluating, and researching, the team members must choose which ideas they want to become recommendations.

It is the role of the change agent to create an environment where idea generation can flourish, where the evaluation of ideas is civil, where the good ideas get supported, and where the final selection of ideas is done through consensus. The change agent can have a huge impact on the quality of the team's ideas.

Generating Ideas

All change processes converge at the idea stage. This is the time when the team stops researching and starts developing recommendations. Figure 7.1 depicts what the team will be generating during the idea phase, depending upon which change process it is using.

In each case, the quality of ideas and their chance of being approved are contingent upon the level of analysis done during the change process. For example, having clear measures of customer expectations, along with the size of the gap between the

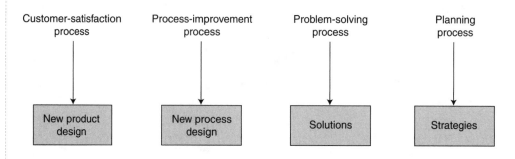

Figure 7.1   Idea phase.

target values and current performance, will yield better ideas than simply brain-storming, "What are all the ways we can make the customer happy?" The structured gap analysis around customer priorities ensures the team is recommending only the solutions that will matter to the customer and will impact results.

Similarly, a new process design will be much more effective if the analysis has been done to identify process bottlenecks, areas where elapsed time greatly exceeds work time, areas with low yields, and so on. The analysis should drive the solutions.

A helpful method for brainstorming is to pose discreet, specific questions such as the following:

- How can we meet the customers' goal of less than five minutes waiting in line?
- How can we reduce errors from 25 percent to 5 percent?
- How can we eliminate this bottleneck?

Generating Ideas for Each Change Process

Customer-Satisfaction Process

Once the team has completed its customer focus groups, has developed objective measures of satisfaction, and has collected baseline data, it is ready to focus on ways to meet the customers' targets.

This can be accomplished in two ways. The first is to actually use the *problem-solving process* to close the gap between the customers' target value and current per-formance. (Table 7.1) That is, you want to find the root cause for the gap and generate solutions to remove the root cause. The other way is to simply brainstorm possible ideas (features) to meet the target. (Consult page 204 for brainstorming variations. Teams have found analogies, opposites, and piling on to be especially effective.) Which route you choose depends on the amount of time you have, the amount of data available, the actual measures themselves, and so on. Many teams end up doing a mix. They brainstorm how to meet many of the targets and problem solve a few key ones when they just do not know how they can meet the goal. Whichever route you take, be sure to factor in the features identified in the customer focus groups.

Another key part of the customer-satisfaction process is generating new product ideas. That is, the team systematically tries to identify better ways to meet the cus-tomers' desired outcomes, including alternatives to replace the existing product. As many of the world's best companies have discovered, it is not enough to continuously improve your existing product. As Deming said, "It is entirely possible to make

Table 7.1 Voice of the customer.

Attribute	Measure	Target	Current perf.	Feature
Easy to complete	Number of minutes to complete	<30	420	Customized form by segment
Accurate	Percentage making mistakes	0	33%	FAQs, top 10 mistakes, caution signs
Simple	Percentage completing taxes themselves	>50%	32%	Web-file, reduce math, plain English instructions

absolutely perfect that which should not be made at all." It is the team's obligation to consider alternatives to its current product that can better achieve the purposes defined by the organization and its customers. The *innovation tool*[1] (Figure 7.2) is a tremendous resource for this.

The *innovation tool* is a variation on the classic Five Whys. Rather than asking "why" to get to the root of a problem (general to specific), however, the team expands the issue to the highest possible purpose for the product (specific to general). The tool simply asks, ***"What purpose does this product serve for the customer?"*** (Answers to this question can come from the focus group question, "A satisfying *product name* is one that results in . . . .") This is followed by, "What is the purpose of the purpose?" That is, why do the customers want that outcome?" Ask it again, again, and again until you have built a hierarchy of purposes.

This method helps the team systematically look at the broader picture. The next step asks the team to choose a level for focus. Essentially, it asks, ***"Which business do you want to be in?"*** (Had the railroads defined themselves in the transportation business, they might have been leaders in trucking and air transport. Had Digital Equipment Corporation defined its business as making people productive, it may have been the leader in laptops or palmtops. Had the slide rule makers defined themselves in the fast, accurate answer business, they may have invented the calculator, then the spreadsheet, and so on.) History is littered with company leaders who defined their businesses so narrowly that they missed the future. (Theodore Levitt called this *marketing myopia* in his groundbreaking article of the same name.) The *innovation tool* ensures your team does not make the same mistake.

Once the team members have selected the level of business they want to be in (one of the purposes in the hierarchy), their next task is to brainstorm all of the possible ways they could better achieve that purpose. This brainstorming is not focused on adding features to the existing product. Rather, the team should be looking for totally new products that are alternatives to the existing product. Essentially, the team is trying to put itself out of business before someone else does.

Once the team members have brainstormed alternatives for one purpose level, they need to go one level higher and do it again. This is what is meant by "getting outside the box." The box is the belief that the product (a flipchart) is here for this purpose (to display information). By elevating the purpose and looking for alternatives, the team gets out of this box.

Most teams struggle mightily with this exercise. This is especially true for people in administrative functions who are absolutely certain their product will always be needed (like an expense account or a sales forecast). Have fun with it. Let those

Where are they now?

- Digital Equipment Corporation
- Stuckey's
- K&E (made slide rule)
- TDK

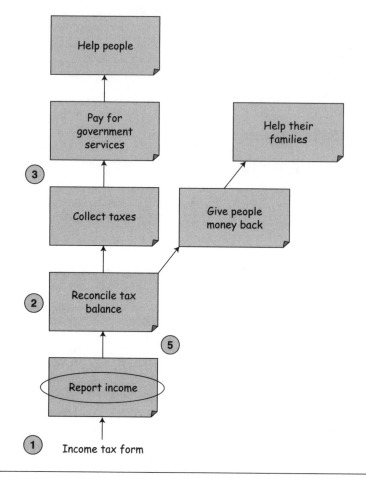

Figure 7.2 Innovation tool.

on the team know they might not end up doing anything with the information, but at least they will have tried. They are not likely to be blindsided by innovation. When I say have fun, I mean it. Get wacky. Look for crazy ideas. Bring in some outsiders. Grab some people from the hallway. Ask children. This exercise should be something the team never forgets.

A change agent whom I admire worked with a government team to improve the state drivers' guide. Using the innovation tool, the team built a hierarchy of outcomes:

Save lives

Reduce accidents

Be safe drivers

Teach rules of the road

The team started brainstorming alternatives to "teach the rules of the road" that were not a driver's guide. They came up with ideas like personal tutors, driving schools, Internet games, simulation software, Public Service Announcements (PSAs), grants to high schools to continue drivers education, and so on.

They then looked at ways other than a driver's guide to create "safe drivers." The team generated ideas such as breathalyzers in all cars, road rage PSAs, full-body bumpers for cars (like bumper cars), raising the driving age, and better lit highways.

You can quickly see the diversity in the ideas. The point was, it got the team to stop thinking that it had to produce a driver's guide. The team opted for several of the alternative ideas.

Process-Improvement Process

Idea generation regarding process improvement is not so much about brainstorming as it is about creating a new process design—that is, rearranging the boxes and players to create a more effective, streamlined process. However, there may be several parts of the new process where the team has to brainstorm some ideas. Additionally, if any of the process improvement deals with reducing errors (increasing yields), the team will need to use the *problem-solving process*. There really is no method for creating a new process. The *FACT* sheet and the *process-analysis checklist* will help the team find the opportunities. From there, it is a matter of mapping out the new process and delineating the changes that will need to be made to accommodate the new process (new measurements, new equipment, new procedures, and so on).

Problem-Solving Process

Idea generation in the *problem-solving process* centers around the question, *"How do we eliminate this root cause?"* Obviously, before you can ask this question, you need to know the root cause. The steps in the *problem-solving process* are a structured way to get you there.

Sometimes, the answer to eliminate the root cause becomes obvious and there is little need to do any brainstorming. That is, when going through the *problem-solving process*, the team stumbles upon the solution to eliminate the problem. In this case, move on to the step of supporting the idea.

One of the best methods for finding the root cause is the *Five Whys* technique. Starting with the problem, you ask, *"Why is this happening?"* You then repeat the question four more times. For example, a problem may be that too many teenagers fail their written drivers license test on the first try.

> *Why?* Because they don't understand the rules of the road.
>
> *Why don't they understand the rules of the road?* Because they don't study them.
>
> *Why don't they study them?* Because they don't have the drivers' guide.
>
> *Why don't they have the drivers' guide?* Because we stopped distributing them to high schools.
>
> *Why did we stop distributing them to high schools?* Because we tried to save money.

When the solution is not so clear, *brainstorming* can be helpful. You can choose the variation that best fits your team. Most problem-solving teams tend to use the free-wheeling method of brainstorming. All of the rules of brainstorming still apply:

- There are no bad ideas.
- Do not evaluate the ideas, good or bad.
- Do not allow debates.
- Do not allow killer phrases.

- Everyone participates.
- The best way to get good ideas is to get lots of ideas.

Brainstorming Variations

Variations on How to Share the Ideas

There is a variety of ways for group members to share their ideas. The method you select should be based on two factors: time and the comfort level of the group with each other.

Freewheel is a very unstructured, open way of sharing ideas. Essentially, the question is asked and members start blurting out answers. It is particularly effective when time is short. This method is not appropriate when there are dominant members in a group, when there are mixed power structures (subordinates will wait until boss speaks before giving ideas), or when there is fear within the group.

Round Robin is a more structured way of brainstorming in which each person is asked to give an idea one at a time. This process continues until all team members have had a chance to contribute their ideas. A person may choose to "pass" at any time. This method is formal and a little slow but is effective when you have dominating participants, quiet participants, or groups that have just come together. While it is structured, it is not anonymous. It may not be appropriate for groups that are afraid to share ideas with each other.

The Affinity Diagram is a very structured, anonymous way of sharing ideas. In this method, participants record their ideas on stick-on notes and place them on a wall. All ideas get mixed together, ensuring total anonymity. Ideas that relate to each other are then grouped together (Figure 7.3). This

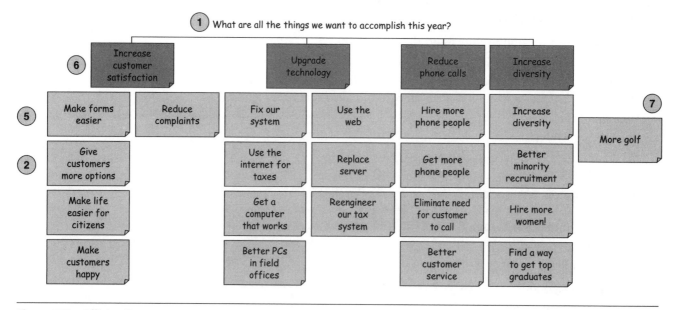

Figure 7.3   Affinity diagram.

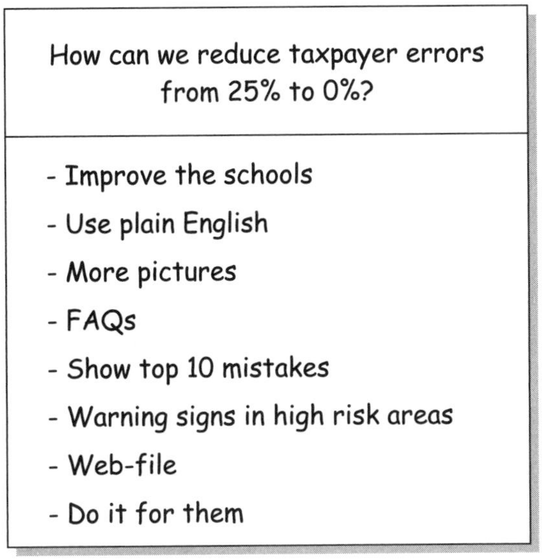

How can we reduce taxpayer errors
from 25% to 0%?

- Improve the schools

- Use plain English

- More pictures

- FAQs

- Show top 10 mistakes

- Warning signs in high risk areas

- Web-file

- Do it for them

Figure 7.4   Pile-on.

method is very effective in large groups where there will be lots of ideas. It is also very effective when anonymity is important and the group needs to see how much consensus there really is. This method is not advised when time is short. Groups will really enjoy this method once. The novelty wears off quickly after that.

Pile-on is a somewhat unstructured, anonymous way of sharing ideas. In this method, team members write on a piece of paper (either at their seat or on flipchart pages on the wall) as many ideas as they can in a given time period (15 to 30 seconds). Each person then passes his or her paper (or moves to a different flipchart page) to the next person. This person must add to and build on the ideas of the previous person (Figure 7.4). This continues until people run out of ideas. The pile-on method is a great way of expanding ideas while still maintaining anonymity. It can also be done quite quickly if necessary. It is especially effective when you are generating ideas for numerous questions.

Variations on How to Spur Ideas

There are numerous ways of spurring ideas, with simple brainstorming being the most basic. Oftentimes, groups will need a kick in the pants to get more creative. Try these options:

Thinking in opposites. In this method, you ask the participants to do the opposite of what they are brainstorming. For example, rather than asking, "How can we make this product easier to use for our customer?" you would ask, "What things could we do to make this product more difficult for our customer to use?" or, "What could we do to decrease employee morale?" The group will get a good laugh and may discover that some of these "opposite" things are currently being done, triggering some more good ideas.

Challenging assumptions. When a team seems stuck in its current paradigm, start asking, *"What assumptions are we making here?"* For example, a team working on a new-employee orientation may be stuck in the following assumptions:

- New employees need to be oriented.
- New employees need to be oriented the first day.
- The only time people need to be oriented is when they are new.
- Human resources has to do the orientation.
- Employees actually care about . . . .

Imagining how someone else would handle the problem/issue (virtual benchmarking). Oftentimes it is helpful to get the team members to stop thinking about the constraints of their own organization; try to help them see how other organizations in totally different businesses approach the same problem.

For example, a team was working on improving the much-loved Department of Motor Vehicle (DMV) offices. The issues they were confronting were long lines, predictable and unpredictable rushes of people, difficult customers, and so on. The team members were struggling with how they could ever solve these problems. Looking at the other DMVs in the country was of little help. Instead, they were asked to think of other organizations that have the same problems. They came up with Wal-Mart, grocery stores, and McDonald's, to name a few. We then asked, *"How does McDonald's handle this, and what can we learn from them?"* The answers became obvious.

When a difficult customer (one who makes a complex order like a cheeseburger with no cheese, extra onions, and three pickles) places an order and goes to the counter or drive-through window, the employee asks the customer to please step aside or park while the order is filled. This gets the customer out of the way so other customers can be helped. This was not the approach at the DMV offices. The team came up with the policy that when a transaction was difficult, the manager would take the customer aside and handle it, freeing up the counter clerk to help other customers. Other lessons learned from McDonald's included staffing up to meet peak periods (which challenged the assumption that all workers have to work the same schedule), converting all back-office staff to counter clerks when lines got long, and helping customers see what is required of them while they stand in line (like McDonald's large menu boards). Wait times in the offices dropped over 50 percent.

Chic Thompson has created a list of the forty killer phrases (Figure 7.5) that ruin creativity and new ideas. During brainstorming these phrases must be avoided at all costs. Chic recommends some form of team punishment (like hurling paper wads at the offender or making the offender contribute a quarter to the team "snack fund") to help curtail the occurrences.

The breakthrough formulas for developing pricing of stock options (and hedging risk) (Black-Schulz method) was adapted from math used to calculate the trajectory of missiles (Ito calculation).

1. Yes, but . . .	21. The boss will never go for it.
2. We tried that before . . .	22. It's too far ahead of the times.
3. That's irrelevant.	23. . . . laughter . . .
4. We haven't got the manpower.	24. . . . suppressed laughter . . .
5. Obviously, you misread my request.	25. . . . condescending grin . . .
6. Don't rock the boat.	26. . . . dirty looks . . .
7. The boss (or competition) will eat you alive.	27. Don't fight city hall!
8. Don't waste time thinking.	28. I'm the one who gets paid to think.
9. Great idea, but not for us.	29. What will people say?
10. It'll never fly.	30. Get a committee to look into that.
11. Don't be ridiculous.	31. If it ain't broke, don't fix it.
12. People don't want change.	32. You have got to be kidding.
13. It's not in the budget.	33. No!
14. Put it in writing.	34. We've always done it this way.
15. It will be more trouble than it's worth.	35. It's all right in theory . . . but . . .
16. It isn't your responsibility.	36. Be practical!
17. That's not in your job description.	37. Do you realize the paperwork it will create?
18. You can't teach an old dog new tricks.	38. Because I said so.
19. Let's stick with what works.	39. I'll get back to you.
20. We've done all right so far.	40. . . . silence . . .

Figure 7.5   Forty killer phrases.

Source: List of 40 "killer" phrases from WHAT A GREAT IDEA! by CHARLES "CHIC" THOMPSON. Copyright © 1992 by Charles "Chic" Thompson. Reprinted by permission of HarperCollins Publishers Inc.

Evaluate the Ideas

The first rule of brainstorming, as advanced by Linus Pauling, is that "the best way to get good ideas is to get lots of ideas and throw the bad ones away." The idea-generation phase took care of the first part of the quote, and the idea-evaluation step takes care of the latter. If you have done your job and have truly pushed the team, they should have tons of ideas—some very practical and some way outside the box. If the team only has feasible ideas at this point, then the team members probably generated and evaluated at the same time.

Now that we have tons of ideas, it is time to evaluate them. The reason I stress using stick-on notes to capture ideas is twofold:

1. It makes the ideas easy to move around.
2. The ideas become anonymous; that is, people will not remember who said what idea, effectively minimizing the issue of people taking too much pride of ownership or getting hurt feelings when their idea gets nixed.

We want to be able to evaluate ideas without evaluating the people who offered them. That is where the *idea filter* comes in. Rather than just going through the list of ideas and rejecting certain ideas, the *idea filter* says that all ideas are good ideas, but the team should prioritize and work on the ideas that have high impact and high feasibility.

The *idea filter* sorts ideas into four quadrants. Take each idea stick-on note one by one, and first ask the group, ***"How high of an impact will this idea have on our goals?"*** Next, ask the group, ***"How feasible is it?"*** The idea is then placed in the appropriate quadrant. (Feasibility is however you want to define it. Some good rules of thumb are that high feasibility means it could be implemented in less than two years without significant resources. Low feasibility means you have to move a mountain to make it happen. Most ideas will fall somewhere along that continuum).

Once all the ideas have been sorted, the team needs to make some decisions. All of the ideas that land in the *high impact, high feasibility* quadrant should be pursued (Figure 7.6). All of the ideas in the *low impact, low feasibility* quadrant should be dropped. The other two quadrants are open for discussion. There might be some high impact, low feasibility ideas that are worth going to the mat. Similarly, there might be some low impact, high feasibility ideas that would be good low-hanging fruit to tackle. The team should decide which ideas in these two quadrants survive. Keep an eye out for "interesting" ideas—the ones that are a little off the wall but still intriguing. If possible, keep them alive for the next stage.

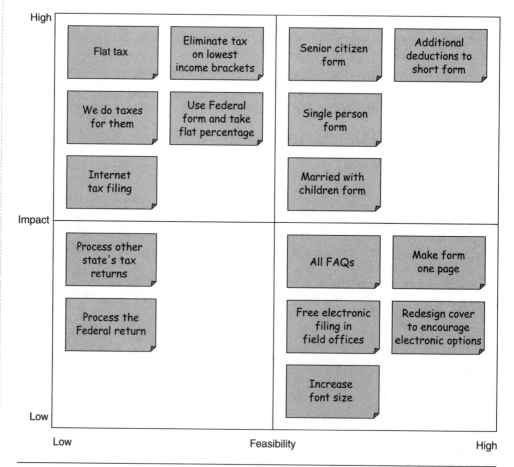

Figure 7.6   Idea filter.

Support the Ideas

The next stage involves finding team members to champion each idea that survives the *idea filter*. That is, they research the idea and make a recommendation to the team whether it should be proposed to the sponsor. This step quickly points out which ideas have little support on the team, thus preventing a further waste of time trying to recommend and implement an idea for which there is no passion. It is one more check on the idea process. If no one volunteers to champion an idea, then pitch it in the trash. (Another benefit of this step is that it also shows which members on the team are carrying their weight and are passionate about the ideas. If a team member does not volunteer to champion any of the ideas, it may be a clear signal that this person has disengaged from the team and could be a hindrance down the road. Intervene immediately to determine why this member does not support any of the ideas.)

The *idea worksheet* (akin to a Force Field analysis tool) is designed to do two things:

- Help the team fully understand an idea and its implications
- Identify ways to sell an idea to the sponsor

The *idea worksheet* (Figure 7.7) consists of the following items:

- **A description of the idea.** The idea champion fleshes out the idea and explains it in a way all can understand. (This also helps the team clarify any confusion about the idea before trying to sell it.)
- **An identification of the people it will affect** (who will have to buy in to the idea and what they value). This helps the team focus proactively on the benefits and potential objections of each person who will need to buy in to the idea.

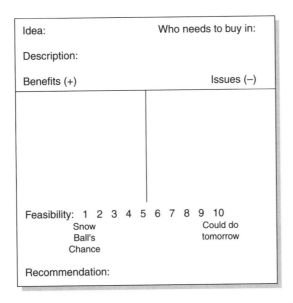

Figure 7.7   Idea worksheet.

- **A description of the benefits of the idea, quantified if possible.** There is an age-old sales adage that says, "Sell the benefits, not the features." I don't care how many micropixels a big screen TV has; tell me what they are going to do for me (a clearer picture). The idea champions delineate the benefits and try to quantify them the best they can. Remember, people do not approve good ideas; they approve increased results. If the team cannot show how an idea will impact things the sponsor cares about, the team will have a tough time getting it approved.

- **A description of the downside or cons of the idea.** The idea champions identify all the reasons why someone would object to the idea and then develop ways to overcome or minimize these issues. (Consult Figure 7.5 for help in anticipating possible objections.) Even if the idea champions think the idea is not feasible, they should still go through this exercise. Too many teams quit on great ideas because they do not see how they are feasible. It is quite possible that the team may be able to discover a way to overcome an obstacle that has never been considered. This tool encourages them to try.

- **A numerical ranking of the feasibility of the idea.** This should be based on the analysis done regarding the objections/obstacles.

- **A recommendation to the team: go or no go.**

The team members work through the *idea worksheets* for each idea they have agreed to champion; they make copies for the team and then present them at a meeting designed for this purpose. It is usually advisable to give the team a couple of weeks to work on these ideas.

Choose the Best Ideas

Once the team has researched the ideas and has made a presentation to the group, it is time for the final decision: they must decide which ideas will become recommendations. Take your time with this, and facilitate an open, deliberate discussion. You want to ensure that the team has fully thought through all the ideas, giving each a fair hearing. It is not uncommon for arguments to develop at this stage as some team members shy away from ideas that others support. This is healthy. You should encourage this discussion and should try to help uncover the source of team member objections. Then the group members need to try to problem solve how they can overcome the objections. Questions like the following can be very effective: *"If we were able to overcome (their concern) would you support the recommendation?"*

After the discussions, the group will need to reach consensus on which ideas they will select. Consensus does not mean that everybody loves the idea 100 percent; rather, it means that everybody can live with it and support it. If someone simply cannot live with an idea and will not support it, then the team has to let go of it (but only after they have clearly uncovered the individual's objections and have tried to work through them).

Consensus can be difficult and time consuming but is far preferable to the alternative: team members disparaging the team or speaking out against an idea to the sponsor. If someone ardently opposes an idea, a majority vote will not silence the criticism. Voting produces winners and losers; steer clear from voting as much as possible.

As a change agent, you should be extra sensitive that the team does not run away from all of the good ideas. If you start to see a pattern emerging that the team is only picking the safe ideas and not really meeting the objectives of the charter, you should intervene. You can either have them all reread the charter and ask them if their ideas are sufficient to meet the objectives, or you can have the sponsor come in and remind the group members that they have permission to get outside the box.

At the least, you should know why the team is backing off ideas, and you should ensure that their fears are not irrational. That is, you might have to do some checking to see if the obstacles they identified are really insurmountable. You can discuss these with the sponsor (take the team spokesperson with you), or invite some advisors into the meeting to discuss an idea's feasibility.

I worked with a team that produced great ideas but was absolutely convinced that the legal staff would never let them be implemented. After much debate, we finally invited the legal counsel to a meeting to discuss the perceived obstacles. As it turned out, the legal counsel not only dispelled many of the objections but worked with the team to remove the rest. Needless to say, the team was surprised. The moral of the story is that many obstacles exist only in the imagination.

Once the team members have finally decided on their recommendations, have them sit back, reflect, and celebrate because the battle is half over. The next step is to get the recommendations approved.

Endnote

1. The *innovation tool* is a conglomeration of excellent tools from GOAL/QPC, the Ralston Group, and IMT.

Brainstorming

What do you think?

Objectives

Generate as many ideas as possible.

Prework

Develop the specific planning question.

Estimated Time

As short or as long as you want it.

How to Introduce It

Review the rules of brainstorming.

Reinforce that no evaluating of ideas is allowed during this stage.

Diagnosis
Organize the project
Change processes
  Customer satisfaction
  Process improvement
  Problem solving
  Planning
Managing ideas
Creating buy-in
Implementation
Evaluation
Celebration

BRAINSTORMING

Action Steps

1. Review brainstorming rules:

   - There are no bad ideas.

   - Do not evaluate the ideas, good or bad.

   - Do not allow debates.

   - Everyone participates.

   - The best way to get good ideas is to get lots of ideas.

2. Clarify the topic (question) being brainstormed; allow time for it to soak in, and ask for clarifying questions.

3. Ask participants for ideas using one of the following methods:

   - **Freewheel:** Everyone just spits them out.

   - **Round robin:** One person gives an idea at a time.

   - **Anonymous:** Use stick-on notes.

   - **Pile-on:** Each person records as many ideas as possible in a specified time interval and then passes the paper on to the next person for additional ideas.

4. Record ideas as generated (as close to verbatim as possible).

5. When the group runs out of ideas, allow a few moments of thinking and reflection, and then ask for more ideas.

6. When you are sure the group is done, discuss the ideas for clarification.

7. Combine similar ideas where appropriate and with permission!

Example

What criteria should we use in making our selection?
Most time consuming
Large source of errors
Source of customer dissatisfaction
Public will notice (2X)
Is possible to change? Y/N
Can be done in 9 months? Y/N

Checklist

❑ The team members did not evaluate the ideas.

❑ Killer phrases were few and far between.

❑ Everyone contributed.

❑ The ideas are out-of-the-box, and beyond "ordinary."

❑ The ideas will help the team achieve its goals.

Multivoting

What are our top priorities on this list?

Objectives

Narrow a long list down to a short one (to prioritize the list).

Prework

Have developed a list using brainstorming.

Estimated Time

5 to 15 minutes

How to Introduce It

Explain that we want to narrow the list.
Explain the voting method.

Diagnosis
Organize the project
Change processes
   Customer satisfaction
   Process improvement
   Problem solving
   Planning
Managing ideas
Creating buy-in
Implementation
Evaluation
Celebration

MULTIVOTING

Action Steps

1. Generate the list using brainstorming.

2. Ensure everyone is clear about the items on the list.

3. Enumerate the items on the list.

4. Explain the voting process:

   - Each person gets X amount of votes.

   - Ten or fewer items—each person gets two votes; add one vote for every five additional items up to eight votes.

   - They may spend them all on one item or spread them across multiple items. (How they spend them is your choice.)

5. Have the participants vote using one of the following methods:

   - They call out their preferences and you tally them.

   - They place tally marks or sticky dots next to the items of their choice.

6. Once the votes are tallied, look for a logical cut-off point and circle the items that have been selected.

7. Do a gut check with the group.

When there are lots of ideas, you might want to consider the following variation: Eliminate items with the fewest votes, and vote again using same process. Continue until list is a manageable size.

MULTIVOTING

Example

What are all the things we want to accomplish this year?

3   (a) - Increase customer satisfaction ✓✓✓✓   **5**

(b) - Upgrade our computers ✓✓✓

c - Reduce turnover ✓

d - Find a new vendor

e - Have fun ✓✓

f - Rewrite the policy book ✓

6   (g) - Reduce phone calls ✓✓✓✓✓✓

h - Obtain necessary funding ✓✓

i - Lower overhead costs ✓

(j) - Increase diversity ✓✓✓✓✓✓

Checklist

❏ The list has been narrowed to a manageable set.

Affinity Diagram

What do we want to accomplish?

Objectives

- Brainstorm answers to a specific question.

- Organize the brainstormed responses into categories.

- Let the team members see the affinity among their ideas.

- Develop broad, shared goals out of specific ideas (from specific to general).

- Develop great ideas/goals without people dominating the process.

Diagnosis

Organize the project

Change processes

Customer satisfaction

Process improvement

Problem solving

Planning

Managing ideas

Creating buy-in

Implementation

Evaluation

Celebration

Estimated Time

45 to 60 minutes

How to Introduce It

Explain that we want to come up with some shared goals.

Explain that we are going to take all of the ideas and look for the consistent themes among them.

Explain that this will take a little while but will produce great results.

AFFINITY DIAGRAM

Action Steps

1. Write the brainstorming question on a flipchart page.

2. Instruct each participant to come up with as many ideas as he or she can (you may give them a quota or time limit) to answer the question. Use the following guidelines:

   - Each idea must be written on a separate stick-on note.

   - Each idea must contain at least four words.

3. When the participants are finished writing, have them place their stick-on notes on the wall in random order.

4. Have each participant read every idea on the wall.

5. Have the group silently sort the ideas into like categories:

   - Two ideas that seem to go together (similar, same theme, and so on) should be stuck together.

   - As more and more ideas are organized together, long chains of stick-on notes should appear.

6. When all of the ideas are sorted, there should be between four and eight categories. Identify a header for each category:

   - Read each idea in the category.

   - Ask the group the general theme to which the ideas point.

   - Ask the group to come up with words (at least a verb and a noun) that capture the gist of the theme. Write this statement on a different-colored stick-on note, and place it atop the category.

7. Find a home for any "orphan ideas."

AFFINITY DIAGRAM

Example

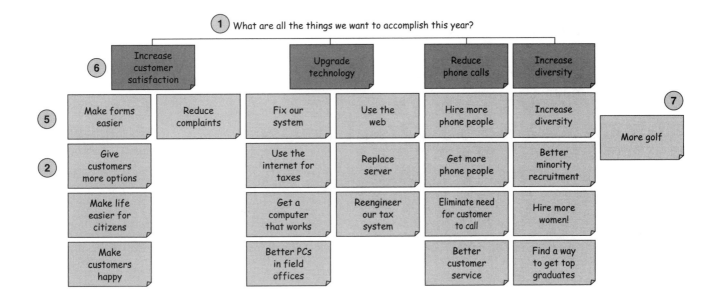

(1) What are all the things we want to accomplish this year?

(6) Increase customer satisfaction | Upgrade technology | Reduce phone calls | Increase diversity

(5) Make forms easier | Reduce complaints | Fix our system | Use the web | Hire more phone people | Increase diversity | (7) More golf

(2) Give customers more options | Use the internet for taxes | Replace server | Get more phone people | Better minority recruitment

Make life easier for citizens | Get a computer that works | Reengineer our tax system | Eliminate need for customer to call | Hire more women!

Make customers happy | Better PCs in field offices | Better customer service | Find a way to get top graduates

Checklist

❏ The ideas have been grouped into between four and eight categories (maybe a few more).

❏ The header cards have been written with at least a verb and a noun.

❏ The team feels good about the identified goals.

Idea Filter

Which ideas would we like to consider further?

Objectives

- Narrow the team's focus to the ideas that will have the biggest impact and are feasible.

- Ensure the team does not waste time on far-fetched ideas.

- Ensure that good ideas that may not be feasible today are discussed and considered.

Prework

Transfer all ideas onto stick-on notes.

Estimated Time

15 minutes

How to Introduce It

Explain to the group that they have lots of great ideas but they likely cannot implement them all. This tool will help identify those ideas that have the highest impact and are the most feasible.

IDEA FILTER

Action Steps

1. Separate a flipchart page into four quadrants like the example on the opposite page. (Do *not* write in the words *long term, just do it,* and so on.) If there are tons of ideas, create the quadrant with four flipchart pages on a wall.

2. Place each idea on a stick-on note.

3. Take each idea, one at a time, and ask the group the following:

   ■ How much impact will this idea have? (High, Medium, Low)

   Visually move the note along the vertical axis until the group tells you to stop.

   ■ How feasible is this idea? (High,* Medium, Low)

   Visually move the note along the horizontal axis until the group tells you to stop.

   High feasibility means the idea could be implemented in a short period of time without significant resources

4. Explain the quadrants as follows:

   ■ High Impact/High Feasibility—Ideas to definitely pursue.

   ■ High Impact/Low Feasibility—Long-term ideas, possibly pursue some.

   ■ Low Impact/Low Feasibility—Forget about these.

   ■ Low Impact/High Feasibility—Low-hanging fruit, maybe pursue these.

IDEA FILTER

Example

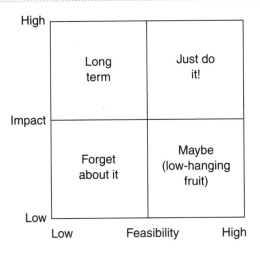

High

Long term	Just do it!
Forget about it	Maybe (low-hanging fruit)

Impact

Low

Low — Feasibility — High

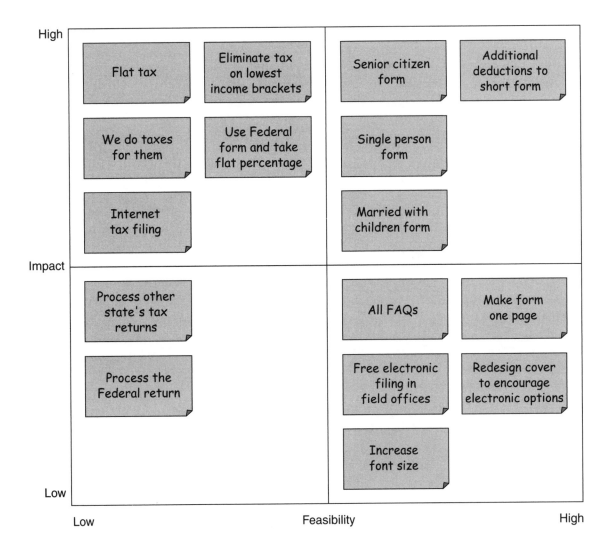

High

Impact

Low

Low — Feasibility — High

Quadrant boxes:

High Impact / Low Feasibility:
- Flat tax
- Eliminate tax on lowest income brackets
- We do taxes for them
- Use Federal form and take flat percentage
- Internet tax filing

High Impact / High Feasibility:
- Senior citizen form
- Additional deductions to short form
- Single person form
- Married with children form

Low Impact / Low Feasibility:
- Process other state's tax returns
- Process the Federal return

Low Impact / High Feasibility:
- All FAQs
- Make form one page
- Free electronic filing in field offices
- Redesign cover to encourage electronic options
- Increase font size

Checklist

❏ The group has some great ideas.

❏ The squirrelly ideas have been eliminated.

❏ Some of the out-of-the box ideas are still under consideration.

❏ The team is excited.

Idea Worksheet

Which ideas do we want to recommend to the sponsor?

Objectives

- Fully think through each possible recommendation.

- Build the compelling case for why the idea should be approved.

- Proactively uncover and plan to deal with any negatives regarding the idea.

- Have the team come to consensus on which ideas it wants to support.

Prework

Have blank copies of the idea worksheets available.

Have completed the idea filter.

Estimated Time

Several days per idea

How to Introduce It

Explain that just because we think we have some good ideas does not mean they will get implemented. For each idea that we want to recommend, we need to have a compelling case that highlights the benefits of the ideas and manages the downsides of the ideas.

Explain that this step will involve research, and everybody needs to pitch in where they can. This step will make or break the project.

Diagnosis
Organize the project
Change processes
  Customer satisfaction
  Process improvement
  Problem solving
  Planning
Managing ideas
Creating buy-in
Implementation
Evaluation
Celebration

Action Steps

For each idea the team wants to consider, do the following:

1. Ask for an idea champion (the person responsible for researching the idea).

2. Give the champion an idea worksheet.*

3. The idea champion is responsible for:

   - Writing a brief summary of the idea

   - Identifying who will need to buy-in to the idea

   - Enumerating the positives or benefits of the idea

   - Quantifying the positives or benefits where possible

   - Enumerating the negatives or issues concerning the idea

   - Identifying ways to prevent or minimize the negatives

   - Rating the feasibility of the idea

   - Making a recommendation to the group about whether the idea should become a team recommendation

4. When the idea champions have completed their worksheets (give them until the next team meeting), have them make copies for the team.

5. Pass out the completed worksheets to the team.

6. Have each champion discuss his or her idea and analysis.

7. Reach consensus on which ideas will become team recommendations.

*Blank idea worksheets can be downloaded at www.changeagents.info

Example

Idea:	Who needs to buy in:
Description:	
Benefits (+)	Issues (−)

Feasibility: 1 2 3 4 5 6 7 8 9 10

Snow   Could do
Ball's   tomorrow
Chance

Recommendation:

Checklist

❑ The champions quantified the benefits of the ideas.

❑ The negatives of the ideas were well thought through, and the team attempted to overcome them (rather than just giving in to them).

❑ The team recommendations have enough compelling case information to get approved.

❑ The final ideas selected by the team are sufficient to fulfill the team charter.

Data-Collection Plan

Who will do what by when to collect the data we need?

Objectives

- Help the team members clarify what information they want before they spend time researching.

- Help the team members get clear on what they plan on doing with the data once they are obtained.

- Ensure the data are collected in a valid and timely manner.

Diagnosis

Organize the project

Change processes

    Customer satisfaction

    Process improvement

    Problem solving

    Planning

Managing ideas

Creating buy-in

Implementation

Evaluation

Celebration

Estimated Time

15 minutes

How to Introduce It

Explain that before we spend time chasing our tails, it is best to be really clear about what we want to know before we set out to collect data.

Explain that the best way to figure out what data we need to collect is to draw the charts first; we can then see specifically what we need.

DATA-COLLECTION PLAN

Action Steps

The data-collection plan can be brainstormed on a flipchart or completed by a team member using the template.* In either case, it consists of the following steps:

1. Define the research question the team would like answered. (For example, "Why are we rejecting applications?" or "How much are we spending on rework?")

2. Specifically define each term in the research question. (For example, what counts as a rejected application? What is meant by rework?)

3. Select how the data should be displayed visually, using one of the following charts:

   - **Bar chart**—Used to show comparisons or to show the frequency of a category (such as most frequently asked questions)

   - **Trend chart**—Used to show a trend over time (such as average phone calls per month)

   - **Pie chart**—Used to show proportions (such as sources of the phone calls)

4. For a bar or trend chart, label each axis. For a trend chart, determine the appropriate time period (scope) to document.

5. Determine the following:

   - Who will collect the data?

   - Who will create the visual?

   - By when?

6. Complete the following statement: "These data will help us decide . . . ."

Note: When complete, each visual should have a footnote at the bottom documenting the data source and the methodology used to compile it. For example, if the measure is the percentage of budget spent on overhead, the methods used to calculate overhead should be delineated.

*Blank data-collection worksheets can be downloaded at www.changeagents.info

Example

How many customers make mistakes?

Definitions: Mistakes—A tax return that has to be
sent back to the taxpayer for correction.
Customers—Can be taxpayers or
their accountants. (Break it out for each.)

Draw visual

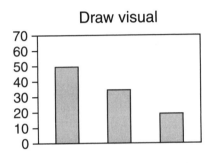

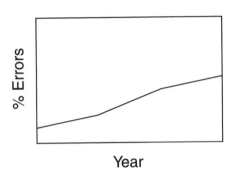

Who collects data: Mary
Who creates visual: Lisa
By when: Next meeting

% Make errors
% Total errors from CPAs

This data will help us decide: Whether errors are significant and if CPAs make
significant errors.

Checklist

❏ It is clear what question the team is trying to answer.

❏ The team knows the specific data for which it will be looking.

❏ All of the terms have been specifically defined.

Creating Buy-In

Once the team has its final recommendations, it is time to begin the buy-in process. The team members will switch modes from being innovators to being politicians. That is, they are now delving into the politics of change. As many teams learn the hard way, people do not do things because "it's the right thing to do." In fact, most people will naturally resist change. Eli Goldratt (1998) offers six layers of resistance to new ideas that must be overcome before an idea will be accepted:

1. **Not agreeing that there is a problem.** Think Alcoholics Anonymous—the team is the intervention. People will not agree to change unless they believe there is a problem.

2. **Believing the problem is out of their hands.** For example, vendors do not always deliver, clients change their mind at the last minute, workers are not properly trained, headquarters makes us do it, and so on. As Eli says, "as long as this layer is not removed, you are talking to the wall."

3. **Arguing that the proposed solution cannot possibly yield the desired outcome.**

4. **"Yes, but . . . ," arguing that the proposed solution will lead to negative effects.**

5. **Raising obstacles that will prevent implementation.** At this point, you are halfway home. Everyone agrees that there is a problem and that your solution could solve it. They are now looking for assurances that you can implement it.

6. **Raising doubts about the collaboration of others.** "This is great, but so and so will never go for it . . . ."

Creating acceptance for new ideas means peeling through each layer of resistance in succession. The steps in the process of creating buy-in are designed to ensure that all six layers of resistance are addressed before they are raised. In order to create buy-in for their ideas, the team will:

1. Build the presentation
2. Invite the participants
3. Make the presentation
4. Secure approval

Build the Presentation

At this stage, the team turns all of its hard work into a short presentation that wins the support of the sponsor. The presentation should cover the following:

- **The team's charter and mission.**
- **The quantifiable benefits** (put these in front of the presentation).
- **The process used.**
- **What was discovered** (either customer priorities, process problems, root cause of problem, and so on). Any compelling data about the problem should be presented here. Even though there has been a charter to work on the project, there will still be people who do not think there is a problem (part of resistance layer one).
- **What is recommended.** Again, the recommendations should sell the benefits. If the team used the *idea worksheet tool,* then this work should already be done. It is a simple matter of creating visuals that describe the recommendation; list the benefits, preferably quantified (resistance layer 3); and list the obstacles and how to overcome them (resistance layers 4, 5, and 6). The recommendations should be clearly enumerated so that the sponsor knows exactly what he/she is being asked to commit to. This also allows the sponsor to reject pieces of the overall proposal without rejecting the whole thing.

The presentation can be done in any number of ways. Teams will commonly use PowerPoint® and supplement it with a handout (sample presentation templates can be downloaded at www.changeagents.info). Other teams have found storyboarding to be effective (large poster boards tracing the team's journey). I have had teams perform skits, reenact customer experiences, play video tapes of botched transactions, sing songs, create a board game, you name it. There is no end to the creative ways teams can get their point across. However, the team needs to ensure it knows its audience. If the sponsor is a "wild and crazy guy (or gal)," have fun with the presentation. If the sponsor is a "suit and tie guy" stick to the PowerPoint®. Regardless of the way the team presents, it should still cover the five areas outlined.

Invite the Participants

This is such a tricky step and one that can make or break a project. Who should be at the team's presentation? As with most things, it all comes down to politics. There is a constant concern about who gets invited and who does not. People who do not get invited feel left out. On the flip side, when everybody gets invited, the team cannot possibly anticipate all of their concerns, and the presentation can get off on obscure tangents.

The best advice I can give is to let the sponsors decide whom to invite. Often they will invite the key staff they rely on to help them make decisions. This is great, so long as at the beginning of the presentation the team takes the time to create the context by explaining the project, its charter, and why the team was formed. If you can have the sponsor set the stage, that is even better. Oftentimes a team will need to make two presentations—one to the decision-makers and after they sign off, one to the various stakeholders.

One of the big mistakes teams make is not knowing who will be at the presentation and, consequently, not building in the compelling case arguments to over-

One of the big mistakes teams make is not knowing who will be at the presentation, and, consequently, not building in the compelling case arguments to overcome the layers of resistance for these individuals.

come the layers of resistance for these individuals. Inevitably, one of these people fires at the team, and if not prepared, the team can go down in flames. For example, a team makes a recommendation to invest in a piece of technology only to find out that the IT manager tried that two years ago and failed.

When the team members are building the presentation, they should consider all of the possible decision-makers who impact the project. Chic Thompson (1992) recommends two specific strategies when trying to create buy-in:

- **Sell up.** That is, identify the hot buttons and describe the benefits that will appeal to the sponsor's boss. If you can appeal to this person, he or she might apply any necessary pressure on the sponsor to accept the ideas.

- **Sell down.** That is, identify the possible objections and concerns of the people who will have to implement and live with the ideas. Having these people on board is one less issue about which the sponsor has to worry.

A quick exercise I like to do with the team is to brainstorm all the possible individuals the team will have to convince and then brainstorm their hot buttons (what do they value? what makes them tick?). This helps the team package their recommendations for maximum effect.

There are three situations that tend to happen with sponsors; all require careful political maneuvering:

- **The sponsor is not really supportive of the project at all.** The sponsor may have chartered the team but really does not want to see big change. This often happens when change initiatives first begin. Someone else has decided that this project is important and tells the sponsor to start a project. Again, politics comes into play. If you are leery of the sponsor's readiness, you might drop a hint to the initiative's champion (if that person is higher in the food chain than the sponsor) that you have an exciting presentation in which he or she might be interested. Your hope is that this person will attend the presentation and upon hearing the team's recommendations, will lean on the sponsor to approve them. Obviously, this is dangerous territory. Keep your head down and do not get shot.

- **The sponsor is shaky, but his or her key advisors are supportive.** In this situation, you (or the team spokesperson) will want to delicately float some of the team's ideas to these advisors (never in writing) and get their support before the presentation. A great way to do this is to "interview" them about their experience and opinions with the idea the team is proposing. During the course of the interview, you will get a feel for whether they are friend or foe and what you will need to do to get or keep them on your side. When the presentation is made and the sponsor sees his or her key people are supportive, he or she is likely to go along. This same scenario can be done after the presentation. That is, if the sponsor is hedging on some recommendations, the team can lobby the sponsor's advisors and hope they influence the decision.

- **The sponsor is supportive, but his or her key advisors are shaky.** You had better hope the team knows this before the presentation. If necessary, meet with the sponsor before the presentation and identify some areas where certain people are likely to object. Get the sponsor's support in these areas before the presentation. When the objections come up, the sponsor can shoot them down, making life easier for the team.

Make the Presentation

The presentation should be no more than 45 minutes plus some time for questions. The whole team can be involved or a spokesperson can handle it. It is not necessary to get a *yes* or *no* immediately following the presentation; rather, the purpose of the presentation is to get the ideas, benefits, and evidence in front of the sponsor so he or she can make good decisions. If the team has done everything right up to this point, the presentation should go quite smoothly. As Sun Tzu said, "the battle is over before it begins."

Secure Approval

During this step, which is usually performed in a separate meeting as soon as possible after the presentation (a week at the latest), the team, sponsor, and invitees of the sponsor's choice meet to decide which recommendations are a go or no-go. The sponsor will decide when this meeting takes place, usually based on his or her comfort level with the recommendations. If the sponsor says, "You've given me a lot to think about, and I'm going to need some time to digest it all," you know that the team has probably not made its case or has missed some obstacles/objections. Offer to have the team spokesperson and yourself available for any questions the sponsor may have. Gently press for a date when the sponsor can discuss implementation of approved recommendations. The more time slips away, the less urgent the team's great ideas become.

There are two resources you can use to make the approval meeting go smoothly:

- An enumerated list of the recommendations. If the team followed the recommended presentation format, this should already be available.
- Copies of a blank action plan for each meeting attendee.

The change agent should facilitate this meeting using the following process for each recommendation:

- Review the recommendation and its benefits and ask the sponsor if he or she has any questions.
- Discuss any issues or concerns related to the recommendation.
- Ask whether it is approved or rejected.
- Have everyone write the approved recommendation down on the action plan.

Once all the recommendations are discussed and decisions are rendered, proceed to the implementation stage and complete the action plan at this meeting.

A word of caution: **A lot can happen in the week or so between the team presentation and the approval meeting.** People who were silent during the presentation may become quite vocal behind the scenes. Different people may lobby the sponsor for or against various recommendations. (In a worst-case scenario, a team member double crosses the team and tries to kill a recommendation.) Be aware that you are likely to walk into a very unpredictable situation. I have seen sponsors who applauded a team during their presentation do a complete 180° turn a week later and shoot down nearly every recommendation. A good change agent will keep his or her eyes and ears open during this crucial time and will help the team stay on top of any emerging issues. This week can be the most critical week of the entire project. Again, it is all about politics—you can either play or be played.

Chapter Nine

Implementation

You mean we actually have to implement all this stuff? This is a common feeling among team members after they make their presentation. They worked so hard to get to this point that they cannot imagine dealing with this project anymore. There are two common problems that affect successful implementation:

- Burnout
- Lack of follow-through

Obviously, the two are related. Burnt-out people rarely have the passion or energy to do the heavy lifting required to implement change. In many cases, therefore, the burden for implementing the team's recommendations may fall on people *not part of the team.* This creates some immediate problems:

- How do we get these people as passionate about the ideas as the original team?
- How do we ensure the spirit and intent of the team's ideas are not lost?
- How do we keep the original team involved?

The steps and tools of the implementation process are designed to address these problems.

Lack of follow-through is a plague that has destroyed any number of great ideas. It can occur for several reasons:

- Steps to implement recommendations are not clear.
- People needed to carry out the implementation are not on board.
- Implementation tasks are not seen as a high priority.
- Accountability is nonexistent or dispersed.
- Obstacles and roadblocks are not planned for or envisioned.

Nothing dooms project number two quicker than not implementing project number one's recommendations. All new team members know how past projects have gone. It is critical for the sustainability of any initiative that ideas become actions. The steps and tools of the implementation process are designed to do exactly that by:

1. Building an action plan
2. Conducting review meetings
3. Creating project plans for complex actions

Nothing dooms project number two quicker than not implementing project number one's recommendations.

Build an Action Plan

At the end of the creating buy-in phase, the sponsor and team reviewed the recommendations and decided which ones would be pursued. From there the team, the sponsor, and people the sponsor chooses should proceed to build an action plan. An action plan is a simple, powerful document that defines the "who will do what by when" to implement the ideas.

Everybody thinks they do action plans. It is one of those things like driving; everybody thinks they are good at it, but in reality most are not. I have seen few people who do action plans well (that is, they lead to results). In most cases, plans are so vague and poorly thought out that the only result is road rage.

There is a missing ingredient in most action plans that I call *the deliverable*. The deliverable makes a squishy action into something very tangible to which we can attach a name and a date. For example, a squishy action might be something like "study the feasibility of adding more phone operators." Actions like these rarely get accomplished. Now, see what happens when we ask, "How will we know we have completed this task?" *Voila*, we have a tangible deliverable: "Feasibility report given to Director" or "Director signs off on feasibility study recommendation." We now have something very specific to which we can attach a name and a date (Figure 9.1).

This simple column makes all the difference between progress and failure.

Action plans can be created on paper using a spreadsheet program, or they can be facilitated using stick-on notes. I like to use stick-on notes because a lot of things

1

Action	Deliverable	Responsible	Due Date	Resources
Redesign 1040 booklet	New 1040 booklet printed	Tom	7/1	–
Create new short form	New short form printed	Mary	7/1	Rebid print contract
Develop Internet filing	First person files on-line	Joe	1/3/next year	Web staff (2 new hires) hardware
Offer free tax assistance in field offices	First customer uses service	Greg	1/3/next year	30 PCs
Redesign refund process	First tax refund goes out	Lesa	1/3/next year	Training We help with hiring New software New PCs
Change performance measures to include customer-satisfaction measures	New performance report	Mike	10/15	Facilitation support
Identify sources of phone calls and reduce them	Call study report with strategies	Dave	8/15	Possible new phone software

3 Review Date: 10/1

Figure 9.1 Action plan.

change while the plan is being brainstormed. Some things to watch out for when creating an action plan follow:

- **The same person gets most of the tasks.** This is a sure way to doom the project. While there may be one person who is excellent or has the responsibility over the area of focus, loading that person up with all of the tasks is unfair and unwise. Intervene when you see this happening and ask, "Is it possible to share some of this burden with others?"

- **Due dates are too far away.** What might we conclude when a sponsor approves all of a team's recommendations and then puts due dates that are three years later? This is a clear sign that the sponsor either has no intention of ever implementing the recommendations or feels they are such a low priority that it does not matter anyway. When the due dates are far away, you can bet money the tasks will never be done.

When the due dates are far away, you can bet money the tasks will never be done.

- **Original team members get shut out.** I hate when this happens. Occasionally it will occur that a sponsor and his or her staff will indirectly say to the team, "Thanks, we'll take it from here." This is like a pin in the team's balloon. Not everybody on the original team will want or need to be part of the implementation. But for those that want to, they should have a role.

- **Too many people are responsible.** When everybody is responsible, nobody is responsible. I am an absolute stickler that there be only one name listed as the person responsible for a task on an action plan. If you want to identify helpers, that is okay, but there needs to be one individual held accountable for progress. Teams or committees may carry out the task, but we still need a name of someone we can tap on the shoulder when time is slipping.

When everybody is responsible, nobody is responsible.

A lot of people are starting to use project-management software such as Microsoft® project. This can be a great resource for tracking the action plan.

Conduct Review Meetings

Progress on the action plan is reviewed in review meetings. These meetings are attended by the original team, the people identified in the action plan, the sponsor, and, if necessary, the sponsor's boss or the sponsor of the change initiative (politics again). The team sponsor or the change agent should run the meeting.

Review meetings serve two purposes:

- **Troubleshoot implementation.** The sponsor works with the implementers to overcome any obstacles that have popped up. The implementers can get additional direction, resources, and so on.

- **Kick people in the pants.** There is nothing like a Spanish inquisition to get people moving. For whatever reason, people tend not to work on their task until right before the due date. If the sponsor is not paying attention to the due date and expecting progress, the team never works on the task. Attention equals progress. By reporting progress on the action plan to the sponsor at regular intervals, there is positive pressure on the team to get things done.

An added benefit of these meetings is that the original team gets to see the progress being made on its ideas. (The number one complaint of team members is that they never know what happened to all of their hard work) Original team members can clarify any questions the implementers may have or challenge the implementers when they feel the original intent of an idea is lost or detrimentally modified.

The frequency of these meetings depends on the scope of the implementation. A project that can be wrapped up in six months may require monthly review meetings. A project with a two-year timeline may need to have a review every quarter. It is a judgment call that the team and the sponsor should make together.

Create Project Plans for Complex Actions

Some parts of an action plan may need a plan of their own. That is, the steps required to complete the task are numerous, complex, and time-sensitive. For example, a task on a team's action plan might say *automate accounts receivable process*. Such a task will need a detailed plan to ensure careful execution. In instances like these, we dip into the body of knowledge called *project management*. Like quality, a whole industry has been created around project management. While there is a lot of useful information out there, it seems that people try to make it harder than it is. At its heart, project management is a method to ensure a project will finish on time and under budget. The good news is that you already know the method. That is, if you can flowchart and analyze a process using the *FACT sheet*, you can build and manage a project plan.

There are a few principles that underlay the project-management methodology I will be describing. These principles greatly impact the way humans behave during a project and explain why few projects are ever completed on time.[1]

- **Murphy's law.** We all know Murphy. He visits often, usually when we least want him to. *Murphy's law states that anything that can go wrong, will.* Murphy attacks projects relentlessly, waiting until the last possible moment to crash the computer or delay the part. (Ironically, this is the last chapter I had to format before a big deadline, and my computer crashed three times! @%$# Murphy!)

- **Parkinson's law.** *Work expands to fill the amount of time allotted for it.* If given two weeks to complete a report, it will take exactly two weeks to complete it. If given four days to complete the same report, it will take exactly four days. Why does this happen? Eli Goldratt refers to it as the *student syndrome*. If you remember your college days, you will recall the process you used to complete a term paper. You read a little bit the first day, did a little research the second day, and then forgot about it until the day before it was due.

Murphy's and Parkinson's laws combine to create a single effect: late projects. That is, if we do not account for either, we will inevitably get behind. Or, if we do account for both, we build in so much "safety" or "cushion" that the project gets dragged out way beyond what is necessary. It is human nature!

When asked how long it will take to complete a step in the project, we know that Murphy is likely to strike (or the boss is going to load up work on us), so we pad our estimate with so much cushion we are not likely to be late. So a task that should take two days gets written on the project plan as two weeks. That way we have plenty of time in case Murphy strikes. But guess what happens? Parkinson's law. We have built in almost two weeks of cushion to do what should only take two days. Guess when we will start working? Two days before the due date. And then what happens? Murphy strikes and we're late anyway, even though we had a two-week cushion. Is it any wonder why projects never finish on time, despite the best of intentions

If you can flowchart and analyze a process using the FACT sheet, you can build and manage a project plan.

Murphy's Law— *Anything that can go wrong, will.*

Parkinson's Law— *Work expands to fill the amount of time allotted for it.*

Murphy and Parkinson combine to create a single effect: late projects.

(and project management techniques)? No project will finish on time unless we account for and change human nature.

There are five steps required to build a project plan. When executed properly, these steps minimize the impact of Murphy and Parkinson.

1. Identify all the tasks required to complete the project, starting with the last one (where the project ends).
2. Create the project flow.
3. Identify task durations.
4. Determine the critical path.
5. Insert time cushions.

Identify All the Tasks Required to Complete the Project

This is done in the same way we create the FACT sheet for process improvement. Using stick-on notes, we generate all the tasks we can think of to complete the project. It helps to first define the end point of the project. A task contains at least a verb and a subject, such as "*create* a *mailing list.*" How detailed should the tasks be? A guide is that every time a resource changes (different person handles the task), there should be a new task. Therefore, if one person will print envelopes, stuff them, and mail them, they could be combined into one task—"mail letters." If these three activities were done by three separate people, then they would be three separate tasks. The size of the project will also impact the specificity of tasks. A small project will have much more detailed tasks, whereas a large project spanning months to years will have much less detail. It is always better to err on the side of being too specific first and consolidating tasks later.

Create the Project Flow

Once the tasks are identified, they need to be sequenced in the order in which they occur. I prefer to use a large dry erase board for this, but a wall of flipchart paper will suffice. In this stage, the following steps are necessary:

- **Sequence the tasks in their logical order.** You may find that there are several paths of tasks going on at once, and that is okay.
- **Determine where tasks are dependent on each other.** A dependent task is one that cannot be completed until another task is done. For example, task B cannot be completed until task A is done. Attach the two dependent stick-on notes together (Figure 9.2).

   A simple way to find the dependencies is to go through each task and ask, "Is A needed before B?" and "Is A the only thing needed before B?" Look hard for any missing tasks.

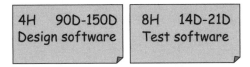

Figure 9.2   Dependent tasks.

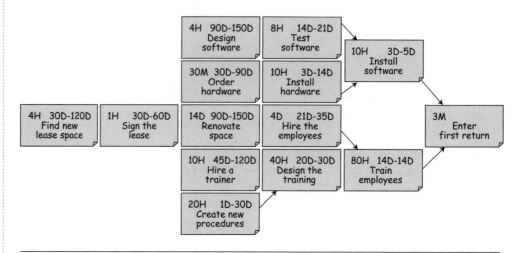

Figure 9.3 Project plan with dependencies.

    After you have found the dependencies, your chart will look a lot like the one shown in Figure 9.3.

- You will remember a key concept from process improvement—*process in parallel*. Use that concept with the project plan. Teams will have a tendency to build a sequential project plan with step B coming after A and step C coming after B, and so on. Any steps that can be done simultaneously should be. Oftentimes step X can come after A and before B. If there seems to be a long chain of sequential tasks, look for opportunities to break them up and do some of the pieces in parallel.

- **Before advancing to the next step, look again for any missing tasks.**

Identify Task Durations

Now that the flow is complete, we need to determine how long it will take to finish the project. This is where we start to deal with our friends Murphy and Parkinson and leave the common practices of project management.

    Remember, in order to finish our projects on time, we have to change human behavior—the desire to pad time estimates to cover all possible contingencies (Murphy). Just as with the *FACT sheet* and process improvement, we want to capture three elements of time for each task (Figure 9.4):

- In the upper-left corner of the stick-on note, record how long it will take to do the task from start to finish as if it was the only thing we were doing. (This is the same thing as *work time* from process improvement.) *Work time* does not count delay times or what-ifs. For example, if the task is to *generate a mailing list*, the *work time* might be one hour if I sat down and kept typing with no interruptions. This calculation will be helpful in determining how many man-hours are necessary to complete the project.

- In the upper-right corner of the stick-on note, record two separate times:
  - **Best-case elapsed time** is "how long it will take to finish the task if everything goes well." It may or may not equal the work time identified. For example, while it may take me only an hour to type a mailing list, best

4H 30D-120D
Find new lease
space

Figure 9.4 Task time estimates.

case with all else that is going on and the disrepair of the client records, it might be two days before the mailing list is done.

- **Worst-case elapsed time** is "how long it will take to finish the task if everything goes wrong." This does not mean a hurricane strikes or an outbreak of Ebola virus but the common stuff that can happen when working on a project (supplies do not show up, people are on vacation, customers change their mind, and so on).

Determine the Critical Path

The *critical path* is the *longest chain of dependent tasks*. We calculate this by adding up the *best-case elapsed time* for each task along each route.

What makes the path critical? Simply stated, any task delayed on this path will delay the project. It is "critical" that these tasks are on time!

Place a stick-on flag on each task that is part of the critical path (Figure 9.5).

If the time to complete the project is too extended, it is time to do some work. Analyze the project just like you would a process:

- **Look for opportunities to do activities simultaneously rather than sequentially.** In some cases, split large tasks into small tasks where some parts of the task can be done earlier.

- **Look for places where there are large best-case elapsed times. These are the time-consuming tasks.** What can be done to shorten them? Do we need to add more resources here?

- **Look for places with large gaps between work time and best-case elapsed time.** This indicates that there is something preventing the task from being worked on and finished immediately. It could be a case of a bottleneck (not enough resources to handle the volume), backlog, batching, and so on. It might be an issue of multitasking (one resource working on several tasks simultaneously and switching between each).

In addition, you will want to pay special attention to places where *the worst-case elapsed time* is significant and highly probable. This is referred to as *risk management*.

> **Critical path—**
> *The longest chain of dependent tasks. Any task delayed on this path will delay the project.*

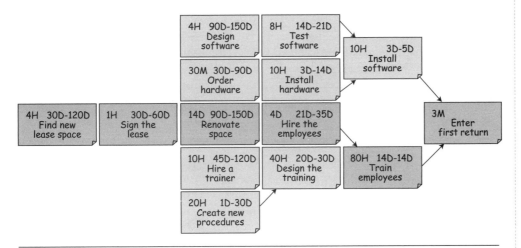

Figure 9.5 Critical path.

Consider developing a contingency plan for each of these tasks (what are we going to do if this happens?).

After discussion, recalculate time, rearrange notes, and refigure the critical path. Determine the start and end dates of the project.

Insert Time Cushions[2]

Insert what? This is where we beat Murphy and Parkinson. I said earlier that people deal with Murphy by adding lots of cushion to their task time estimates. When this entire cushion is added up, the result is a very long project. This would not be much of a problem if people did not use their entire cushion and passed on their part of the project as soon as they were done. But they do not. The giant cushion gets wasted! This is either because of the student syndrome (they wait until the last minute to do the task, wasting all of the cushion) or because the next people in line do not start their task early because the project plan said they did not have to begin until next week.

The way to counteract this instinct to overpad task estimates is to use *the best-case* and *worst-case* task estimates from step three. The *best case* is what we really want; it should be virtually cushion-free (you will know it still has cushion if the estimate is much larger than the *work time* estimate). The *worst-case* task estimate is where they have added the entire cushion. We are going to use the *best-case* task estimates to calculate the total project time.

As you can imagine, the team will protest—"There's no way we can meet that timeline!" So we make a deal. We are going to add a big cushion at the end of the project (at the end of the critical path). However, that cushion will be only 50 percent of the size of the cushion from each task on the critical path.

For each task on the critical path, we will subtract the *best-case* estimate from the *worst-case* estimate, reduce it by half, and throw it in the project cushion. What does this do? It does the following?

- It takes the cushion out of individual tasks. People will not have the luxury of Parkinson to wait until the last minute. To meet their target, they will have to start work immediately.

- It places the cushion at the end of the project, where it does not matter if any cushion is wasted. The project will be done early! Remember—task cushion gets wasted. Project cushion does not.

In the example shown in Figure 9.6, the total of the differences between best-case and worst-case task estimates was 194 days. Divide that in half to get a project cushion of 97 days.

Whenever Murphy strikes an individual task and delays it, the project loses some of its cushion. So long as there is cushion left, it is acceptable.

So now the critical path is protected from Murphy and Parkinson. There is still one more potential culprit: *other paths or feeding paths. Feeding paths* are noncritical paths that meet or integrate with the critical path.

While the critical path is protected from its own task delays, it is not protected from delays along the feeding paths. For example, suppose the hardware for the tax process takes forever to arrive, is the wrong stuff, and has to be reordered. Upon installation, the programmers discover a glitch in the software. These tasks are not on the critical path, but they all have to be done before the first return is entered. The project could be on time on the critical path and still be late on the project because a feeding path was delayed. Why do feeding paths get delayed? They are delayed due to Parkinson and Murphy, of course.

The remedy is to do to each feeding path what has been done to the critical path. For each task on the feeding path, subtract the *best-case* task estimate from the *worst-case*, cut it in half, and throw it into a cushion at the end of the feeding path. (Write the size of the cushion on a stick-on note, and place it between the last task on the feeding path and the critical path—the integration point.)

Repeat this process for each feeding path. When finished, the project plan should look like the one shown in Figure 9.7.

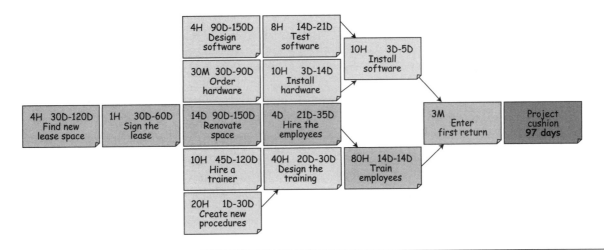

Figure 9.6   Project cushion.

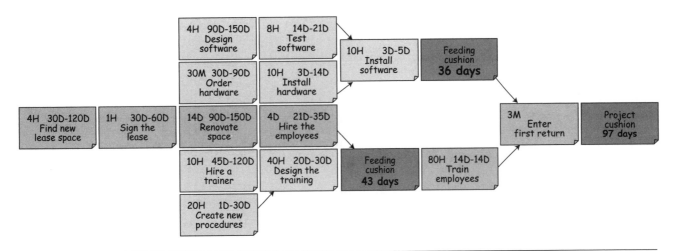

Figure 9.7   Completed project plan with feeding cushions.

Assign Resources to the Tasks

Once the team is comfortable with the project plan, it is time to assign responsibility for each task. Responsibility should be placed with one person at all times. This person may have helpers, but one name needs to be on the task (so we know whom to tap on the shoulder when time is slipping). Look for places where one individual is overloaded, as this inevitably causes delays. Try to prevent any bottlenecks.

Manage the Project

It is difficult to carry large sheets of paper with stick-on notes from meeting to meeting. Most teams prefer to convert their plan to a software program. Microsoft Project® works fine; even a simple spreadsheet can be used to track progress. For advice on how to convert a project plan to popular project management software programs, visit www.changeagents.info.

Once the plan is complete and in a usable form, all that is left to do is manage it. How does one manage a project of such complexity? Simple—manage the cushions.[3] The size of the cushions will tell you how well the project is progressing. It is helpful to mentally divide the cushions into three equal parts, as shown in Figure 9.8.

As we watch the project, any delay on the path eats into its cushion. For example, a two-day delay (a delay is anything over the *best-case* estimate) on task one leaves the cushion size at 25 days. Another delay of five days at task two and the cushion is down to 20 days. Should we panic? Not yet. By dividing the cushion into three equal parts, we create a panic button:

- If delays have used up less than the first section of the cushion, we do nothing.
- If delays have used up the entire first section of the cushion and are into the second, we prepare a contingency plan (what are we going to do to get back on track?).
- If delays have used up the entire second section of the cushion and are into the third, we implement the contingency plan (push the panic button).

Cushions can shrink and grow. Suppose task three is done seven days early; what do we do? We simply add seven days to the size of our cushion. We made up time!

> *How does one manage a project of such complexity? Simple—manage the cushions.*

9 days	9 days	9 days
	Cushion = 27 days	
Do nothing	Draft contingency plan	Implement contingency plan

Figure 9.8 Managing the project cushion.

Table 9.1   Multitasking.

A 10		B 10		C 10	
A 5	B 5	C 5	A 5	B 5	C 5

The success of running a project this way hinges on a few key rules:[4]

- **Work must begin as soon as it is assigned.** The cushion has been taken out, so there is no time to waste.

- **Work without interruption until done.** This gets best-case time as close as possible to actual work time. Multitasking is the death of projects. For example, see Table 9.1 for a comparison of working on three tasks one at a time versus working on them simultaneously (multitasking).

    In the first case, A is done in 10 days from start of project, B is done in 20 days, and C is done in 30 days. In the second case, A is done 20 days from the start of the project, B is done in 25 days, and C is done in 30 days. People waiting on A and B are delayed 10 days and 5 days, respectively.

- **Announce finish immediately when the task is complete.** Projects are a relay race. We do not want to waste time even if we are done early. We may need that extra time later on when Murphy strikes. Everybody on the critical path needs to be alert to the fact that they may have to start earlier than they planned. The start dates on project plans are only estimates. If a task can be started sooner, it should.

As with all plans, regular review meetings are essential to keep the team on track. These review meetings can be short and sweet and as frequent or infrequent as the project demands. The purpose of the meetings is to:

- Troubleshoot any problems (Murphy)
- Review cushion sizes and plan accordingly
- Alert people about possible start dates for their tasks (because of early or late finishes)
- Reallocate resources
- Celebrate

Endnote

1. The principles of the interaction between Murphy's Law and Parkinson's Law were first articulated by Eli Goldratt in *The Critical Chain*, North River Press, 1997.
2. The concept of adding time buffers or cushions to the critical and feeding paths of a project plan come from Eli Goldratt's *The Critical Chain*, North River Press, 1997.
3. The concept of managing a project by tracking the size of the cushions/buffers comes from Eli Goldratt's *The Critical Chain*, North River Press, 1997.
4. The rules for individuals in a project come from Eli Goldratt's *The Critical Chain*, North River Press, 1997.

Action Plan

*Who will do what by when to implement
the team's recommendations?*

Objectives

- Ensure that good ideas actually get implemented.

- Help the team understand what it will take to implement the ideas.

- Enlist the help of others in implementing the team's recommendations.

Prework

The sponsor has indicated which recommendations he or she would like to see implemented.

Estimated Time

20 to 30 minutes

How to Introduce It

Explain that we are going to put in writing all the things we need to do to implement the recommendations.

Explain that action plans usually only work if:

- Specific deliverables are identified

- One person is responsible for the deliverable (others can help, but we want one person we can tap on the shoulder when time is slipping)

- A specific due date is identified

Diagnosis

Organize the project

Change processes

   Customer satisfaction

   Process improvement

   Problem solving

   Planning

Managing ideas

Creating buy-in

Implementation

Evaluation

Celebration

ACTION PLAN

Action Steps

1. Identify the actions necessary to successfully complete the project.

2. For each action, identify the following:

   ■ The deliverable (how we know when the action is complete; that is, if the action is *find new office space*, the deliverable would be *lease signed or last person moves in*)

   ■ The person responsible for the deliverable

   Tip: When everyone is responsible, no one is. You are better off assigning responsibility to one person.

   ■ The date when the deliverable is due

   ■ Any resources needed to produce the deliverable

3. Set a date to review action plan progress.

ACTION PLAN

Example

Action	Deliverable	Responsible	Due Date	Resources
Redesign 1040 booklet	New 1040 booklet printed	Tom	7/1	–
Create new short form	New short form printed	Mary	7/1	Rebid print contract
Develop Internet filing	First person files on-line	Joe	1/3/next year	Web staff (2 new hires) hardware
Offer free tax assistance in field offices	First customer uses service	Greg	1/3/next year	30 PCs
Redesign refund process	First tax refund goes out	Lesa	1/3/next year	Training We help with hiring New software New PCs
Change performance measures to include customer-satisfaction measures	New performance report	Mike	10/15	Facilitation support
Identify sources of phone calls and reduce them	Call study report with strategies	Dave	8/15	Possible new phone software

3 Review Date: 10/1

Checklist

❏ There are clear deliverables for each action. (It is easy to see how we will know if each step is done.)

❏ The due dates are realistic (not so far away that people will die before they are done and not so soon that people will die trying to implement them).

Project Plan

Who will do what by when to complete this project on time and under budget?

The project plan is useful on complex projects where tasks are dependent on each other. The project plan contains much more detail than a simple action plan. The tool allows you to organize tasks into a logical flow that minimizes project delays.

Objectives

- Clearly lay out all the tasks that must be completed.
- Sequence the tasks in the most productive manner.
- Assign responsibility for task completion.
- Allow everyone involved to see who needs to be doing what by when.
- Minimize the impact of Murphy's law (anything that can go wrong will) and Parkinson's law (work expands to fulfill the amount of time allotted for it).
- Actually finish a project on time and under budget.

Prework

Prepare a sufficient work space.

Estimated Time

2 to 6 hours, depending on the scope of the project

How to Introduce It

Explain Murphy's law and Parkinson's law.

Explain that this rather lengthy exercise is designed to minimize the impact of Murphy and Parkinson and to help us finish our project on time.

PROJECT PLAN

Action Steps

1. Identify the *end point of the project* (when is the project finished?), write it on a stick-on note, and affix it to the far right-hand side of the work space.

2. Identify all the *tasks* necessary to successfully complete the project, placing each on a stick-on note. (The task must contain at least a verb and a subject.)

3. *Sequence the tasks* in their logical order:

   - First, create paths of sequential events (A comes before B, which comes before C, and so on). Place these stick-on notes side by side. Several paths may exist at this point.

   - Find the integration point in the paths by determining if there are any tasks in path 1 that are dependent on tasks in path 2, and so on. Draw an arrow between the tasks to reflect the dependency. You may want to rearrange the notes to make the flow easier to understand.

4. Identify *task durations:*

   - Record in the upper-left corner of each stick-on note the actual *work time* required to finish the task.

   - Record in the upper-right corner of each stick-on note estimates of the *best-case and worst-case elapsed times* to finish the task.

5. Determine the *critical path* by adding up the best-case elapsed time for *each* task along *each* possible route. Each route should have a total best-case time estimate. The critical path is the longest chain of dependent tasks—the route with the longest *best-case elapsed time.* Place a stick-on flag on each stick-on note on the critical path.

6. Insert the *project cushion:*

   - For each task on the critical path, subtract the *best-case elapsed time* estimate from the *worst-case estimate.*

   - Add up all of these figures and divide by two.

   - On a stick-on note, write the size of the cushion and place it to the right of the project end point.

   - You should now know how long the project will take. Select an appropriate start date.

7. Insert cushion at the end of each *feeding path* (where a noncritical path integrates with the critical path).

   - For each task on the *feeding path,* subtract the *best-case elapsed time* estimate from the *worst-case estimate.*

   - Add up all of these figures and divide by two.

   - On a stick-on note, write the size of the cushion and place it where the *feeding path* integrates with the *critical path.*

8. Assign *resources* to each task.

9. Input the project plan into project-management software. (Visit www.changeagents.info for specific instructions on converting project plans to popular project-management software programs.)

Example

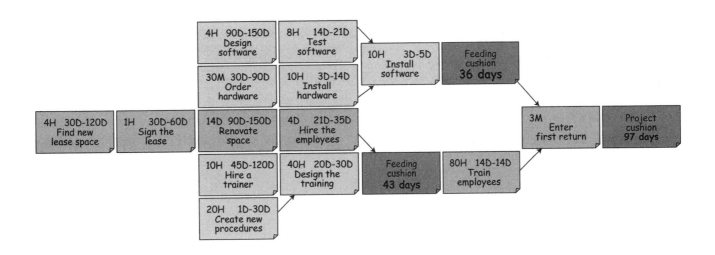

Work time—The amount of time to complete a task if you sat down and completed it from start to finish with no interruptions

Best-case elapsed time—The actual time it will likely take to complete a task if everything goes well

Worst-case elapsed time—The actual time it will likely take to complete a task if everything goes wrong

Checklist

❑ The team identified the critical path (the longest chain of dependent tasks).

❑ All of the task dependencies are identified.

❑ There are cushions at each place where noncritical path activities merge with the critical path.

❑ The time estimates seem correct.

❑ Everyone understands who will do what by when.

❑ The team believes it can complete the project on time.

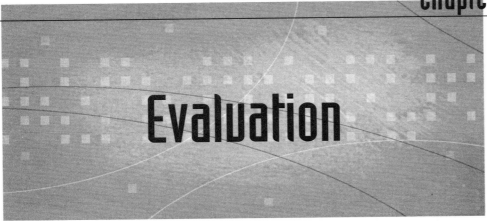

Chapter Ten

Evaluation

hile evaluation appears after implementation in the change agent model, the groundwork for it is laid early on. When the team completes its *implementation plan*, it should also complete a *measurement action plan* that clearly identifies the following:

- How will we know the project was successful?
- When will we know the project was successful?
- Who will collect the data?
- To whom will the data be reported?
- How will the data be presented?
- What decisions will we be trying to make?

The success of some projects can be measured shortly after implementation, while others can take years. Regardless, without a plan to do so, the evaluation rarely takes place.

Evaluation closes the loop on the DNA of change (Figure 10.1). The team members have recommended a plan to improve performance; they need to review whether their plan has made a difference. The purpose of the evaluation

Figure 10.1 DNA of change.

is not to punish but to learn. Several key questions should be answered during the evaluation:

- What worked?
- What did not work? Why?
- What could we have done to make the change operate more smoothly?
- What did we learn that we could share with others?
- If we had it to do over again, what would we do differently?
- What actions do we need to take to sustain the improvement?
- How should we celebrate?

The evaluation discussion should include the team sponsor, the change agent, the implementers, and the original team. It should be a positive event and a chance to reflect on all of the great work done by so many.

Measurement Action Plan

How will we measure this?

Objectives

- Help the team develop performance measures.

- Help the team members clarify what information they will need before collecting data.

- Determine who will report the measure, to whom it is reported, how often, and in what format.

- Ensure the data are collected in a valid manner.

Diagnosis

Organize the project

Change processes

　　Customer satisfaction

　　Process improvement

　　Problem solving

　　Planning

Managing ideas

Creating buy-in

Implementation

Evaluation

Celebration

Estimated Time

20 minutes per measure

How to Introduce It

Explain that developing performance measures can be easy or quite painful. This tool is designed to make it easy.

Explain that all measures must begin with a number or percentage.

Explain that after we develop the measures, we are going to actually draw the charts (how we will display the data) before we collect the data to make sure we know exactly what we are seeking.

Action Steps

The measurement action plan can be brainstormed on a flipchart or completed by a team member using the template.* In either case, it consists of the following steps:

1. Define what the group would like to measure. All measures must begin with either a number or percentage (for example, the *number* of lost-time accidents, or the *percentage* of repeat customers).

2. Specifically define each term used in the measure (for example, what is meant by lost time? What counts as an accident?).

3. Select how the data should be displayed visually, using one of the following:

   ■ **Bar chart**—Used to show comparisons or to show the frequency of a category (such as most frequently asked questions)

   ■ **Trend chart**—Used to show a trend over time (such as average phone calls per month)

   ■ **Pie chart**—Used to show proportions (such as sources of the phone calls)

4. For a bar chart or trend chart, label each axis. For a trend chart, determine the appropriate time period (scope) to document.

5. Determine the following:

   ■ Who will collect the data?

   ■ Who will create the visual?

   ■ Who will review the data? (Who will look at the data to make decisions?)

   ■ How often does the reviewer need to see the data (daily, weekly, monthly, and so on)?

6. Complete the statement, "This measure will help us decide . . . ."

Note: After complete, each visual should have a footnote at the bottom documenting the data source and the methodology used to compile it. For example, if the measure is the percentage of budget spent on overhead, the methods used to calculate overhead should be delineated.

*Blank measurement action plans can be downloaded at www.changeagents.info

Example

1. **Measure:** #/% decrease in error rates

2. **Definitions:** Error—tax return sent back to taxpayer for correction.
   Error rate—tax returns sent back/total tax returns submitted

3. **Draw visual:**

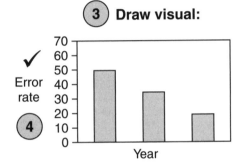

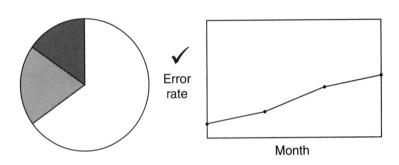

5. **Who collects data:** Greg
   Who creates visual: Lisa
   Who reviews the data: Stan
   How often: Quarterly

6. **This measure will help us decide:** Whether our changes had any impact on errors.

   Methodology: Tax Information System generates monthly report of total returns received and total returns processes. The difference is the error rate.

Checklist

❏ The performance measures are actually measures (beginning with *number* or *percentage*).

❏ The chart type selected adequately portrays the information.

❏ The team is clear about what the measure will help them decide.

❏ The data are possible to collect in a timely and cost-effective manner.

❏ It is clear who will do what by when.

Chapter Eleven

Celebration

Where's the party?

You will not find celebration as a key component in any academic model about performance improvement. Yet it is the fuel that sustains change initiatives. Sure, people want to do great things, but they also want to have fun doing it. In Frederick Herzberg's (1968) seminal article on motivation, "One More Time, How Do You Motivate Employees," he identifies achievement, recognition, and growth as among the top employee satisfiers. Successful team projects deliver all three. Aubrey Daniels (1994), a leader in applying behavioral science to management practices, identifies celebration as one of the most critical things management can do to improve motivation. People want to feel that they have made a difference, that people notice, and that people care. What better way to do this than to celebrate?

Celebrations do not have to be elaborate events. They do not have to be black-tie affairs at the Ritz Carlton. Instead, as Aubrey Daniels recommends, the best thing you can do to make people feel good about their accomplishment is to let them relive it. Celebration should be a time for the team members to recount their experience, to revel in the old inside jokes they had, to share the ups and downs, and to rekindle relationships lost to the firefighting of daily work life.

Kristin Arnold (personal communication), a master facilitator, has a saying: "Management sucks the fun out of fun." Celebration events should be fun to the team. They should be what the team wants. Some teams want to be praised by mucky-mucks. Some just want to go have a beer together (after hours) and laugh about their experience. Let the team decide.

A great way to let teams revel in their accomplishment and relive their experience is to have them present their accomplishment to others. While most people hate public speaking, they will enjoy getting to talk about what they have done. For each team I work with, I try to find a way for them to share their message. Perhaps it is a presentation to another work unit struggling with the same problem. Maybe it is a national award or an award from a professional association. These events keep the enthusiasm alive and let it spread, which is the planned side effect of celebration. Celebration is like a virus. When people see one group having fun and getting recognized, they want a piece of the action as well. Perhaps the most rewarding thing you will ever hear as a change agent is for a former skeptic or cynic to approach you and say, "When can you help work on a project in my area?" That is music to my ears.

Never forget to celebrate. You can't celebrate too much or too often. And you don't have to wait to the end of the project to do it.

Chapter Twelve

Leading a Large-Scale Change Initiative

Hop on the bus, Gus . . .

Most of this book has been written as if the change agent were playing a reactive role; that is, something is clearly broken and the change agent is brought in to fix it. However, more often than not, the change agent role is a proactive one—where the agent is asked to start and support large-scale change initiatives. For example, the Big Kahuna goes to a conference and hears a presentation about how an organization saved a million dollars using the latest management fad. Naturally, the Big Kahuna comes back and asks you to implement this whiz-bang concept throughout the organization . . . by next month. What is it? How do I do it? Why are we doing it? These are questions you are not supposed to ask.

The unfortunate part of being a change agent is that often you are thrust into the position of having to carry out an initiative that has not been thought through properly. With each new flavor of the month, the organization develops a thicker layer of cynicism, and the change agent has a more difficult time. There are effective ways to run large-scale change initiatives, but they require clarity of thought, word, and deed.

Three Places to Focus Improvement

You will remember Figure 12.1 from chapter 1. Again, there are three places to focus improvement efforts, and each will produce different results. In the long run, improvements must be in place at all three levels. However, there is some strategy as to where to start.

Organizational-Level Change

Organizational-level change initiatives focus on the "big" stuff—the vision, the mission, the strategic plan, and the "culture." All of this stuff is important. However, most organizational-level change initiatives tend to focus in one place: the organizational structure.

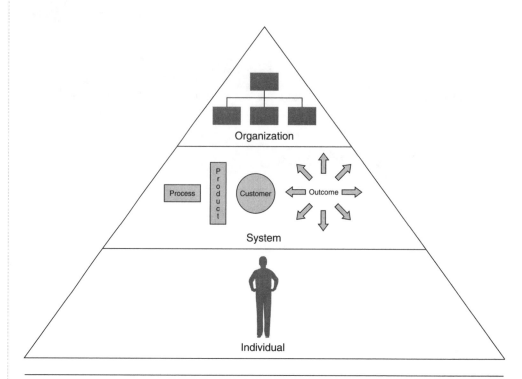

Figure 12.1   Three levels of change.

It is as if moving the boxes on the organization chart (an exercise I call Executive Legos) will suddenly increase customer satisfaction, reduce cycle time, and drive up employee morale. Restructurings are immensely painful to all involved and usually have little impact on the results of the organization. (I have worked with countless organizations that have a "consultant's report" on the book shelf. All the "efficiency" ideas were consolidations and restructurings with no fundamental changes in the systems of work inside the organization.)

There are times that restructurings are important:

- When accountability and authority are out of whack
- When it serves a new process design
- When there are fundamental strategy shifts in the organization (for example, going from a centralized organization to a decentralized one or switching from a functional to a geographic structure)

My strong advice to anyone who asks is to not make restructuring the first play of the game. People want to come in and "shake things up." Well, change a core business process, redesign a core product, innovate a new one—that will shake the place up.

Often, restructurings are a tremendous act of cowardice. Rather than confronting a difficult manager or making a necessary personnel move, organizations "restructure themselves out of the problem." Nobody is fooled by this. The lousy manager is still there (and now feels more powerful as a martyr), and the new management has lost credibility with the people that were praying for the lousy manager's removal. I am not advocating mass firings, but if the choice is between removing a couple of people or reorganizing 600, I will take the former.

We trained hard . . . but it seemed that every time we were beginning to form up into teams, we would be reorganized. I was to learn later in life that we tend to meet any new situation by reorganizing; and a wonderful method it can be for creating the illusion of progress while producing confusion, inefficiency, and demoralization of our subordinates.

— Petronious Arbiter, Grecian Navy, 210 B.C.

Individual-Level Change

We are all familiar with this type of change strategy; it is the "we're okay, you're not" philosophy. That is, "the organization would be doing great if you all could just get your act together and do a little more a lot better." These types of initiatives (performance appraisals, performance management, training, personal development plans, suggestions systems, and so on) make the assumption that improved individual performance will lead to better organizational results. There are some cases where this is so (sales organizations, for example), but in many cases it reveals a fundamental ignorance of how work is done. Individuals work in systems. Poor performance usually can be traced to the system first. W. Edwards Deming's famous estimate was that 96 percent of problems can be attributed to the system and 4 percent to the people. Let's fix the system first.

Perhaps an example will help illustrate this point. Figure 12.2 shows five sequential steps in a process and how much output the employees can produce in a day. Because of the complexities of the jobs, each step differs in length. At the end of the day, how many units can the organization produce? 75. Now, let's implement a popular individual-level change initiative—performance management. We sit down and meet with each person individually to develop his or her goals and performance plans for the year (carefully linking them to the strategic plan of the mother ship). Now how many units can the organization produce? 75. What happened to all of the increased productivity? It is sitting in a pile in front of Jennifer. So what do we do next? Well, of course, we create a performance goal for Jennifer to reduce the size of her backlog. This ridiculous cycle continues in perpetuity. Rather than focusing on the individual performers in the process, the focus should have been on how to eliminate the process bottleneck, reduce process cycle time, and so on. Then the focus can shift to the skills and productivity of the individuals.

Individual-level change is built on Theory X (Figure 12.3). At its heart is the belief that employees only give their all if there are incentives to do so. It assumes that employees are naturally withholding effort. When confronted with this, most managers would never say they subscribe to Theory X, yet their actions speak louder than words. Before focusing on individual performance, let's fix the system.

A slightly different twist on individual change initiatives is the flavor-of-the-month programs. This is where senior management declares (insert flavor of the month) to be important, so "everybody must get trained." Robin Lawton refers to this as the sheep dip approach. We line everybody up, run them through training, and expect that fabulous things will happen. Like sheep dip, it wears off after the first rain.

> *96 percent of all problems can be attributed to the system and 4 percent to the people.*
> *— W. Edwards Deming*

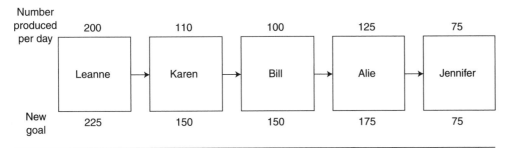

Figure 12.2 Performance management fallacy.

> ### Theory X Assumptions about Workers
> *The traditional view of direction and control*
>
> 1. The average human being has an inherent dislike of work and will avoid it if he or she can.
> 2. Because of this characteristic of dislike of work, most people must be coerced, controlled, directed, or threatened with punishment to get them to put forth adequate effort toward the achievement of organizational objectives.
> 3. The average human being prefers to be directed, wishes to avoid responsibilities, has relatively little ambition, and wants security above all.
>
> ---
>
> ### Theory Y Assumptions about Workers
> *The integration of individual and organizational goals*
>
> 1. The expenditure of physical and mental effort in work is as natural as play or rest.
> 2. External control and the threat of punishment are not the only means for bringing about effort toward organizational objectives to which they are committed.
> 3. Commitment to objectives is a function of the rewards associated with their achievement. The most significant of such rewards, the satisfaction of ego and self-actualization needs, can be direct products of effort directed toward organizational objectives.
> 4. The average human being learns, under proper conditions, not only to accept but to seek responsibility. Avoidance of responsibility and lack of ambition are generally the consequences of experience, not inherent human characteristics.
> 5. The capacity to exercise a relatively high degree of imagination, ingenuity, and creativity in the solution of organization problems is widely, not narrowly, distributed in the population.
> 6. Under the conditions of modern industrial life, the intellectual potentialities of the average human being are only partially utilized.

Figure 12.3   Theory X vs. Theory Y.

Source: Douglas McGregor. *The Human Side of Enterprise.* New York: McGraw-Hill. 1960.

> *All of the empowered, motivated, teamed-up, self-directed, incentivized, accountable, reengineered, and reinvented people you can muster cannot compensate for a dysfunctional system. When the system is functioning well, these other things are all just foofaraw. When the system is not functioning well, these things are still only empty, meaningless twaddle.*
>
> —*Peter Scholtes*

This approach was immensely popular with Total Quality Management (TQM). The word *total* led organizations to assume that everyone in the organization needed to be improving. So organizations spent outrageous sums of money training every employee how to use statistical process control tools in the ridiculous hope that somehow, if all of these individuals were collectively monitoring control charts, the organization would improve. The success of these initiatives is usually measured by the number of people trained. There is one state in our fine Union that trained every employee in state government (60,000) on how to use quality tools. This goes back to the hammer and nail analogy. When organizations hear about something that works, they naturally want to apply it to their organization—whether it makes sense or not.

Training-driven change makes two false assumptions:

- Individuals can improve the system.

- Once people are trained, they will apply what they have learned (successfully).

There is a time for training, but the beginning of a change initiative is not necessarily it.

System-Level Change

As I have advocated throughout this book, to change an organization you have to change its vital systems (processes, products, and so on). Organizational change initiatives that do not fundamentally change how work is done rarely succeed. An effective large-scale change initiative should be focused on identifying and improving the organization's key systems.

What does system improvement look like? Suppose an organization just produced one product. For example, IBM makes a ThinkPad 600. If this were the only product in the organization, the change initiative would consist of measuring and improving the following (Figure 12.4):

- Customer satisfaction
- Quality (process produces product correctly)
- Process yield
- Process cycle time
- Supplier quality
- Cost

In addition, IBM would want to do some long-range planning to ensure the success of the ThinkPad 600. The company would also want to focus on ensuring that employees that work in the process are satisfied, challenged, and continuously improving their skills.

IBM would be continually striving to achieve better results by making the right product that fully satisfies customers—better, faster and cheaper.

Roughly, that is how system change happens. However, no organization produces just one product. Inside each organization are hundreds of products (and their associated systems). Each unit in the organization has multitudes of products and systems. Each one of these systems needs to do all of the things outlined in the IBM example. But how? You cannot improve a hundred things at once.

This is when Mr. Miagi's[1] key principle for organizational change comes in: *FOCUS!* You cannot improve everything at once, so focus your efforts on the vital

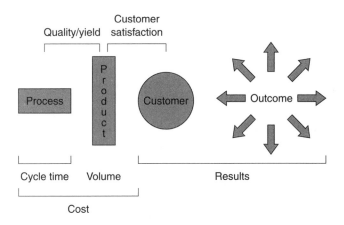

Figure 12.4 What to measure and improve.

Source: Adapted from IMT's workshop, "Creating a Customer-Centered Culture."® Used with permission. (See appendix A.)

It is not important that we do everything well but that we do the really important things really well.

I have seen strategic plans so voluminous and all-encompassing that they made the Kremlin look like a DOT.COM.

Service product[2]—
A deliverable created as a result of work activity. It is:

- *A noun*
- *Countable*
- *A unit of output that is given to a customer*
- *Packaged in discrete units*
- *Expressed as something that can be made plural (with an s)*

Examples:

PC Repairs
Purchase orders
Financial audit
reports
Grant applications
Strategic plans

few. What are those systems that if you fundamentally improved them, would have a dramatic impact on results? A wise person (whose name I cannot remember) once said, "It's not important that we do everything well but that we do the really important things really well." This principle has guided every successful change initiative with which I have been involved.

How do you pick the vital systems? What are the key ones to focus on? The answer lies in the organization's strategic plan. Simply, what is the organization trying to achieve? (Call these goals, objectives, outcomes, whatever.) The key systems are the ones that are the most critical to achieving the results. (Note that they do not have to be broken to improve. Remember: Do the really important things really well.)

Starting a large-scale change initiative consists of four key steps:

1. Define the desired results of the organization.
2. Identify the key systems most vital to achieving those results.
3. Prioritize systems for improvement.
4. Form teams to improve the key systems.

Define the Desired Results of the Organization

In most cases, organizations already have some kind of plan in place that provides direction (supposedly). If you do not think your organization has one, look on some bookshelves or behind doors; you will find one. Strategic plans should also follow the principle of *focus.* I have seen plans so voluminous and all-encompassing that they made the Kremlin look like a *DOT.COM.* Strategic plans are not designed to dictate the individual actions of every employee. Rather, they are there to say, "Here's how we see the future, here's the results we want to achieve, and here's what we're going to do *differently* to get them." It makes little sense to write a strategic plan that explains what you already do.

A good strategic plan should have a handful of goals for the organization to accomplish. I have seen plans with 25 goals and over 100 objectives for a staff of 1000 people! (Less than 1 percent were implemented.) If your organization has an existing plan with a few key priorities, you are off to a good start (skip to step two). If your organization has a plan but no clear priorities (too many goals, for example), it is time to do some prioritization. (Then advance to step two.) If no plan currently exists, it is time to create one. (See chapter 6.)

Identify the Key Systems Most Vital to Achieving the Results

The organization needs to identify the key systems before prioritizing them. Again, the definition of a *system* is a process that produces a product that is delivered to a customer to achieve some desired outcome(s). The easiest way to identify these systems is to inventory the key products (deliverables) the organization produces. Each participant in the planning session should come equipped with the products his or her unit produces that impact the organization's desired results. You may need to provide extensive coaching on how to complete this task.

Prioritize the Key Systems

Once the systems have been identified, it is time to narrow them down to the vital few. I prefer to use a two-stage process—one to narrow the list to 10 and the other to prioritize the top 10. Both stages, however, start with a clear set of selection criteria. The following are possible selection criteria to use when prioritizing key systems.[3] You can have the group pick from these or simply let them brainstorm their own and ask if any of these are relevant.

We want to pick systems that:

- Are a potential cause of dissatisfaction, complaints or defection of customers
- Will yield a high return on the project's investment
- Will show noticeable improvement within 12 months
- Are central to the mission of the organization
- Are a source of error, complexity, cost, or dissatisfaction inside the organization
- Are a cause of time consumption and high cost for others external to the organization
- Are time-consuming to create, fix, maintain, and so on
- Are created earliest in the relationship with customers

Some additional rules of thumb follow:

- Cross-functional products provide the best opportunities for improvement.
- Enterprise products (the main products the organization produces) are the hardest to change.
- Products produced earliest in the chain are the easiest to improve and can have a huge impact (for example, an application form, an order form, a standards document, or a design document).
- If the project does not deal with a product or process, it is not going to be easy to get your arms around it.
- The project can focus on a product that does not yet exist. That is, the lack of a certain product or system may be what is holding the organization back.

Once the criteria have been identified, solicit from the group members the products from their list that they feel best meet the criteria. Write each of these on a flipchart. If the number is greater than 15, multivote to get down to at least the top 10. From there, use the *project-selection matrix* to rank each of the priority systems against the criteria. A clear set of priorities should pop out.

Form Teams to Improve the Key Systems

From this point forward, it is a matter of how many projects to tackle and who will be their sponsors. For most organizations, three to five projects at a time are plenty. The main constraint on how many projects an organization can handle is the number of skilled change agents. A full-time change agent can run three projects simultaneously at the *maximum*. (Three is almost too much, and two is not quite enough. Two

The main constraint on how many projects an organization can handle is the number of skilled change agents.

Malcolm Baldrige Criteria for Performance Excellence

1. *Leadership*
2. *Strategic planning*
3. *Customer and market focus*
4. *Information and analysis*
5. *Human resource focus*
6. *Process management*
7. *Results*

and a half works best; run two projects and advise or assist on another.) If your organization has one change agent—you can do the math.

A change agent and sponsor should be appointed for each project selected. From there, the change agent begins the steps in the change agent model, starting with diagnosis. Working with the sponsor, the change agent determines what needs to be changed, who needs to be involved, and so on. Then the team is chartered, formed, and off they go.

Expanding the Initiative

The process just described can be repeated over and over again until the organization has exhausted its key systems. That is, the core business—the systems most vital to the organization's results—have been identified, dramatically improved, and continuously measured and planned for. Many organizations choose to use this selection process as part of their annual strategic planning process. Figure 12.5 shows the leadership system of a state quality award-winning organization. If you are familiar with the Malcolm Baldrige criteria for performance excellence, you will see the tight integration of categories 2, 3, 4, 6, and 7.

Figure 12.6 depicts the common reasons change initiatives fail. Most of us can relate to many items on the list. The methods outlined in this chapter and the entire book are designed to prevent failure. However, there are some additional factors vital to the success of any change initiative.

Involve top management. I have yet to encounter radical organizational change that was "bottom up." Granted, some good improvements can happen in parts of an organization. But truly creating large-scale change demands leadership from the top. People will always look up to see what the leaders are doing (not saying). Change initiatives without leadership involvement become low priorities.

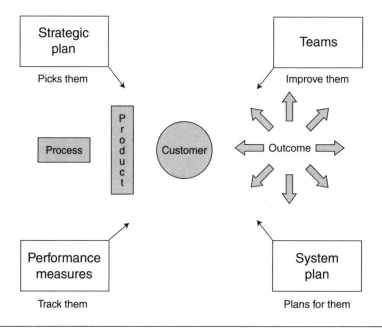

Figure 12.5 Leadership system.

Source: Adapted from IMT's workshop, "Creating a Customer-Centered Culture."® Used with permission. (See appendix A.)

1. The initiative's purpose is ambiguous or not agreed to by those affected.

2. The tools and methods are not personally practiced by top management.

3. The conceptual framework for the initiative is either absent, inadequate, or not clearly applicable to knowledge/service work.

4. The scope, pace, and manner of deployment do not match expected results.

5. The tools provided do not change values, assumptions, and behavior.

6. Activity is treated as an end in itself.

7. The initiative is not integrated into the business plan and organizational objectives.

8. Strategic business priorities, measures, and incentives do not support or are in conflict with the initiative.

9. Successes do not have a clear impact on improving the customers' experience or the producer's competitive position.

10. The current improvement effort is perceived as the best and final solution.

Figure 12.6   Why change initiatives fail.

Source: Adapted from chapter 7 of *Creating a Customer-Centered Culture* by Robin Lawton (Milwaukee, WI: ASQC Quality Press, 1993).

Do not just involve top management. You do not want the change initiative to be "*that thing* that *they* are doing to *us*." The solutions and the truth are buried two to three levels deep in the organization. The faster you get to them and engage their hearts and minds, the quicker you will see change happen. The use of teams to improve high-priority systems is a great way to expand the reach of the initiative.

Place customers at the center of the change initiative. Wow, this is important! I cannot begin to tell you how important this is. I have run across so many change initiatives that start with a steering team of managers and employees tasked with identifying the "issues" effecting the organization. These well-meaning folks identify numerous internal concerns (synchronizing the time clocks, faster expense account processing, better company vehicles) and set about forming teams to work on them. These teams work on these items, as well as things like "improving communication" or "increasing morale." At the end of the day, an employee newsletter is created that nobody reads. Finally, senior management pulls the plug because the initiative is taking up too much time and is not producing any results. Does this sound the least bit familiar? Focus the change initiative on customer satisfaction first. You will be amazed at the impact. During the course of improving things for customers, you inevitably make life better inside the organization. Further, by directing the attention outward, you avoid the petty bickering over inconsequential internal issues. Employees want to make their customers happy. Help them make that possible, and you have friends for life.

During the course of improving things for customers, you inevitably make life better inside the organization.

Link the change initiative to the business plan. Senior management cares about results. Results are articulated in the business plan (or strategic plan). If the change initiative will not directly lead to improvements in those priority areas, abandon ship.

Have a coherent change philosophy that fits the work and culture of the organization. TQM failed miserably in nonmanufacturing organizations. Its practitioners continually glossed over the differences between manufacturers, health care providers, educators, and other service organizations. Many folks could not see how drawing a control chart would lead to better results for their organization. Do not try to fit a square peg into a round hole. If customer satisfaction is not critical to your organization's success, then do not do a large customer-satisfaction initiative. If your organization does not have routine, repetitive, cumbersome processes, then do not try to start a reengineering effort. If your organization is comprised of highly technical professionals, keep the funny hats and silly trinkets in the drawer.

Focus. Start small and expand. Pick a few key processes to improve, and focus on a few key products to make better. Work on unleashing intrinsic motivation in a few work units. As always, when picking the few, make sure they are the *vital few*.

Low visibility of activity, high visibility of results. Advertise your accomplishments, not your intentions.

You cannot train your way to change. Most change initiatives start with a massive initial investment in training. They do not have to. Use just-in-time training to give people the skills and tools at the time they will need it. Simply telling everyone what is expected of them and showing them how to do it does not mean they can or will do it. Consider the following example:

> An organization I worked with developed a knockout leadership-development program that turned middle managers into change agents. During the course of the program, these managers were leading teams in their work areas to improve customer satisfaction, to streamline processes, and to solve problems. They learned exactly what they needed to know to make system changes right when they needed it. For instance, they learned the customer-satisfaction process, and before the next class convened a month later, they conducted focus groups with their end users. They learned by doing. Once the teams improved the systems in their work area, they began working on removing the barriers to pride and joy in the workplace and developing employees' potential. The program produced remarkable results. However, the program was not step 1. It came along 18 months into the organization's improvement journey. It came along after the key systems in the organization had been improved and after folks had faith that the principles they were being taught could make a difference. The leadership-development program was a means of expanding the initiative, not starting it.

Focus capacity building on change agents, top management, teams, and middle management, in that order. Change agents are the biggest constraint to the success of change initiatives—either because there are not enough of them or because they do not have the skills to do the job. The change agents are often the coaches to the top management team. Invest in them first, and you will go a long way to improving the performance of the top management team. Before any teams are formed, top management needs to understand the philosophy and methods associated with the change initiative. Before expanding the initiative too far, try numerous methods to expand the knowledge of the leadership team (for example, send them to a seminar, give them an article to read, facilitate a discussion). As mentioned before, once there is success and there is trust in the organization that the change initiative is a positive thing, invest in the middle managers. You can make some significant changes without their buy in, but you will never sustain the change without them. Many change initiatives stall once they get to the middle managers. You need a way to engage their hearts and minds and turn them into change agents.

Celebrate all the time.

Guerilla Warfare: How to Create Change When You Are Not in Charge

Many of you who read the previous section are probably thinking, "Great, the top leadership in my organization will never be enlightened. Now what do I do?" Probably the question I get asked the most after addressing an audience is some variation of the following: "How do you create change when you're not in charge?" When top leadership is not supportive of a change initiative, there is only one recourse left—go underground. The following points explain how.

Find a supportive manager. Guerilla warfare starts with two people—a brave change agent and an enlightened manager. No matter how backward your organization may be, there is at least one manager who "gets it"—who wants to make her unit the best it can be. Find this person and indoctrinate her. Take her to lunch, give her an article, a book, a website—something to peak her interest. Discuss how the proposed change initiative (its concepts and methods) will impact the things she cares about. Attend a seminar or conference together.

Implement the change initiative in one unit. Once you have found your comrade in arms, it is time to get to work. Together, draft a game plan for how to implement the change initiative in her unit. Involve others she trusts in the discussion. Obviously, I would encourage you to follow a similar change strategy to the one outlined in this chapter:

- Define the priority results.
- Identify the key systems.
- Prioritize the key systems.
- Form teams and improve the key systems.

You will probably want to start with one team. Again, the same criteria apply: high impact, high visibility, high probability of success, and so on. Work on and dramatically improve a system that makes everybody notice, including customers inside the organization and out, employees, upper management, and so on. The response you want is, "How did you do that?" *Don't make the mistake of piloting the concepts on low-hanging fruit.*

Create a buzz. Ideally, the results of the project(s) will be evident to all. That is, if you have selected a high-impact, high-visibility system (not moving the water cooler closer to the break room), you will not need to broadcast the results; people will notice. The desired result you want from your guerilla operation is a "buzz"— a shot across the bow or conversations at the water cooler such as, "Did you hear what they pulled off in Mary's unit?" Here are some strategies for creating that buzz or helping it grow.

- **Celebrate the employees' accomplishments wildly.** Celebrate in a way that everyone will notice. Make noise, trash the place, or hang a huge banner with the results on it. Have a party outside and invite others in the organization. You are trying to create interest—"Why are they celebrating? What did they do? Why are they having so much fun?" Invite the Big Kahuna to the celebration. You want that person to see the results and feel the energy. The Big Kahuna will have one of two reactions: 1) get back to work, or 2) where can I get more?

- **Obtain external recognition for accomplishments.** An organization I was working with was one part of a much larger organization. It was clear that no direction was going to come from the mother ship on performance improvement. So, the enlightened leader of the unit decided to go underground. With no fanfare and no pronouncements, the leader set about radically remaking the organization using the methods I have described. A year into the effort the organization held a wild celebration of team accomplishments where everybody from the mother ship could see what was going on. The buzz began. A year later, several of the organization's teams were recognized by professional organizations for their outstanding accomplishments. The buzz grew. At the end of the third year, the organization won a state quality award. All of this was accomplished using guerilla warfare. How did the story end? The enlightened unit leader was placed in charge of improving the entire organization.

Long-term Strategies

Much of this chapter has been about turning the direction of a misguided ship. I have outlined ways to make dramatic change happen in a short period of time. It would be misleading to stop there. Any seasoned organizational change agent knows that truly changing an organizational culture is a long-term endeavor. There are some key strategies to sustain cultural change in the long haul that build on the methods I previously described.

Organizational Level

Many keys to the long-term success of any change initiative are at the organizational level. There will come a point when system changes are not enough to ensure the long-term viability of the enterprise. To supplement targeted system changes, you will likely need to do the following:

Ensure DNA is present (Figure 12.7). The organization needs a balanced set of metrics that it can use for analysis, planning, and celebration. These metrics should give the leadership team a comprehensive view of how well the organization is performing on its priorities. In addition, there need to be some leading or predictive metrics they can use to better see the future. You cannot lead an organization by always looking in the rear-view mirror. While many organizations have metrics, they often do not do anything meaningful with them. For each measure there needs to be a process for receiving feedback, setting goals, creating plans, and reviewing progress. The absence of any of these components leads to stalled progress. Measurement is merely a tool to start a discussion. Without the discussion, the measurement is meaningless. Without a plan, the discussion is meaningless.

Adjust structure to align responsibility and authority and to accommodate new process designs. There will come a point at which the structure of the organization is the main constraint to further improvement. (This point is usually not at the beginning of the change initiative.) New process designs may dictate new structures and new jobs. Old divisions might not make sense anymore. Performance measures might reveal a disconnect between what someone is accountable for and what that person has the power to change. These are times to adjust the organizational structure. When changing the structure, remember three things: communicate, communicate, and communicate. Let people know why you are doing it, when you are

. . . [A]ggressive measuring changes the learning and behavior of a human being to the same extent as meteorology can change the weather.

—Peter Block

Measurement is merely a tool to start a discussion. Without the discussion, the measurement is meaningless. Without a plan, the discussion is meaningless.

Figure 12.7   DNA of change.

doing it, what will change, what will *not* change, how it affects them, and so on. And communicate all of this even before you are done! Large withdrawals in the trust account will be made if people feel that they did not have a role in the change or that it was done behind their backs. Structural changes should be done *with* people and not *to* them.

Develop executives. Surprise! The current change initiative you are working on will not be the last one or even the best one. It should not be. The organization should be continuously learning and continuously searching for better ways to do things. If the executives are not learning, chances are the organization is not either. Executives are busy people, but that is no excuse. And while you are developing the executives, develop the future executives as well.

Focus on innovation. No system change would have saved Smith Corona or Stuckeys. It is not enough to continuously improve existing products and processes. Organizations have to continuously discuss the future:

- What results are we here to achieve?
- What results do our customers want to achieve?
- What could we do completely different to achieve those results?
- Are we in the right business?
- Although impossible today, what one thing, if it could be done, would fundamentally change our business? (Barker 1993)

Senior management needs to be thinking about the asteroid that could wipe out the planet or the medicine that will save the world, and they must have an idea what they are going to do about it.

System Level

Sustaining system-level change for the long term involves continuous attention and strategic expansion. The effort shifts from creating dramatic performance improvements to sustaining the gains, incrementally improving over time, and cascading improvement efforts down to the processes and subsystems that feed the key systems. (For example, after improving the tax refund process, numerous subsystems were identified for improvements, including the funds transfer process, the computer maintenance system, the forms design process, and so on.)

The following are some key elements to sustaining and enhancing system-level change.

Ensure DNA is present for each key system. Improvement is not a one-time event; it is a continuous process. Even if you have radically improved a key system, you need a mechanism to continuously improve it for the long haul. The DNA of change is critical for this. The key systems in the organization should have a balanced set of metrics that encompass customer satisfaction, effectiveness, efficiency, and employee satisfaction. Regular review cycles, goal setting, and planning will help to ensure the system is better tomorrow than it is today.

Benchmark and stretch. So, you are pretty good. Are you the best? A great way to achieve the next breakthrough is to get outside the organization and see who is better than you and why. Do not limit yourself to your industry. Similar processes exist in state prisons, Ford Motor Company, patient billing centers, and consulting firms. Some of the best ideas come from the strangest places. A progressive organization I worked with required each system to find the best in their industry and the best in another industry with which to benchmark. Their performance helped set stretch targets for the system, and the field trips produced new ideas and better ways of doing things.

Turn managers into change agents. The role of managers is to continuously improve the system for the betterment of the organization, its customers, and its employees. These people are not paid to keep the employees from stealing the furniture. Managers need to know how to change the systems for which they are responsible. All managers should know how to:

The role of managers is to continuously improve the system for the betterment of the organization, its customers, and its employees.

- Determine customer expectations
- Develop performance measures
- Analyze data
- Improve a process
- Solve a problem
- Manage a project
- Develop their people

As an organization matures and its managers become change agents, your role as a change agent starts to evolve. You no longer have to lead the projects; you become a coach for all of the people who are trying to create change in their unit. Managers will look to you for help, because you are already skilled at what they are now struggling to do. There are few things more rewarding than when middle managers "get it." They do get it, given the proper approach.

Individual Level

Individual-level change is a subject that requires a book of its own. In fact, there are countless books on the topic. There are numerous theories, many of them competing, but all with something to add to the discussion. I will not pretend to give you the solution for developing individual performance. Rather, I will direct you to the sources that I have found provide the greatest insight and inspiration:

William Byham and Jeff Cox. *Zapp! The Lightning of Empowerment.* New York: Harmony Books. 1998.

Frederick Herzberg. One More Time: How Do You Motivate Employees? *Harvard Business Review* (January–February 1968).

Peter Scholtes. *The Leader's Handbook.* New York: McGraw-Hill. 1998.

At the heart of my philosophy of individual-level change are two principles:

- Fix the system first.
- Focus on intrinsic motivation. People want to do the best job they can. It is our job to remove the barriers that prevent people from having pride and joy in the workplace.

Having said that, here are some basic elements necessary to sustain change at the individual level:

Ensure DNA is present for each work unit and individuals where appropriate. I hate to sound like a broken record, but this is crucial. People work all day. They would like to know how they are doing. Imagine playing basketball every night for three hours a night and never keeping score. It gets boring after a while. It is incumbent on managers to share with their employees some critical elements:

- Lee Iacocca said that all employees needs to know the big picture and their place in it. Share both with them.
- Employees must know the goals of the unit long and short term and how they apply to them.
- Explain the values of the organization and what that means to them.
- Define how the unit is performing, and seek their ideas to make it better.

Weekly staff meetings should be about more than dress code policies and doughnut ceremonies. Where are we headed? How are we doing? What can we do differently? The emphasis should be on the unit or the system.

In addition, employees may want to have their own goals. If they want a manager's help in setting them, great. If not, don't. It does not have to be the manager's guidance and feedback that develops an employee. Teach them how to use the DNA of change, and get out of the way.

Redesign jobs and training to accommodate new process designs. Nothing can be more frustrating for employees than to change the system and not provide them with the new skills to succeed in the new job. With new processes typically come more advanced jobs. People need the time and attention to adapt.

Provide career-development opportunities for those who want it. Not everybody is in the rat race. Some people want to keep doing what they do forever. Let them. However, ensure that is a choice they are making and not the only option. For those who want to advance in their careers, hook them up with the resources to do it. Build career paths; make visible the skills necessary to hold the different jobs in the organization. Invest in training for the job they have and the job they want to have. If they ask, help them find a job that better suits their interests. Too many managers treat their units like the former East Germany; they want to build a giant wall

Imagine playing basketball every night for three hours a night and never keeping score. It gets boring after a while.

Good managers know that the goal is not to get the most work out of people but to help people get the most out of work.

around it to make sure nobody defects. The end result is what you saw in East Germany—people with little motivation, passion, or hope for their lives. Good managers know that the goal is not to get the most work out of people but to help people get the most out of work.

Continually involve employees in change efforts. People support what they help create. Never stop asking for help.

Finally, all long-term change initiatives need fuel. Celebration and recognition are the fuel that keeps people going. A three-year transformation needs a six-month goal and a six-month celebration. Take the time to relax, reflect, and have fun. Involve the employees in designing the fun. When at all possible, management should delegate away celebration activities. As a change agent, you should try to help the organization find ways to recharge its batteries.

While I have tried in this book to cover what is needed to initiate, implement, succeed, and sustain a change initiative, I cannot begin to do justice to all of the wonderful techniques and concepts that exist. This book should in no way be the end of your journey. A change agent should be continually learning and constantly seeking new methods and tools. I hope you will do so and will share your discoveries with your fellow change agents and myself.[4] Go forth and do great things.

Endnotes

1. Mr. Miagi is a veteran instructor of martial arts and sculptor of bonsai trees.

2. Adapted from *Creating a Customer-Centered Culture* by Robin Lawton (Milwaukee, WI: ASQC Quality Press, 1993).

3. Adapted from IMT's workshop, "Creating a Customer-Centered Culture."® Used with permission. (See Appendix A.)

4. I welcome any feedback regarding the *Change Agent's Guide to Radical Improvement*. If you have new tools and methods to offer, suggestions for improving the book, or success stories you would like to share, drop me a line at www.changeagents.info.

Project-Selection Matrix

What projects should we work on?

Objectives

Reach consensus on the best projects to work on to achieve the organization's desired results.

Prework

You have identified the organization's desired outcomes (or the desired outcomes of the improvement initiative).

You have identified a list of possible projects (preferably systems) on which to work.

Create the prioritization matrix on flipchart paper ahead of time.

Decide how many projects the organization can handle at once.

Estimated Time

60 minutes

How to Introduce It

Explain that we cannot work on everything and that it is important to pick the vital few with which to start.

Explain that they will decide what criteria to use in picking the projects.

Explain that after the projects are picked, we will need to do some work to identify the right sponsors (define sponsor for them) and to form the right team.

Diagnosis

Organize the project

Change processes

Customer satisfaction

Process improvement

Problem solving

Planning

Managing ideas

Creating buy-in

Implementation

Evaluation

Celebration

PROJECT-SELECTION MATRIX

Action Steps

....

1. Brainstorm the selection criteria by asking, "What criteria should we use in making our selection?"

2. Ask if any of the criteria are yes/no. That is, if the option does not meet the criteria, it is immediately disqualified. (For example, can it be completed in six months?) If the team has not identified any yes/no criteria, ask if there are any criteria that would automatically disqualify an option.

3. Ask if any of the criteria are twice as important as the others. Write 2X next to these criteria.

4. Create a matrix like the one on the example page, with the project options down the left side and the criteria across the top. Write 2X next to the criteria identified in step 3.

5. At this point, you have two options for ranking:

   1. Working *horizontally*, score each option one at a time against all of the criteria. You can use a scale of 1 (Low) to 5 (High); 3 (Low), 6 (Medium), and 9 (High); or any other scale you deem appropriate. Multiply the score in any 2X column by two. When complete, total each row. The *highest* scores are the top selections.

   2. Working *vertically* with one criteria at a time, rank order the options in terms of how well they meet the criteria. The option *that best meets the criteria receives a one, the next a two, and so on.* Divide the score in any 2X column by two. When complete, total each row. The *lowest* scores are the top selections.

   I recommend using the second method only when there are 10 or fewer options to be ranked.

PROJECT-SELECTION MATRIX

Example

(1) What criteria should we use in making our selection?

Most time consuming

Large source of errors

Source of customer dissatisfaction

(3) Public will notice (2X)

(2) Is possible to change? Y/N

Can be done in 9 months? Y/N

(4)

	Option	Possible to change? Y/N	<9 months? Y/N	Public will notice 2X	Time Consuming	Lots of errors	Customer dissatisfaction	Total
	Accounting System	N						
(5)	Performance appraisals	Y	Y	1 / 2	3	1	1	7
	Tax forms/refunds	Y	Y	5 / 10	4	5	5	(24)
	Field office	Y	Y	4 / 8	1	2	2	13
	Tax regulations	Y	N ⟹					
	Website	Y	Y	4 / 8	1	1	2	11
	Error notices	Y	Y	3 / 6	3	5	5	19
	Budget report	Y	Y	1 / 2	4	4	1	11
	Phone answers	Y	Y	5 / 10	5	4	5	(24)

Checklist

❏ The projects picked are actually systems.

❏ The projects picked do not resemble solving world hunger (we can get our arms around it).

❏ The projects picked are not the subject of another improvement initiative (including an automation project).

❏ The projects picked, once improved, will have a noticeable impact on the organization and its customers (it is not "low-hanging fruit").

❏ The projects picked are vital to the mission of the organization.

❏ The projects picked are in areas where there is likely to be a ready sponsor.

References

The following are resources that have fundamentally shaped my worldview. I hope they have as big an impact on your life as they have on mine.

Barker, Joel. *Paradigms, the Business of Discovering the Future.* Harperbusiness. 1993.

Bens, Ingrid. *Facilitating with Ease!* San Francisco: Jossey-Bass. 2000.

Byham, William and Jeff Cox. *Zapp, The Lightning of Empowerment.* New York: Harmony Books. 1998.

Daniels, Aubrey. *Bringing Out the Best in People, How to Apply the Astonishing Power of Positive Reinforcement.* New York: McGraw-Hill. 1994.

Goldratt, Eliyahu M. *The Critical Chain.* Great Berrington, MA: North River Press. 1997.

Goldratt, Eliyahu M. *My Saga to Improve Production.* Avraham Y Goldratt Institute. 1998. [www.goldratt.com/saga.htm]

Goldratt, Eilyahu M. with Jeff Cox. *The Goal.* Great Berrington, MA: North River Press. 1984.

Herzberg, Frederick. One More Time: How Do You Motivate Employees? *Harvard Business Review* (January–February). 1968.

Keirsey, David and Marilyn Bates. *Please Understand Me: Character and Temperament Types.* Del Mar, CA: Gnosolgy Books. 1984.

Kroeger, Otto with Janet M. Thuesen. *Type Talk at Work: How the 16 Personality Types Determine Your Success on the Job.* New York: Dell Publishing. 1992.

Lawton, Robin L. *Creating a Customer-Centered Culture, Leadership in Quality, Innovation, and Speed.* Milwaukee, WI: ASQC Quality Press. 1993.

Scholtes, Peter. *The Leader's Handbook.* New York: McGraw-Hill. 1998.

Thompson, Charles "Chic." *What a Great Idea! The Key Steps Creative People Take.* Harperperennial Library. 1992.

Here are some additional resources worth checking out:

Arnold, Kristin J. *Team Basics, Practical Strategies for Team Success.* Hampton, VA: QPC Press. 1999.

Coens, Tom and Mary Jenkins. *Abolishing Performance Appraisals, Why They Backfire and What to Do Instead.* San Francisco: Berrett-Koehler. 2000.

Hammer, Michael and James Champy. *Reengineering the Corporation, A Manifesto for Business Revolution.* New York: HarperBusiness. 1993.

Kyle, Mackenzie. *Making it Happen, A Non-Technical Guide to Project Management.* Ontario, Canada: John Wiley and Sons. 1998.

Miller, Ken. Are Your Surveys Only Suitable for Wrapping Fish? *Quality Progress* (December): 47–51. 1998.

Rummler, Geary A. and Alan P. Brache. *Improving Performance, How to Manage the White Space on the Organization Chart.* San Francisco: Jossey-Bass. 1995.

I would like to thank my friend and colleague Robin Lawton for his special contribution to this book. His Customer-Centered Culture© model provides a critical framework for the business knowledge all change agents must possess. In addition, Robin has contributed a process, method, and tools to help change agents improve customer satisfaction. His book, *Creating a Customer-Centered Culture, Leadership in Quality, Innovation, and Speed*, is available from ASQ Quality Press. To learn more about the work of Robin Lawton and International Management Technologies, visit www.imtc3.com.

The copyrighted or trademarked content in these three figures is included in this book in either its original or a modified format and is reprinted with the permission of IMT, Inc. and Robin Lawton.

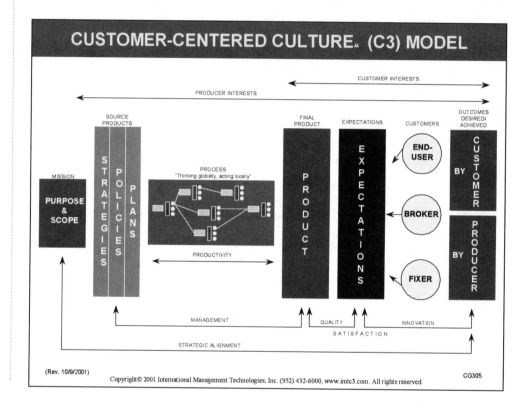

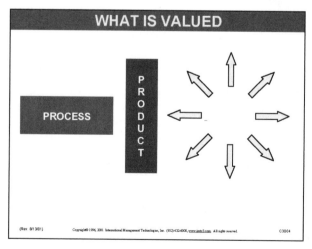

10 STEPS TO ALIGNMENT WITH CUSTOMER PRIORITIES

1. Articulate priority outcomes wanted.
2. Determine how each outcome will be measured.
3. Set numerical improvement objectives and due dates.
4. Select the few products most likely to enable or constrain outcome success.
5. Identify end-users, brokers & fixers for chosen products.
6. Uncover customers' priority expectations for each product.
7. Measure seemingly immeasurable expectations.
8. (Re)Design products to best achieve outcome priorities.
9. Map and shorten fulfillment response times by 80%.
10. Implement and CELEBRATE SUCCESS!

Frequently Asked Questions

Where do I find a change agent?

This question is most often asked by senior managers who realize the need for a change agent but do not know where to look to find them. As I mentioned in the introduction, change agent is not a recognized profession. You cannot advertise for a change agent and expect to have one show up at your door. However, inside every organization are people with great potential to lead change efforts. Again, there are five bodies of knowledge in which a change agent must be proficient. Three are easy to train for (facilitation skills, change processes, and tools), while two are a little more difficult (business knowledge and political skills). In most organizations, when any change initiative is launched (and after the consultants have left), things generally get turned over to human resources or training staff. This usually occurs because they have demonstrated proficiency for facilitation, using tools and group techniques, and so on. This might work, but in many cases I have found that some of these folks lack the business knowledge to lead improvements that matter to the bottom line or have not been high enough in the organization to experience the politics of change. I would first seek to find somebody with keen business acumen and exceptional political skills (they find a way to get things done, with and through people). From there, evaluate whether you think that person has the people skills, presence, and respect of the organization to facilitate teams through change processes. In any case, all five skills can be learned! Do not limit your search to senior managers, quality professionals, or training and development staff. Here are some other places you can look:

1. Personality types are discussed in chapter 2. Each personality type will yield a different change agent with different strengths and weaknesses. I like to look for people with intuitive personality types. That is, they are imaginative, challenge the status quo, explore new ideas and concepts, and are fascinated with making things better. How do you find these people? It is not hard. They are usually the ones coming up with suggestions to make things better, challenging policies and procedures, and going around the bureaucracy (in some cases, they are labeled the *troublemakers*).

2. You are not likely to find the people you are looking for in compliance functions. Rules-oriented procedure writers rarely make ideal change agents.

3. Look at past team members. Some people really shine when put on a team or special project. Talk to past team leaders or participants, and ask about people they think have potential to lead teams.

4. Look at the middle managers that produce phenomenal results and have the total admiration of their staff.

5. Look for the volunteers in the organization. There are some people, no matter what the initiative, who step up and want to be a part of things. You can probably name three of these people right now.

How do I become a change agent in my organization?

It is unlikely that your organization will be posting a want ad for a change agent anytime soon, so it is not a job you can seek and find. Rather, it is a job you have to create. Here are some suggestions:

1. Volunteer to help with the existing improvement initiative. I imagine that your organization has some type of change initiative occurring right at this moment. And someone is running this thing who may or may not have the skills identified in this book. In fact, the change initiative may be way off base in its philosophy or execution, but that is okay. The key is to get involved, display your wisdom and skills, and start to shape the future of the next change initiative. Essentially, this is how I got started. I knew I wanted to be a change agent but was stuck in a pretty uneventful job. One day I heard that the parent organization of which my unit was a part was going to begin implementing Total Quality Management (TQM). I did some sleuthing to discover who was leading it, an outside consultant from academia, and wrote him a letter volunteering my services in any way (including stapling papers). I helped prepare the binders for the senior management training and was invited to attend their session to help with any logistics. During the training, I got to know senior management and they got to know me. Within a month, I was helping to train the rest of the organization. Within six months, the consultant left and I was put in charge of the initiative. The rest is history.

2. See chapter 12, especially the section on guerilla warfare. The key is to find someone who trusts you and will let you start an initiative in his or her area. Achieve enormous success, celebrate it, advertise it wildly, and wait for the calls to come in.

3. Make dramatic improvements to your work. You can model all of the principles in this book in your work area or with your work specifically. Conduct focus groups to determine customer expectations. Redesign your work products to better satisfy customers. Cut 80 percent of the time out of the process in your area. Develop an entirely different, innovative way of doing what you already do. When people notice, tell them how you did it, and offer them help.

4. What are senior management's priorities? Find out all you can about them, and make improvements in your unit or other units that directly relate to those priorities. Make sure senior management finds out about them, and hopefully you will get to present on how you did it.

5. If you cannot seem to break through in your own organization, try to become a change agent somewhere else—your church, a volunteer association, a charity, and so on. For example, lead a strategic planning retreat for the United Way, or facilitate some focus groups with new church members. Word about you will spread to other organizations, and soon enough you will be living the change agent life.

One piece of advice I would offer is that you should not expect to be a full-time change agent. In the organizations I work with, I try to stress that the change agents also have some other line responsibility. It helps keep you connected to the work of the organization and keeps you part of the "team." Managers and employees often view internal consultants with the same affection as they view external consultants.

Project Maps

What follows are the ways typical projects tend to flow for each change process, including the typical meeting agendas, tools used, and time. Again, the beginning and end of projects are usually the same, with the middle varying depending on the change process required. These maps are designed to show you the quickest, straightest route from beginning to end. Your projects will inevitably take varying paths. Group dynamics, availability of data, and the complexity of the project all impact how long certain steps take. In addition, your project may bounce back and forth between customer satisfaction, process improvement, and problem solving.

Try to finish your projects (not including implementation) in four months or less. The energy and passion deplete quickly thereafter.

Customer-Satisfaction Process

Meeting	Week	Agenda	Tools	Time
1	1	• Sponsor shares charter • Team mission • Ground rules/values • Team roles • Future meeting dates	• Team Charter • Team Mission • Ground Rules/Values	120 minutes
2	2	• Achieve consensus on the "product" • Determine customers/roles • Segment customers into relevant groups • Plan focus groups	• Customer Roles Matrix • Customer-Segmentation Matrix • Focus Group Action Plan	10 minutes 20–40 minutes 20–40 minutes 10 minutes per focus group
3	3–5	• Review progress on focus group	• Focus Group Action Plans	60 minutes
4	6	• Focus groups (typically takes three weeks)	• Focus Group Tool	90 minutes each
5	8	• Debrief focus groups • Measure the degree to which customers' expectations are achieved • Discuss need for data collection on current performance	• Voice of the Customer • Data-Collection Action Plan	30 minutes 60 minutes
6	9	• Develop innovative, alternative products to better achieve customer outcomes • Brainstorm ways to meet customer targets (close the gap between existing and customer-desired performance) • Evaluate ideas • Identify sponsors for each idea selected • Set date and make arrangements for final presentation to sponsor	• Innovation Tool • Brainstorming or Problem Solving • Idea Filter • Idea Worksheet (to be done after meeting)	20–40 minutes 60 minutes (brainstorming) to several meetings (problem solving) 15 minutes 10 minutes
7	11	• Team members present idea worksheets including their recommendations • Team selects which ideas will become recommendations • Assign roles for preparing presentation	• Idea Worksheet	10 minutes per idea 30 minutes and up (depends on level of consensus) 10 minutes
8	13	• Team presentation		90 minutes
*9	14	• Sponsor discusses which recommendations are approved • Implementation plan is drafted	• Action Plan	30 minutes 60 minutes
*10	15	• Team develops success measures against which to evaluate project • Plan dates for review meetings	• Measurement Action Plans	45 minutes 15 minutes
11	16	• Celebrate		Until closing time

Process-Improvement Process

Meeting	Week	Agenda	Tools	Time
1	1	• Sponsor shares charter • Team mission • Ground rules/values • Team Roles • Future meeting dates	• Team Charter • Team Mission • Ground Rules/Values	120 minutes
2	2	• Observe the process (process walkthrough) • Record observations		45–90 minutes
3	3	• Flowchart the process (to the best of your ability) • Assign responsibility to collect missing elements for flowchart • Assign responsibility to collect data about process	• FACT Sheet • Data-Collection Action Plan	2–3 hours
4	5	• Finish flowchart • Analyze flowchart/data for opportunities	• Process-Analysis Checklist	2–3 hours
5	6	• Create new process flow • Enumerate major changes (recommendations) necessary to create new process • Identify sponsors for each recommendation • Set date and make arrangements for final presentation to sponsor • Assign roles for preparing presentation	• Idea Worksheet	90–120 minutes
6	8	• Team members present idea worksheets including their recommendations • Team selects which ideas will become recommendations	• Idea Worksheet	10 minutes per idea 30 minutes and up (depends on level of consensus)
7	10	• Team presentation		90 minutes
* 8	11	• Sponsor discusses which recommendations are approved • Implementation plan is drafted	• Action Plan	30 minutes 60 minutes
* 9	12	• Team develops success measures against which to evaluate project • Plan dates for review meetings	• Measurement Action Plan	45 minutes 15 minutes
10	13	• Celebrate		Until closing time

Problem-Solving Process

Meeting	Week	Agenda	Tools	Time
1	1	• Sponsor shares charter • Team mission • Ground rules/values • Team Roles • Future meeting dates	• Team Charter • Team Mission • Ground Rules/Values	120 minutes
2	2	• Define the problem • Determine what data are needed to better understand the problem	• Know/Don't Know • Data-Collection Plan	30–60 minutes
3	4–8?	• Analyze the data • If ready, write the problem statement (may repeat meeting agendas of weeks 2 and 4 repeatedly until problem statement is done) • Determine root cause	• Problem-Statement Template • Know/Don't Know • Five Whys • Root Cause Chart	10 minutes 45 minutes and up
4	5	• Generate possible solutions • Evaluate solutions • Identify sponsors for each idea selected	• Brainstorming • Idea Filter • Idea Worksheet (to be done after meeting)	60 minutes 15 minutes 10 minutes
5	6	• Team members present idea worksheets including their recommendations • Team selects which ideas will become recommendations • Assign roles for preparing presentation	• Idea Worksheet	10 minutes per idea 30 minutes and up (depends on level of consensus) 10 minutes
6	7	• Team presentation		90 minutes
7	8	• Sponsor discuss which recommendations are approved • Implementation plan is drafted	 • Action Plan	30 minutes 60 minutes
8	9	• Team develops success measures against which to evaluate project • Plan dates for review meetings	• Measurement Action Plans	45 minutes 15 minutes
9	10	• Celebrate		Until closing time

Sponsor's Guide to Teams*

Thank you for agreeing to be a team sponsor. As the team sponsor, you play a vital role in ensuring the team's success. What follows are things you should know about the team, how the project will work, and what things you can do to help.

About the team. An improvement team is a group of people who use a guided, structured process to arrive at excellent recommendations that will be agreed upon using consensus. They are much more informal than committees and much smaller than work groups or task forces. The teams do not use Roberts Rules of Order and rarely, if ever, vote. Instead, they use proven improvement tools and methods to accomplish their tasks. Because of their intense work, the ideal team size is between six and eight people.

The role of the change agent. The change agent serves you and the team. This person is in charge of the process the team will use—not the content! The change agent has been trained in structured methods to improve processes, to increase customer satisfaction, and to solve problems. This person runs the meetings using methods and tools specific to the type of project being worked. The change agent is specially trained to keep meetings and teams on track, while ensuring that great ideas surface and survive. The change agent will work closely with you to set up the team project and is your resource for project status.

The role of the team spokesperson. This person is the team's primary contact when any problems are encountered. The team spokesperson will accompany the change agent in any discussion about the team with you. With the exception of these duties, the team spokesperson should be no different than any other team member. While he or she might be a content expert, the team spokesperson does not have veto power or any other power over the ideas and recommendations of the team. During a team meeting, it should be impossible to distinguish whom the team spokesperson is! The team spokesperson does not run the meetings or decide what process the team will use; these are the domains of the change agent. However, it has proven to be quite successful for the change agent and team spokesperson to collaborate on meeting agendas and to work together when problems with the team arise.

The role of the sponsor. The sponsor is the person with the authority to say *yes* to a team's recommendations. You are the person to whom the team will pitch their ideas. The sponsor plays critical roles in the beginning, middle, and end of the project.

*To be distributed to team sponsors. Clean copies (without the book formatting) can be downloaded at www.changeagents.info and may be shared freely.

The Beginning

Help the Change Agent Scope the Project

Once the project is selected, a change agent will meet with you to better understand the project and to get a feel for its scope. This meeting is for the benefit of the change agent so he or she can best determine how to organize the project and what methods to use to bring the project to swift completion. Things you should be prepared to discuss include background about the issue, previous attempts to work on the issue, time constraints, and the overall scope of the project (for example, where does the process start and end?).

Charter the Team

The *team charter* is a powerful document that serves two purposes:

1. It helps you to clarify your expectations of the project and to understand what will be necessary to achieve them.

2. It provides direction and guidance to the team, proactively answering the most important questions team members have of a project, namely the following:

   - What results are expected of us?

   - How long will the project last?

   - How much time can I spend on it, and who is going to do my real work?

The *team charter* consists of the following components:

- **The current situation** (what is going on that makes us want to work on the project?)

- **The desired outcomes of the project** (what does success look like?)

- **The undesired outcomes of the project** (what do you not want to have happen from the project?)

- **The scope and boundaries of the project** (what is off the table? where does the process start and stop?)

- **The team members** (what functions need to be represented, and who should represent them?)

- **The amount of time and resources the team can dedicate to the project**

Team projects should be wrapped up in four months or less. That is, you should be prepared to receive recommendations roughly four months after the team begins. Experience has shown that teams lose their momentum after this time period. In order to accommodate such an aggressive schedule, it is usually necessary for team members to devote four hours per week to the pursuit of project goals. Two to three of the hours will be spent in team meetings, while the rest will be spent doing research and supporting team tasks. Experience has also shown that teams are more effective if they meet weekly for at least two hours. Meeting every week encourages commitment from the team and allows for continuity of the project.

The following are observable effects of meeting too infrequently or for too short a time period:

- High team turnover results.
- There is high absenteeism among team members.
- Members "withdraw" (lose interest but continue to show up).
- One or two people carry most of the load.
- The team feels like it is "spinning its wheels."
- Little data are collected to present a compelling case for change.
- Final recommendations are "simple," with little depth of analysis.
- Final recommendations do not get very far "outside the box."

Preapproving the time commitment for team members is an excellent way to show your commitment to the project.

The change agent can help facilitate the creation of the *team charter*. Many sponsors find it helpful to invite other people (usually not the likely team members) in to help draft the charter. During the course of one meeting, the change agent can help you and whomever you invite come to consensus on the critical elements of the charter. From there, the charter will be typed up and ready for you to share with the team.

After the *team charter* is drafted, the change agent will work with you to form the team and to notify the participants. On cross-functional teams, you as the sponsor may need to do some work to secure commitment from other managers in the organization to use their people on the team. Once the participants have been notified, a meeting is held to orient the team.

Orient the Team

The team orientation is your chance to share the charter with the team. In addition, you will want to cover or keep in mind the following during this meeting:

- Explain your role with the team.
- Explain how the project fits into the larger initiative, the strategic plan, and so on.
- Show the team why the project was picked and how important it is.
- Maintain the self-esteem of the people in the area being improved.
- Discuss the time commitment asked of team members.
- Make the team members feel special and honored to be part of the project.
- Introduce the change agent and explain his or her role. A ringing endorsement from the sponsor about the change agent will make the change agent's job much easier.

You should also encourage the team members to ask you questions and to state any concerns. In addition, make the offer to them that if they do not feel that they are up to the project or have other concerns, they can come see you privately.

The team members will be looking for verbal and nonverbal clues to gauge your sincerity and commitment to the project. How you handle this orientation will set the tone and tenor for the rest of the team project. *The team should be fired up when you are finished.*

The Middle

During the course of the project, the change agent will be leading the team through a structured process to produce excellent recommendations for your consideration. Depending on the scope of the project, the process may include:

- Flowcharting
- Customer focus groups
- Data collection
- Site visits to other organizations
- Brainstorming
- Innovation exercises
- Research
- Performance measurement

Again, the team will be working for approximately four months. During this time, your role becomes one of *troubleshooter.* That is, if the team has some obstacles they need cleared (such as a supervisor who will not let a team member devote the time or a piece of data that information systems will not produce), they will come to you for help. Unless the team members are encountering difficulties or need some clarification of direction, do not expect to hear much from them until they are done. The team will not keep traditional minutes and will not be sharing the outputs of its meetings with anybody outside of the team. We are not trying to keep the team's work secret. Rather, we are trying to foster an environment where the team is free to work through and discuss *preliminary* ideas, good and bad, without worrying about how others will react. The change agent and team spokesperson will keep you abreast of the team's progress and team dynamics issues and may fill you in on certain content discussions. The team charter and the change agent will keep the team inbounds. At this point, do not worry *what* the team members are doing; rather, worry about *how* they are doing.

What follows are common team issues where the sponsor may need to get involved:

- A team member misses a lot of meetings.
- A team member's supervisor will not give him or her the time to devote to the team.
- A team member's supervisor is pressuring him or her for details of what the team is discussing.
- The team has hit on something entirely new and wants your direction before it expends any energy on it.
- Someone in the organization is not cooperating with the team on an information request.
- The team needs to get input from others outside the organization and needs you to clear the way.
- The team dynamics have broken down, and certain team members are hampering the group effort.
- The team is getting out of bounds and needs your subtle redirection.
- The team members are unnecessarily constraining themselves and will not consider new or different ways of doing things.

When any of these or other situations arise, the change agent and team spokesperson will bring them to your attention.

The End

Once the team has completed its work, it will make a presentation to you and whomever you would like to invite. The presentation will consist of recommendations that are well thought through and supported by data. You will clearly be able to see the following:

- The team's mission
- The process they went through
- The discoveries they made
- What they recommend
- The benefits of the recommendations
- Any issues or obstacles to successful implementation

It is not necessary at this time to make decisions on the recommendations. That will come later. Rather, use this time to fully understand what the team is recommending and why.

After the presentation, the onus is on you to decide which recommendations you would like to approve. Hopefully the team has made a compelling case to support each one, but there may be some that you just do not think will work or that simply need more thought. In any case, the change agent will set up a meeting for you to sit down with the team and discuss their recommendations.

During the next meeting, the change agent will facilitate a discussion between you and the team about which recommendations are approved. After reviewing each recommendation, a go/no-go decision will be made. Each of the approved recommendations will then be placed on the *implementation plan*, where a due date and responsible person will be identified. *You are in charge of implementation!* The *implementation plan* can serve as your management tool to ensure things are happening.

The team members may or may not have a role in the implementation, depending on the tasks identified. Periodic review dates should be set to review progress on the implementation plan.

Finally, once the *implementation plan* has been drafted, the team will convene one final time to draft success measures that can be used to evaluate the project once it is complete.

A nice touch at this point is for the sponsor to host some form of celebration activity for the team. This is a chance to show your appreciation and to let the team members revel in what they have accomplished.

If at any time you have a question regarding how the team process works, do not hesitate to contact the change agent.

About the Author

Ken Miller is an experienced change agent, having led, facilitated, trained, or supervised more than 100 performance-improvement teams.

Ken is the founder of the Change and Innovation Agency, a firm committed to helping change agents and organizations radically improve performance.

He is the former Director of Performance Improvement for the State of Missouri, where he is leading a group of change agents to help all state agencies achieve performance excellence.

Prior to this, Ken was the Deputy Director of the Missouri Department of Revenue, where he led the initiative to improve customer satisfaction and to reduce the burden on citizens to pay taxes and to register motor vehicles. Working with great employees and terrific management, he accomplished the following:

- Reduced the time to issue tax refunds by 80 percent at less cost
- Reduced the time to issue motor vehicle titles and registrations by 80 percent at less cost
- Cut wait times in motor vehicle offices by half
- Moved 50 percent of tax filers off the 1040 long form to simpler, shorter, customized forms and filing options
- Became the only government organization to win the prestigious Missouri Quality Award, the state award for performance excellence modeled after the Malcolm Baldrige award (only three other government agencies in the country have ever won such an award)

Before joining the Department of Revenue, Ken was a partner in the customer-satisfaction consulting firm of International Management Technologies (IMT). IMT helps clients achieve results by focusing on their customers. Some of IMT's clients have included Motorola, AT&T, Eastman Kodak, 3M, Microsoft, Northwest Airlines, and the Department of Defense. Ken worked with numerous clients in diverse industries on measuring customer satisfaction, customer-centered product design, radical process improvement, and innovation.

Ken received his MBA from Northwest Missouri State University.

Ken can be contacted at www.changeagents.info

Index

Page numbers in **Bold** indicate figure or table entry